The Signature Quilt

Traditions, Techniques and The Signature Block Collection

Pepper Cory
Susan McKelvey

Copyright 1995 by Pepper Cory and Susan McKelvey.
All rights reserved. Published in the United States of America
by Quilt House Publishing.

Editing and production direction by Mary Coyne Penders.
Technical editing by Darlene Zimmerman.
Title page illustration by Susan McKelvey.
Cover and book design by Hani Stempler, Character Place, Inc., Atlanta.
Production and illustrations by Character Place, Inc., Atlanta.
Photography by Sharon Risedorph, San Francisco.
Printing and color separations by Regent Publishing Services, Limited, Hong Kong.

First edition.

Library of Congress Cataloging-in-Publication Data

Cory, Pepper, 1951 –, and McKelvey, Susan, 1942 –
        The Signature Quilt: Traditions, Techniques and The Signature Block Collection

1. Signed Quilts   2. Quilting/Patchwork Patterns   3. Quilting/Appliqué Patterns
4. Crafts and Hobbies

ISBN 1-881588-14-9

Quilt House Publishing
95 Mayhill Street
Saddle Brook, NJ 07663

Dedication

❧

To our husbands,
Doug McKelvey and Rod Magyar,
our best friends.

Acknowledgements

❧

We wish to thank our editor, Mary Coyne Penders, for her faith in our vision; our designer, Hani Stempler, for her creative touch; and our printer, Jamie Draluck, for his sound advice. Special thanks to Joe Mishkin and Chuck Sabosik of Quilt House Publishing for their support throughout the production process.

We are grateful to all our friends who made the beautiful quilts which grace the pages of this book. Our thanks to the Chester County Historical Society Museum of West Chester, Pennsylvania, for allowing us to study and photograph the quilts in their collection. We extend a particular thank you to Jodi King, Barbara Rasch, Nora Reedy and Phyllis Foust, whose quilts could not be included because of space limitations.

Finally, we are extremely grateful to our fellow quiltmakers, whose interest in signature quilts provided the enthusiasm and inspiration that made our work possible.

Table of Contents

BOOK III: THE COLLECTION

Oak Leaf, maker unknown, New Hampshire, 1854. 52 x 76 inches. Collection of Pepper Cory and Susan McKelvey.

Belonging to the Past, Present and Future

Pepper's Perspective

I began to write on quilts because I needed to make labels to identify my quilts. Susan McKelvey's books on the subject were my guides to label-making. After reading Susan's books, I decided to experiment with writing and inking on the fronts of my quilts as well. Then after joining a friendship quilting bee, where it was presumed that every block I made for someone in the group would be signed, I soon acquired a lot of practice in writing on quilts.

Signature quilts intrigued me at once because they represented the most complete documentation of the quiltmaker's art. To know those quiltmakers of old, I looked at their quilts and read what they had written.

After assembling a pattern library of close to one hundred blocks used in signature quilts, I realized a book was begging to be written. At a chance meeting at a quilt show, Susan McKelvey asked, "What are you working on?" I replied, "I'm thinking of writing a book about signature quilts." Her face was a study in controlled dismay. "Me, too," she said quietly. We parted, each puzzled about what to do.

Susan took the first step. In a letter that would have taken first prize in the Diplomacy Olympics, she asked if I would consider a collaborative work. Little did Susan know at the time how relieved I was to receive her offer! Apart from the daunting news that my friend was working on the same subject, I was laboring to improve my writing-on-quilts skills. Susan's invitation was the obvious solution. I immediately telephoned and said with wholehearted enthusiasm, "Let's write *the* book on signature quilts!" And so it began.

Susan's Perspective

When I see an old quilt, I ache to know its story, but the quilt yields up little of its history. My longing to know is frustrated because, although the quilt may sing part of its story in clear colors with strong design, it hides the essential story of its maker.

Would an artist work so long and hard on a painting and not sign it? What modesty controlled these women of the nineteenth century who did not think of their quilts as more than simply bedcovers? They labored for months and sometimes years to add beauty to utility. Yet their vision was limited, and they could not foresee that we, their descendents, would appreciate and want to document their efforts.

Fortunately for us, the signature quilt tradition of the nineteenth century not only encouraged these modest women to sign quilts, but required them to do so. They weren't signing as proud quiltmakers; they were friends giving solace to family, friends and strangers, which made signing quilts an acceptable activity.

Our knowledge of nineteenth century quiltmaking would be scant had there not been signature quilts. Begun in the 1830's and lasting, with ups and downs, well into the twentieth century, the tradition of signing quilts provides information on women which otherwise would have been lost. As Linda Otto Lipsett observes in *Remember Me*, signature quilts are "the only remaining records of the women whose names are inscribed on them."[1]

We quilters of the late twentieth century are fortunate to be able to participate in the revival of the signature quilt tradition and to look back at the world of the nineteenth century women who began it. That world, although fraught with change and hardship, included at least touches of gentleness, color and beauty. These touches are recorded in their quilts.

As Pepper and I have worked on the book and the quilts, our friendship has grown. We offer *The Signature Quilt* as a gift to you, our fellow quilters. May you use the information and patterns provided to make signature quilts which cement friendships of your own and mark our generation's place in the history of both women and their quilts. Pepper and I are honored to be part of this tradition.

The Signature Quilt Timeline

Friendship Quilts 1840 – 1945	Fund-raising Quilts 1834 – 1920	Presentation Quilts 1870 – 1920
Most popular 1840 – 1865	Anti-Slavery Quilts 1834 – 1861 Women's Rights Quilts 1848 – Early 1900's Temperance Quilts 1874 – Early 1900's Civil War Quilts 1861 – 1865	Most popular 1880 – 1900

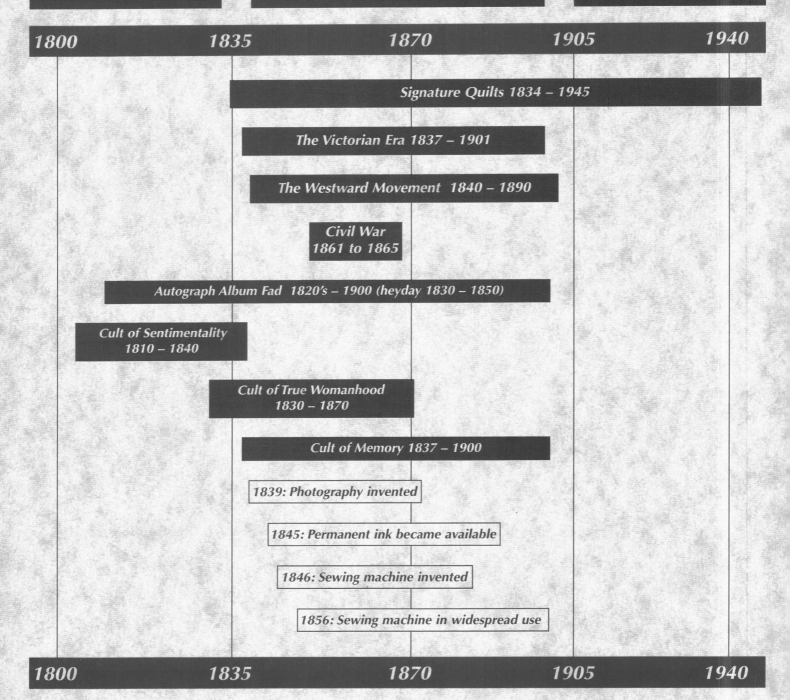

1800   1835   1870   1905   1940

Signature Quilts 1834 – 1945

The Victorian Era 1837 – 1901

The Westward Movement 1840 – 1890

Civil War 1861 to 1865

Autograph Album Fad 1820's – 1900 (heyday 1830 – 1850)

Cult of Sentimentality 1810 – 1840

Cult of True Womanhood 1830 – 1870

Cult of Memory 1837 – 1900

1839: Photography invented

1845: Permanent ink became available

1846: Sewing machine invented

1856: Sewing machine in widespread use

1800   1835   1870   1905   1940

Book One
The
Traditions

We have chosen to begin The Signature Quilt with an historical overview of the traditions of writing on quilts because we believe this will enhance the making of your own signature quilts. Understanding our connection to the past helps us to perpetuate these traditions. We hope you will enjoy reading about what our quiltmaking ancestors accomplished, and appreciate how valuable their legacy is to our efforts today.

Founders' Quilt by The Annapolis Quilt Guild, Annapolis, Maryland, 1980. 56 x 56 inches.
Collection of the Annapolis Quilt Guild.

The Legacy

As we begin to consider the traditions of the signature quilt, questions arise about the role we play as inheritors of these traditions, particularly as the end of the twentieth century approaches. In the midst of a resurgence of quiltmaking unimaginable forty years ago, we may wonder how women of this enlightened age can return to the very domesticity they and their mothers fought to escape. Perhaps the answer lies in the fact that people must react to the age in which they live. Finding themselves surrounded by unprecedented change, many women today find quilting to be a haven, a return to the comfort of a practical yet beautiful craft. Quilting connects us to the women who preceded us and binds us to our contemporaries, a connection without conflict and filled with the joy of beauty, creativity, and friendship.

The phenomenon of signature quilts is part of this movement. Signed quilts fill many needs, from affirming relationships and marking momentous occasions to raising funds for worthy causes. Friendship quilt groups, which make quilts for every conceivable occasion, are springing up all over the world.

The reasons for the enormous appeal of signature quilts at the end of the twentieth century echo the reasons for their popularity beginning over one hundred and fifty years ago.

Life for women at the end of the twentieth century is, at best, confusing. Consider some of the pressures we are experiencing:

• Society is rapidly undergoing great changes.
• The role of women in the family and in society continues to change.
• Old values are under debate and attack.
• The mobility of society means families and friends are constantly moving in and out of each others' lives.

In the face of all of this, women find comfort in affirming family, friendship, and love. They feel the need to celebrate and commemorate life's events, and they strive to preserve the worthwhile rituals that are disappearing.

Without realizing it, we have chosen methods of coping with our lives which echo those used by our ancestors. There is a focus today on sentimentality or *sensibility* as the Victorians called it, just as there was one hundred and fifty years ago. Many sentimental activities, popular in both eras, serve to strengthen relationships. These include the exchange of such remembrances as calling cards, gift books of sentimental phrases, greeting cards, and small tokens. Today there is a revival of the journal-keeping popular in the last century. At that time, journals, called *commonplace books*, were described as "treasuries to save poetry, prose, observations, and clippings."[6]

The first signature quilts developed as one way of coping with the loss of friends. Lipsett states that a signed quilt owned by a pioneer woman was different from her other quilts because "it had names on it, names of her loved ones, some of them no longer living, and it held memories. That made it special. It was her personal treasure."[7] It is no coincidence that we are once again making signature quilts.

Signature quilts made today are and will remain equally special as symbols of love and friendship. They are evidence of how women can create beauty in adversity and of how quilting can offer refuge and hope in disturbing times.

Classic Friendship Sampler by Pepper Cory, Lansing, Michigan, 1995. Quilted by Lois Miller, Ohio; finished by Ada Miller, Ohio. 55 x 72 inches. Collection of the quiltmaker.

The Signature Quilt Defined

When we refer to *signature quilts* in this book, we include all quilts which contain signed blocks, whether the signatures are inked, embroidered, cross-stitched or otherwise applied. These quilts may celebrate relationships or special occasions (friendship, leave-taking or reunion, marriage, birth, freedom, retirement, mourning). They may have been made to help raise money for worthy causes. This broad definition allows us to include the many different kinds of signed quilts and the great variety of blocks found on them.

Most signed quilts have been called *friendship quilts* by quilt historians writing in recent years. For our purposes, we prefer to include *friendship quilts* as a category within the larger group of *signature quilts*.

When studying antique signed quilts, some researchers have distinguished between *friendship* and *album* quilts by the way in which they were constructed. Jessica F. Nicoll defines *friendship quilts* as those made by repeating one block, while *album quilts* combined many different blocks, both pieced and appliquéd.[2] However, according to Jane Bentley Kolter, although *friendship quilts* made early in the nineteenth century were one-pattern quilts, by the end of the century they too might have included both pieced and appliquéd blocks. Kolter prefers to distinguish between *friendship* and *album quilts* by their intentions: "While the album quilt was competitive, the friendship quilt was less so," and their sophistication: *friendship quilts* were simpler, less elegant, and more primitive or "more homey, in both senses of the word."[3]

The fact that there was usually very little quilting on friendship quilts contributes to their primitive appearance. Lipsett believes that friendship quilts did not contain large amounts of fine quilting because the quilting was considered unimportant; they were made "primarily for [their] sentimental value, not for use."[4] The blocks used were frequently simple patterns as seen on "everyday, scrap-bag quilts."[5]

We prefer to define the various categories of signature quilts by purpose.

Friendship quilts are quilts made to bind friends and loved ones. They include both single block quilts and album quilts.

Presentation quilts from the nineteenth century were made to be given to important people such as ministers or teachers, often at leave-taking or to celebrate special occasions. They were constructed in both single-block and album designs, although most were single-block.

Fund-raising quilts were made to raise money for worthy causes. These causes included the abolition of slavery before the Civil War, the Temperance Movement throughout the nineteenth century, Civil War efforts on both the Union and Confederate sides, and social, political and church-related activities throughout the nineteenth and twentieth centuries. Fund-raising quilts were made in both single-block and album designs, but most seem to have been single-block.

Although these distinctions are useful, our interest lies in all signed blocks. We will use the term *signature quilts* to describe all quilts containing signed blocks. We consider any block which contains a designated place on which to write a signature block.

We present to you the traditional blocks found in all categories of signed quilts, as well as new blocks specifically designed to hold signatures. This collection of fifty signature blocks will provide you with wonderful variety and will enable you to create your own versions of these enduring quilts.

Now let us examine the signature quilts of the past, so that their traditions may inspire us to create a personal record of the times in which we live, making this legacy our very own.

The Historical Background

SOCIETY CHANGES

Signature quilts first appeared on the quilting scene in the early 1830's. The height of the quilt-signing fad lasted through the Civil War, but signature quilts continued to be made "in one guise or another...well into the twentieth century."[8] Why did these quilts become popular at this time? Many factors coalesced to encourage this first wave of signature quilts, including societal changes and new inventions of the Industrial Age.

In the mid-nineteenth century, society began to experience a powerful change from an agrarian, rural society to an industrial and urban one. For the first time in history, a majority of men were working away from the home and family, leaving the women to hold the family together. This was a major change for women, who found themselves almost entirely responsible for their children's education, values, morals, and traditions. At the same time, extended families were dispersing, removing another traditional avenue of support. Women turned to other women for support, and friendship became a vital part of their lives.

The Westward Movement

The Westward Movement affected one of the most dramatic changes in American society. At its height from 1840 to the Civil War, it tore familes and friendships apart forever. When loved ones went west, it was almost certain they would never return. Women found solace in quilting. They kept their loved ones in their hearts and memories by taking friendship quilts with them. Made by family and friends, and frequently containing scraps of clothing and names and phrases of remembrance, friendship quilts became *the tie that binds* for the women moving westward.

Looking at the timeline on page 8, you will see that the heyday of signature quilts was exactly the same thirty year period as that of the Westward Movement.

Between 1840 and 1870, a quarter of a milllion Americans crossed the continent to Oregon and California in what was considered one of the greatest migrations of modern times. . . . Women went West because there was no way for them not to go once the decision was made by their husbands and fathers.[9]

The first signature quilts were friendship quilts made in the east to be taken west. They first appeared "in the early 1840's"[10] in the "mid-Atlantic area from Trenton, New Jersey down through Philadelphia and Delaware to Baltimore, Maryland,"[11] and by the middle of that decade had spread "north to New York and New England and south to Virginia and the Carolinas, and later to the rest of the country."[12]

In the months before a woman left her home for the west, friendship quilts were created as farewell gifts. Sometimes the future traveler participated in the making of the quilt, as did Miriam Davis Colt, who recorded in her diary that her friends

held two bees for her prior to her departure from New York state for Kansas in 1856. One was for the elderly ladies, one for the younger, and both... "united pleasure with business."[13]

Sometimes the quilts were surprises. Jane Nugent Hart, when getting ready to leave Wisconsin, was surprised by a knock on her door one evening.

Jane opened it to friends and neighbors who had come to bring a farewell gift, a Friendship Album quilt. . . . The center of each block contained ink signatures of friends and neighbors who hoped to be remembered.[14]

"Quilting bees often served as ceremonial leavetakings. Women might be seeing friends and kin for the last time, severing ties with a female world inside which they had lived all their lives."[15]

Friendship quilts were made on the trails as well. Women used quilts to maintain a semblance of stability on the long trip. They made both blocks and full quilts. Some even made quilts containing the names of their fellow travelers.[16]

Thousands of friendship quilts were made during the period of the Westward Movement. These quilts were carried by their owners from the east to the west

> over the Appalachians and Alleghenies, over the Wilderness Road and the National Road, into states such as Ohio and Michigan, Wisconsin and Kansas, by wagon, stage, train, canal boat and steamboat. And, although patterns, fabrics, and inked inscriptions varied from one region to another, American's friendship quilts are remarkably similar to each other.[17]

The Changing Role of Women

In addition to the upheaval of American culture caused by the Westward Movement, another dramatic change in society led to the popularity of signature quilts. Women's roles were changing as nineteenth century society moved from an agrarian to an urban industrial society. In the former predominantly rural society, women worked alongside their men, producing tangible goods for survival. Children worked alongside both parents. But in an industrial society, men left the homes, leaving women to hold families and traditions together. Middle-class women were most affected by this change, and for support in this awesome task, they turned to each other. They

> found security in a family-based female world characterized by strong ties of mutual need and deep affection.... They broadened their definition of family to include an extensive network of female relatives [and] friends.[18]

In the mid-nineteenth century, as a result of the changes in society, there emerged what historians refer to as the *Cult of True Womanhood*, the *Cult of Domesticity*, the *Cult of Sentimentality*, or the *Cult of Memory*. The values espoused in the new Cult emphasized home, family, kinship, friendship and memory, all designed to maintain old values and traditions. This ideology "was a conservative reaction to profound changes that were...occurring."[19] Many quilts of this period memorialized relationships and the rites of passage in women's lives. This was also a time when death was a frequent if unwelcome companion, especially for women and children. Quilts also served as lasting memorials to lost loved ones.

Prior to the development of the signature quilt, women displayed affection for each other with autograph albums. They served the same purpose as quilts, acting as "tangible links to absent sisters"[20]

and recording the thoughts of friends and relatives, both men and women, for reading and remembering.

A remembrance in an Autograph Album.

Gift books were the rage from the 1820's to the 1860's; they were the source for much of the writing we see on signature quilts and in autograph albums. These little books contained poems and phrases of love and affection, written especially for people who didn't know quite how to express themselves. Called *autograph writers*, they had titles such as *Token of Friendship*, *Fifteen Hundred Selections in Prose and Verse for Autograph Albums*, *Memorial*, and *The Gift*.[21] The popular magazine, *Godey's Lady's Book*, also published poems and quotations on friendship and remembrance.[22]

As tokens of friendship, calling cards were "exchanged and collected by the millions."[23] They contained the same kinds of sentiments and symbols which appeared on quilts and in autograph albums: phrases of love and affection and pictures of such things as hands, flowers, and doves.

Calling Cards

Gift giving among women was popular. The gifts were generally small, inexpensive, domestic items such as bookmarks, pincushions, needlecases, valentines, and little gift books.[24]

All of these activities, inspired and encouraged by the *Cult of True Womanhood*, served serious purposes: to mark life's milestones and transitions, to hold families and friends together, and to emphasize traditions that were worth keeping in times of change.[25] "Women used their needles to make quilts that reflected the passages in their lives...birth, childhood, coming of age, marriage, death, and involvement in church and community activities."[26]

Signature quilts played a significant role in defining and achieving these goals. They provided tangible and beautiful links from generation to generation at a time when women legally owned nothing, and therefore could not bequeath anything to their daughters.[27] They provided links to friends who would be remembered long after time and distance had taken them away. They provided the quiltmakers with a reason to create items of great beauty shrouded in the cloak of usefulness.

THE PURPOSES OF SIGNATURE QUILTS

Fund-raising Quilts

From their beginnings in the 1830's, signature quilts were used to raise funds for chosen causes and to make political statements. Women saw their reform activities "as the logical extension of their duties as protectors of the home."[28]

One of the major causes for which women created signature quilts was the Temperance Movement. From its inception in the 1830's and throughout the nineteenth century, this was "one of the largest of all nineteenth century women's reform movements."[29] It was more than just a crusade against alcoholism. When women worked for temperance, they worked for other women's rights issues as well.[30] The Women's Christian Temperance Union (WCTU) chapters used quilts "extensively as fund-raisers, especially the ten-cent signature quilt."[31]

Money was made from the fund-raising quilts in two ways: the members of a community or organization "donated a dime or a quarter to have their names embroidered or inked into the quilt's design,"[32] and later the quilt was auctioned or raffled.

From the 1830's until the Civil War, women used their needles to fight against slavery as well. They held Anti-Slavery Fairs beginning in 1834 where they sold needlework of all kinds, including quilts. Many signature quilts were made for this cause.[33] Some were fund-raising quilts; others were simply statements of political sentiment, as was a wonderful baby quilt in the collection of the Chester County Historical Society (pictured on page 21). Made by the Herrick Sewing Circle of Lancaster County, Pennsylvania, the quilt contains the following inscription:

Do thou, sweet babe, in safety sleep
Beneath this canopy so fair.
Formed [sic] thy fragile limbs to keep
Protected from the chilling air.

Formed in love for Freedom's Fair
To aid a righteous cause
To help its advocates declare
God's unchangeable and equal laws.[34]

During the Civil War, women from the North and South made signature quilts to raise money for the war effort and to pay tribute to their loved ones who were fighting.[35] Even children made signature quilts. In *The American Quilt*, Roderick Kiracofe describes a friendship quilt made, signed, and donated to the war effort by northern school children and inscribed, "For any soldier who loves little children."[36]

The Civil War exhausted and sobered the nation. After the war, "sentimentalism in art and literature changed to a more realistic point of view."[37] This change is reflected in women's activities as well as in the national focus. The earlier sentimental exchanges declined in popularity and were replaced by the zeal for social reform.

Fund-raising quilts continued to be made throughout the rest of the nineteenth century and well into the first quarter of the twentieth century,[38] but as the century closed, quilting declined in popularity. Many women were now working, educational opportunities had improved, inexpensive commercially-made blankets were available, and quilting was not considered fashionable.

By the early 1900's, fund-raising efforts were focused locally. Most fund-raising quilts were made to raise money for civic groups and church-related causes such as building campaigns and missionary work.[39]

Red and white or blue and white, usually in solid fabrics, were popular color combinations for fund-raising quilts, and after the 1880's most signatures were embroidered. The red and white embroidered quilt detail shown here is typical of fund-raising quilts of the time. Made in 1912 by the Order of the Eastern Star in South Bend, Indiana, it contains wheels of names, all purchased by helpful donors.

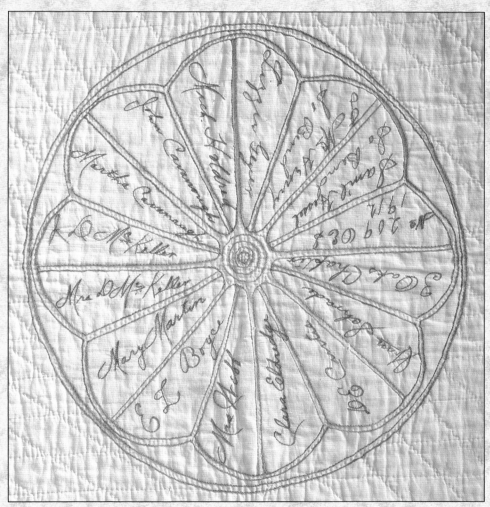

Embroidered signatures.

From 1925 to 1959, fewer fund-raising quilts were made, "although there were still seamstresses willing to embroider hundreds of names on a quilt for a good cause."[40]

Friendship and Presentation Quilts

Friendship quilts and friendship-album quilts, so popular in the mid-nineteenth century, declined by the mid 1870's[41] and were passé before the country's Centennial in 1876.[42] Although signature quilts continued to be made, inked until the end of the 1880's and embroidered after that, they were usually either fund-raisers or presentation quilts.

During the late nineteenth century, presentation quilts were popular, made by admirers for important people such as ministers and teachers, and for special occasions such as departures and retirements. The patterns were usually simple ones like the *Schoolhouse* and the *Fan,* although the *Chimney Sweep* continued to be popular.[43] The colors, as with the fund-raising quilts of the time, were often solid red and white, with lots of white on which many people could write. (See *The Monument* on page 22.)

A few friendship quilts were made in the 1930's and 1940's. Quiltmakers were encouraged by periodicals such as the *Kansas City Star,* which printed patterns weekly, and once in a while presented a friendship block. The captions on the four clippings presented on the next page illustrate this decline.

On May 3, 1933, the writer offered a pattern called *Friendship Star,* saying that quilting was bringing back "an old custom, that of exchanging blocks with friends."

The July 4, 1934 block, *Friendship Quilt,* was described as a "name quilt made by the women of the Central Presbyterian Church, Kansas City, nearly fifty years old."

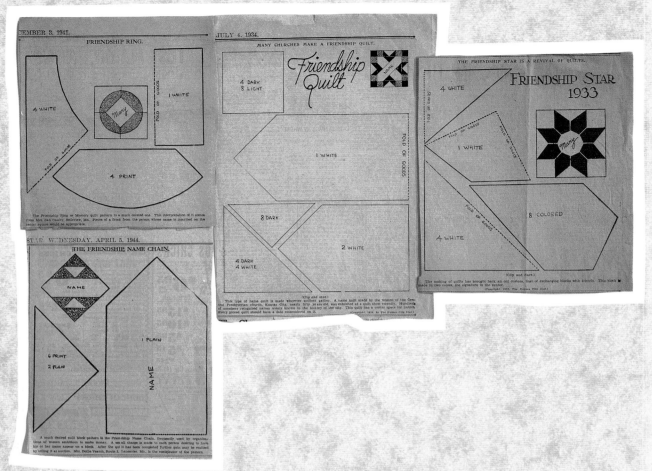

Four Friendship blocks offered by the *Kansas City Star*.

The *Friendship Ring*, from the December 3, 1941 edition of the paper was also called the *Memory* block and was described as a "much-coveted one."

In presenting *The Friendship Name Chain* on April 5, 1944, the writer referred to the history of how fund-raising quilts were made. She said that the block was

frequently used by organizations of women ambitious to make money. A small charge is made to each person desiring to have his or her name appear on a block. After the quilt has been completed further gain may be realized by selling it at auction.

References to signature quilts after the 1920's are infrequent, and after the fund-raising fad died out, few signature quilts were made. The quilting groups which existed were often social in nature, and the signature quilts they made were friendship quilts.[44] We often see embroidered signatures on these quilts.

A few presentation quilts were inspired by the war effort for World War II, but these were usually tied, not quilted.[45] By mid-century, the signature quilt had faded gradually into obscurity, not to be seen again until its revival in the late 1980's.

Snowflake, maker unknown, Connecticut, 1850. 80 x 80 inches. Collection of Susan McKelvey.

1840-1865 *Friendship Quilts*

The first signature quilt fad began in the 1840's. This *Snowflake* quilt, dated 1850, illustrates several characterisics of quilts of the period. The combination of turkey red and green was a popular quilt color scheme at the time, and the *Snowflake* block was a popular signature quilt block. The inking is minute and as fine as that found on the best Baltimore Album quilts of the same era. Oddly, only three blocks were inked, and although the names are different, the inking was done freehand and by the same writer.

The Primitive Hall Quilt Top, 1842-1843. 66 x 66 inches. Collection of the Chester County Historical Society, West Chester, Pennsylvania. Photograph by George J. Fistrovich.

1840-1865 Friendship Quilts

The *Primitive Hall Quilt Top*, from the collection of the Chester County Historical Society and dated 1842 and 1843, is a superb example of an early signature quilt. It contains fine inked drawings and freehand writing typical of mid-nineteenth century signature quilts, and the two completely inked blocks are rare. The fabrics and soft brown and pink color scheme are also typical of the period, but the accents of gold and chartreuse are unusual. Constructed in the English piecing method over paper templates and still containing the paper, the quilt top was made for Sarah Pennock, born in 1840, the daughter of Casper Pennock, a prominent Quaker physician and his non-Quaker wife, Caroline Morris. Two blocks, *Sarah's Star* and *Friendship Rosette*, are included in the Signature Block Collection.

Abolitionist Baby Quilt by the Herrick Sewing Circle, Lancaster County, Pennsylvania, c. 1830's. 56 x 56 inches. Collection of the Chester County Historical Society, West Chester, Pennsylvania. Photograph by George J. Fistrovich.

1834-1920 Presentation and Fund-raising Quilts

Throughout the nineteenth century, women made presentation quilts as expressions of all kinds of sentiments. This Abolitionist quilt from the Chester County Historical Society was made to be presented to a baby. The inscription in the center block (see p. 16) indicates it was made for "Freedom's Fair," probably an anti-slavery fair. This quilt is a poignant reminder of how strongly-held beliefs permeated every aspect of womens' lives. Made in the popular madder browns of the period, and inked and signed with anti-slavery admonitions by a group of women, it represents many quilts made from the 1830's until the Civil War. It is touching that the makers felt strongly enough about the issue of slavery to begin a baby's life under such a quilt.

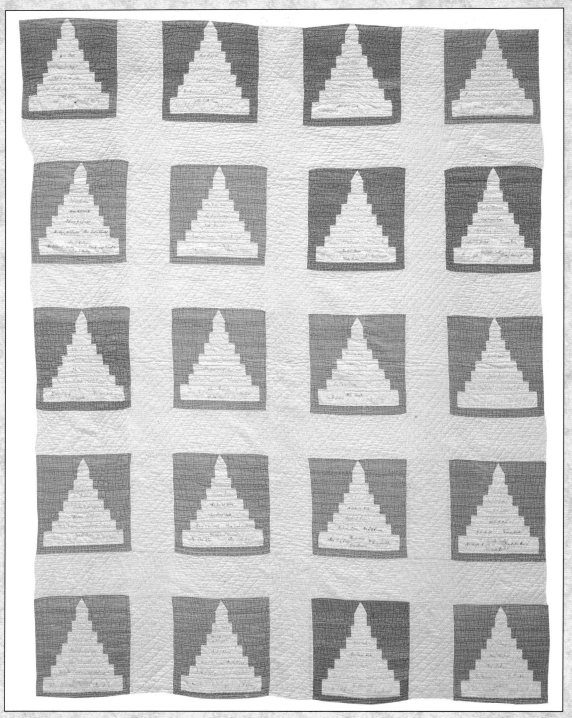

The Monument by The Ladies of The Baptist Aid Society, Eastport, Michigan, 1888. 72 x 80 inches.
Collection of Susan McKelvey.

1834-1920 Presentation and Fund-raising Quilts

Presentation quilts and fund-raising quilts were often intertwined. This red and white quilt is dated 1888, the height of presentation quiltmaking, and was made by The Ladies of The Baptist Aid Society in Eastport, Michigan for presentation to Mrs. M. Melvin. The red and white color scheme in solid fabrics is typical of both kinds of quilts at that time. The quilt is entitled *The Monument*, and provides many spaces in which to sign. Each block is filled with names, and the inking seems to have been done by several people.

Checkerboard, maker unknown, c. 1900. 76 x 76 inches. Collection of Mary and Tom Sharp, Georgetown, Texas.

1900-1920 Fund-raising Quilts Remain Popular

Fund-raising quilts remained popular through the first decades of the twentieth century. They were usually made in solid red and white color schemes, but in contrast to the inked signatures on the 1888 Baptist Ladies Aid Society quilt, they were usually embroidered in the color to match the fabric. Fund-raising was done for every kind of cause from church projects and charities to political efforts. The embroidered signatures are unusual in this quilt because they are large satin-stitched words, white on the red fabric and red on the white fabric.

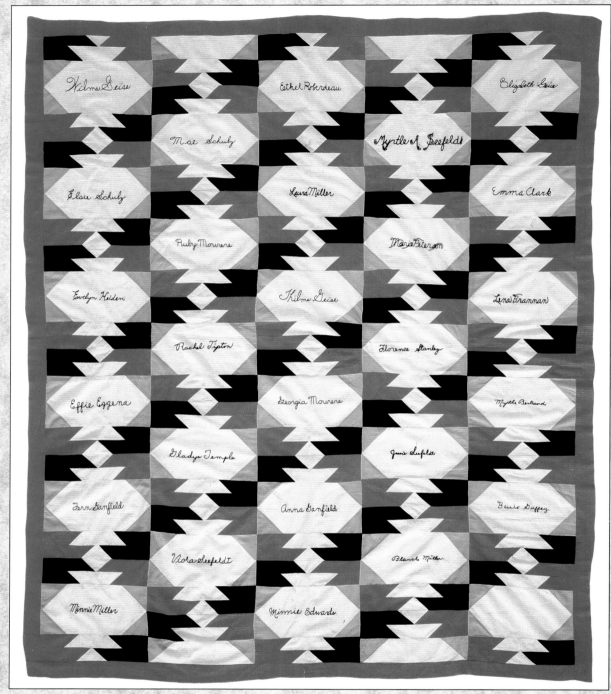

The Chief, maker unknown, c. 1931. 62 x 76 inches. The pattern was published in Ruby McKim's *Parade of States for 48 Quilts* in 1931. Collection of Pepper Cory.

Early 1900's-1930's The Craftsman and Art Deco Influence

In the early 1900's, quilt styles and patterns were greatly influenced by newspaper and magazine articles which regularly produced patterns. In reaction to the unbridled clutter of the Victorian period, the Craftsman and Art Deco styles emphasized simple lines and vivid colors. While floral appliqué quilt kits were popular at this time, they were rarely used as signature quilts. The blocks promoted by the publications of the time were simple, and this quilt top exemplifies the style. Probably made in South Dakota in the 1930's, the bold, black embroidered signatures complement the architectural quality of the pieced pattern.

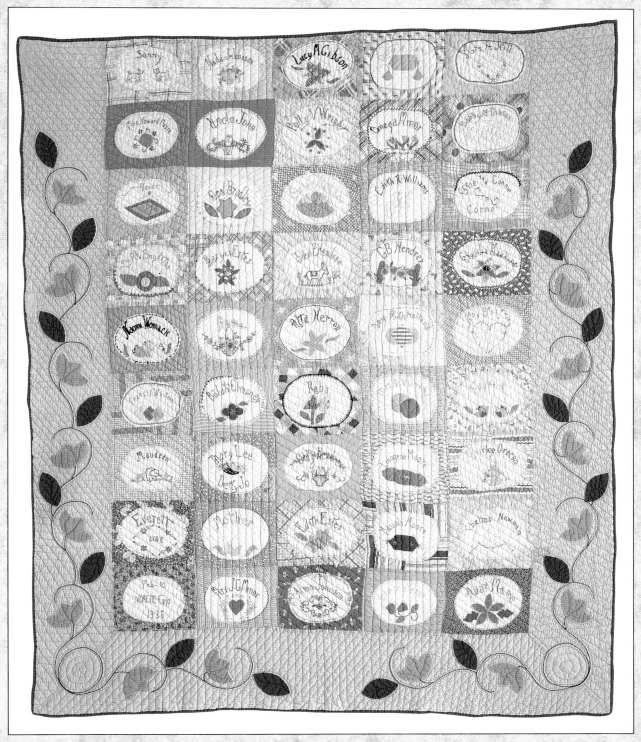

Embroidered Friendship Quilt, makers unknown, Claymore, Oklahoma, 1936. 62 x 60 inches.
Collection of Pepper Cory.

The 1930's and 1940's Friendship Quilts

By the 1930's, fund-raising quilts were much less popular, but some friendship quilts were still made. Their style had greatly changed, however. This charming example is typical of the period in both style of construction and in color and fabric. The block is simple. The signatures are large, embroidered, and embellished with embroidered flowers and vines. The fabrics are feedsacks and period prints in bright pastels, the batting is thick, and the quilting is simple. From an estate in Claymore, Oklahoma, the quilt is dated 1936.

Friendship Links, makers unknown, c. 1950. 71 x 92 inches. The pattern is from the *Chicago Tribune*, December 24, 1933. Collection of Pepper Cory.

1940-1980 Friendship Quilts

We see relatively few signature quilts from the 1940's until their revival in the late 1980's. This quilt top was made in the 1950's. The pattern, *Friendship Links*, was printed in the *Chicago Tribune* quilt column in 1933. There are no signatures on the quilt; the theme of friendship was symbolized by the choice of pattern and by pairing fabrics donated by friends. The unlikely fabric combinations bear out this theory. The quilt was discovered in Houston, Texas.

The Traditions

Leslie's Graduation Quilt by Susan McKelvey, Millersville, Maryland, 1991. 56 x 70 inches. Collection of Leslie McKelvey, Beaufort, North Carolina.

1980-Today The Signature Quilt Revival

Signature quilts returned to popularity in the late 1980's, and today they are well represented at every quilt show. No one style predominates. *Leslie's Graduation Quilt* is a pieced friendship quilt typical of the period. Susan made it in 1991 for her daughter as a college graduation present and invited her sorority sisters to sign it. The pattern is an old one, which Susan calls *Betsey Wright's Block* after the quilt in *Remember Me*, where she first admired it. A favorite signature quilt pattern being used today, this traditional block is made contemporary through the use of bright marbled fabrics.

Holiday Houses by members of The Sunbonnet Sues in Canoes, Lansing, Michigan: Gayle Cain, Enola Clegg, Daisy DeHaven, Edna Eckert, Jan Gagliano, Barbara Hawkins, Gail Hill, Mary Hutchins, Jane Johnson and Carol Seamon, 1995. Arranged by Pepper Cory and quilted by Loyola Dysinger, Perry, Michigan. 58 x 74 inches. Collection of Pepper Cory.

1980-Today The Signature Quilt Revival

Holiday Houses, made by Pepper and the members of her friendship bee, The Sunbonnet Sues in Canoes, was the result of Pepper's challenge to her friends to use the *House* Block to portray any holiday except Christmas. This quilt illustrates how tradition may be used as a springboard to creativity. The colors, styles and settings of the signed quilts of the 1990's display many new images rooted in tradition.

Book Two
The
Techniques

How were quilts signed in the nineteenth century, and how can we replicate them today? In Book Two, we acquaint you with early methods for signing quilts, and demonstrate exciting new methods for writing on and decorating them. Helpful suggestions for color selection and working together in groups are also discussed. The easy, practical techniques presented here will enable you to enhance your quilts with lovely signatures.

My Little House in the Big Woods by Barbara Hawkins, Lansing, Michigan, 1995. 45 x 51 inches. Collection of the quiltmaker.

Tools For Making Early Signature Quilts

In the mid-nineteenth century, the skills for signing quilts developed as the useful tools became available.

Ink

Permanent ink became commercially available in 1845, making writing on cloth easy and reliable. Before that time, if quilts were signed at all, they were signed in minute cross-stitch or embroidery, as were all the linens in a family. Very little inking was done, and the available inks were homemade. Not only was the process for brewing homemade ink time-consuming, but the resulting ink was hard on fabric, causing it to deteriorate rapidly. This early 1800's recipe for homemade ink shows what a potent potion it must have been:

> Take one gallon of soft water, and pour it boiling hot on one pound of powdered galls. . . . Set in sun in summer, or in winter warm by any fire and let stand 2 or 3 days. Add to them half a pound of green vitriol powdered; let stand again 2 or 3 days; add further 5 ounces of gum arabic dissolved in a quart of boiling water and lastly 2 ounces of alum; after which the ink should be strained through a coarse linen cloth for use.[46]

This thick ink contained "gall-nuts, copperas and gum" and

> minute particles of...iron and tannin in it that caused cloth to rot quickly, leaving only a ghostly silhouette of the inked inscriptions, as well as giving those inks brown and yellow tints, instead of good blacks.[47]

Indelible ink containing no iron had been patented in both France and America by the 1840's. At last, women could apply ink with confidence that their precious quilts would not be damaged.[48] The availability of good permanent ink probably contributed to the popularity of signature quilts.

Pens

At the same time, there was a dramatic change in pen points from gray goose quill to steel[49] and even silver points. These new pens allowed greater control than the quill pens, and the beautiful writing and drawing we see on signature quilts of the time is the result.

Penmanship Instruction

In the nineteenth century, middle class women of all ages placed an increased emphasis on penmanship. This was a contributing factor to the beauty of signature quilts. Although elegant handwriting had been important in the hiring of men for clerical work, no such situation existed for women until this time. "Fine handwriting, an attribute prized in England, was another important feature of an American girl's education. Some girls...attended special schools for writing."[50] During this period, "a fancy Spencerian script and other calligraphic squiggles and flourishes were taught in the schools."[51] For those who could not attend classes, "*self-instructors* – manuals in fancy pen-drawing – provided motivation and instruction on how to accomplish feats of embellishment with the tip of a pen."[52] One such manual from the 1880's, *Hill's Manual of Social and Business Forms*, advised that

Autograph books and covers

"good writing is a fine art, and is to the eye what good language is to the ear."[53]

Women of the time were expected to keep commonplace books filled with collections of "poetry, prose, observations, and clippings,"[54] and autograph books were popular throughout the nineteenth century. Both kinds of books were expected to be enhanced with "calligraphic scrolled drawings."[55] These pen and ink drawings, often detailed and realistic, were popular just before the invention of photography in 1839 and were "a common way for untrained artists to make detailed observations of life around them."[56] Women who were accustomed to drawing with pen and ink, and embellishing their handwriting with squiggles and calligraphic pictures, applied these skills to their quiltmaking,

leaving us a legacy of exquisitely inked signature quilts to admire and replicate.

A remembrance in an Autograph Album.

Signing Quilts in the Nineteenth Century

Throughout the history of quiltmaking, women have signed quilts in many ways, including inking, stenciling, embroidery, quilting, and cross-stitch. Before the advent of signature quilts in the 1830's, quilt signing was usually done with a needle in minute cross-stitch or embroidery.

With the availability of commercial ink, inking immediately became popular because it saved time and allowed women to use their writing skills on fabric just as they did on paper.

Inking remained popular after the Civil War and into the twentieth century, but by the 1890's embroidered signatures re-emerged. They were now large, showy, and frequently in vivid color. The block on the right contains embroidered signatures from a fund-raising quilt. The use of many colors is unusual. The *Crazy Quilt* fad and the resulting availability of a variety of embroidery threads certainly contributed to its increased usage.

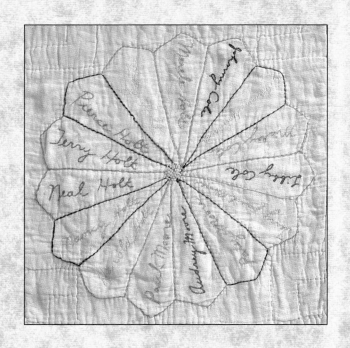

Inked signature on **Snowflake** block.

Stencils

INKED SIGNATURES

By examining quilts from the mid-ninteenth century, we know that inked signatures were applied to quilts in three ways: stenciling, stamping, and freehand writing.

Stenciling

Stencils of the time were made from tin, nickel and copper. Because they were much thinner than the metal and acrylic stencils available today, these stencils could produce fine signatures on fabric. They were custom-made for individuals, with names in script or block lettering. Some were probably used to mark linens as well as quilts. Stencil-making was a craft form in its own right at that time. "Plates were typically cut by tinsmiths for use in labels and decorations of all sorts."[57] The seven stencils which follow are from the nineteenth century. Notice the undecorated stencil with three names on it. It was probably a linen marker.

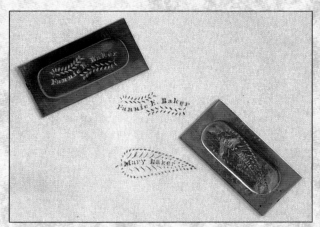

Stenciled signatures.

Stamping

Metal stamps became available about the same time as metal stencils, but stamps seem to have been more widely used. The handles of the stamps were made in both wood and metal, and some were exquisitely decorated. The stamping mechanism was made of lead. Each stamp came with a box of changeable type so letters could be combined to spell different names. Many stamps contained lovely medallions filled with some combination of flowers, angels, lyres and doves. On one quilt we might see a different name in each block, but all the names are surrounded by the same stamped design. This kind of quilt was signed with the same stamp, but the type was changed for each signature.

This block from an early twentieth century quilt is unusual in the way it was stamped. The names were stamped one letter at a time with large stamps which filled the entire block.

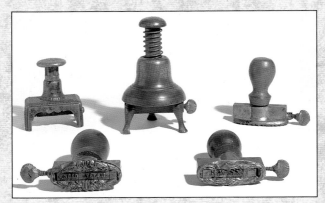

Nineteenth century signature stamps

Detail of bottom of a stamp

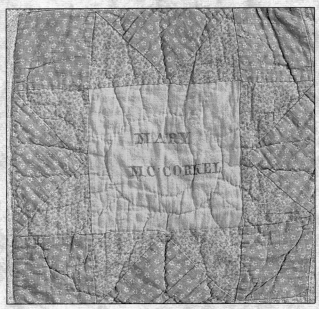

A twelve inch block from **Stamped Stars.** Collection of Eileen Schamel.

A stamped quilt block.

Freehand Writing

The most popular method of signing quilts in the nineteenth century was freehand writing. Sometimes the signatures on a quilt are all so different that we are fairly certain they were signed by different individuals. On other quilts, however, the handwriting throughout the quilt is the same. Perhaps on those quilts someone whose handwriting was particularly fine, either a member of the group or an outsider, was asked or hired to do the writing. On some quilts, as in the sample block on the following page, names were written in fancy script by a calligrapher and also signed below by the maker. Judging from the quilts we have studied, the most popular way of signing in the nineteenth century was freehand.

The Techniques

Small piece of twice signed fabric.

Occasionally, we see pieces of paper basted onto antique blocks or a quilt top. According to Lipsett, "When all the blocks were to be signed by one hand...it was a common practice to baste a small strip of paper with the intended person's name to each block, so that no one would be accidentally omitted. Many times these names were cut from signatures on letters, to be sure of the spelling."[58]

The Hours of the Day by Susan McKelvey, Millersville, Maryland, 1995. 40 x 40 inches. Collection of the quiltmaker.

Signing Quilts Today

❧

Quilters have always used the tools available to them to reach their creative goals. This is as true today as it was in the 1840's, when permanent ink was invented, prompting great interest in making signature quilts. The methods of today echo the interest and popularity of past efforts at signing quilts. Quiltmakers of the 1990's sign their quilts in a number of ways, including three used on antique quilts: stenciling, stamping, and freehand drawing.

WHEN TO WRITE

No matter which kind of embellishment you choose, it is best to decorate the fabric before putting the quilt together. It is possible to write on the blocks at any time before quilting. After that, the puffiness of the quilting makes it difficult, although not impossible, to write nicely. We frequently are asked whether to write on the fabric before or after constructing a block or an entire quilt. You may do either, but there are obvious advantages to writing first, because at any time in the inking process you might make a mistake. It happens. Susan found the antique block below in a shop in Connecticut. We love it because it reminds us that our forebears had bad days too. The quiltmaker pieced the block and then set out to sign it, but things went awry! In those days, writers used split point pens and liquid ink. Inking with these pens was difficult because pressing too hard as one wrote might split the pen point too wide and lead to a blotch, which is what probably happened to this quilter. Rather than waste the block, she then used it for practice, writing several times in different directions.

Badly inked block.

Keeping our frustrated forebear's experience in mind, prudence dictates that we do the inking before sewing the block. It may seem odd to sign an appliqué block before the many hours of sewing, but it is easy to plan. Just as you plan and mark the layout of the fabric pieces to be applied, you can plan where and how to sign the block. Then, after basting or marking for appliqué but before beginning to sew, take the time to ink. If you make a mistake at this point, you have lost only a square of background fabric.

STENCILING

Stenciling designs on signature quilts is a wonderful way to enhance their beauty. The many attractive stencils available today complement both pieced and appliquéd quilts, and they may be combined with inked signatures to create stunning effects. Try stenciling some signature blocks, and you will be eager to add stenciling to your repertoire of quilting skills.

Stenciling is easy, quick and fun. There are two kinds of stenciling paints which work well on fabric: *water-based acrylics*, and *oil-based paints* (which come in liquid, cream, and stick form). Water-based paints are familiar to many stencilers because of their quick drying time and the ease of clean-up. Pepper prefers oil-based paints in their most convenient form, the oil-stick. Whichever you choose, it is worth taking the time to pre-test both paints and fabrics.

Pre-Test the Paint on Fabric

Making samples does more than test the durability of the paint. It lets you practice your stenciling technique before actually touching the quilt.

1. Test the paints on small pieces of the same fabrics used in your quilt.
2. Set the paint as directed by the manufacturer.
3. Gently wash the samples to see if they hold up to your satisfaction. Subject them to the kind of cleaning your quilt will likely encounter.

The Advantages of Oil-Sticks

The advantages of stenciling with oil-sticks are numerous. Unlike smelly, old-fashioned oils, which were the consistency of thick syrup, oil-sticks are virtually odorless. There is little waste with oil-sticks. They are made in the form of enormous, paper-wrapped crayons. Before using them, the stenciler peels back the paper and scrapes off the protective skin on the tip of the stick. This skin re-forms from exposure to air (after about a day), so the stick automatically re-seals itself.

Designs on fabrics stenciled with oil-sticks remain soft and pliable. Delicate shading is possible by stenciling sparingly with a second color oil-stick over the primary design. With the new odorless turpentine-based cleaners, both the stencils and brushes come clean quickly. Finally, oil-stick stenciling, when set as recommended by the manufacturer, is permanent on fabric.

Supplies for Stenciling with Oil-Sticks

Prewashed 100% cotton fabric
Stencils
Masking tape
Spray adhesive
Oil-sticks
Stencil brushes, one for each color stick used
A pad of clean paper towels
Turpentine-based cleaning solvent

Directions

- Wash the fabric with detergent in warm water. Dry and iron it. Thorough washing is necessary to break down the sizing, thus allowing the paint to bond with the fibers.
- Apply pieces of masking tape over any parts of the stencil you do not want in the design.

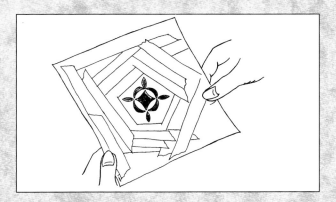

- Hold down the stencil on top of the pad of paper towels and draw a thick line of oil-stick around the holes on the stencil.

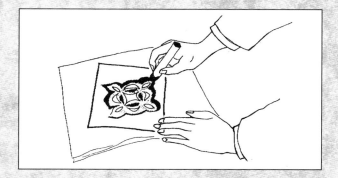

Try not to smear paint into the holes. Think of a little girl playing with Mommy's make-up who gets the lipstick all around but not on her lips. That is how the oil-stick on the stencil looks prior to stenciling.

- Lift the stencil from the towels and lightly spray adhesive on the back.
- Position the stencil over a double thickness of fabric, taking care that the surface under the fabric is clean and free from nicks or bumps that would show later in the stenciled design.
- Holding the stencil brush perpendicular to the stencil, bear down slightly and swirl the brush in a circular motion, gently bringing the paint into the stencil's openings.

Do not swipe the brush sideways; instead, continue in a swirling motion. Pay special attention to defining the edges of the stenciled design, and stencil more lightly when filling in large areas. Lift the stencil away from the fabric when you think the design is complete.

- Clean the stencil by placing it on the towel pad and wiping it with a rag or towel soaked in cleaner. Put the brush in a glass half-filled with cleaner, vigorously swirl it around, and pounce it on the towel pad until no color shows.
- Let the stenciled fabric air-dry at least twenty-four hours, and then set according to the manufacturer's directions.
- When ironing stenciled fabric, use a hot, dry iron. Place a clean pressing cloth between the fabric and the iron's surface.

Combining Stenciling and Inking

Combining stenciled designs and inked details creates wonderful effects. After stenciling a design, *add details* with a permanent pen. *Introduce shading* with lots of tiny dots. Use the pen to *draw fake quilting* or appliqué stitches. They can be real eye foolers, especially when inked in colors darker than the stenciled designs.

Pepper's **Shakertown Quilt** (on the facing page) combines a simple pieced block, *Puss in the Corner*, with alternate stenciled squares on a pale parchment color. Pepper stenciled the *Reel* blocks (using her own commercially available stencil) prior to teaching quilt classes at Shakertown, the restored Shaker village at Pleasant Hill, Kentucky. All forty students individualized their squares. Some wrote around the stenciled designs and others right through them. The designs were outlined with a Pigma™ pen after stenciling, and the signatures were rendered in different colored pens. While some of the signers accepted the stenciled designs as frames for their signatures, others considered them challenges! After piecing the blocks, Pepper added more stenciling and writing in the parchment top and bottom borders.

Stenciling to the Rescue

When people are signing blocks for the first time, they are sometimes timid about filling an entire patch. If someone places a signature in the corner of a patch, a little theraputic stenciling may greatly improve the block. Look over your stencils and find a small design such as a tiny heart or a flower which you can add to the space. Mask off the rest of the stencil, and stencil the decorative detail. Be careful when stenciling at this stage because the block or quilt top has already been completed.

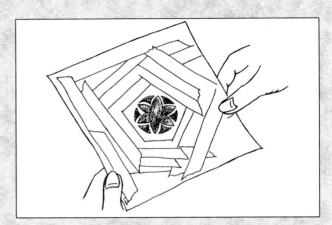

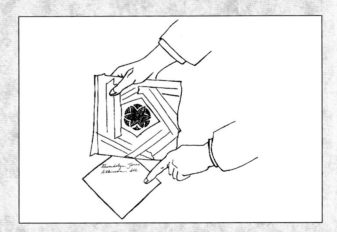

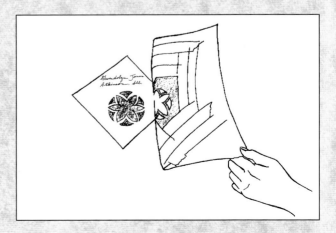

The Techniques

Shakertown Quilt by Pepper Cory, Lansing, Michigan, 1995. Quilted by Corona Weldy, Indiana. Block signatures by members of The Kentucky Heritage Quilt Society. 60 x 70 inches. Collection of the quiltmaker.

A block from the **Shakertown** quilt.

RUBBER STAMPING

Rubber stamps are good tools for embellishing fabric and therefore, quilts. Many decorative stamps are available for stamping on fabric, including Signature Stamps© Susan has designed especially for signing quilts in antique style. (See *Sources*.)

Supplies for Stamping on Fabric

Stamps. Not all stamps work as well on fabric as on paper. The designs must have clear lines and be deeply cut. Stick to stamps made especially for fabric.

Fabric ink. Many different kinds are widely available. Look for quick drying, non-acidic, easy-to-use, permanent ink. Authentic antique colors are black and brown. For variety, many colors are available.

Prewashed and ironed fabric.

Stamp pad or make-up wedge (available at any cosmetic counter) and *flat dish*. You may find you prefer one over the other. Susan uses both the pad and the wedge.

Masking tape to anchor the fabric.

Directions

- *Practice*. Stamping is unreliable. Sometimes the image is clear and complete, sometimes not. Practicing with the ink and stamp of your choice is essential before putting stamp to fabric.
- *If you use a stamp pad*, pour a little paint onto the pad. Then use a toothbrush to even it out and spread it into the corners.

- *If you use a make-up wedge*, spoon a little paint onto a plate or plastic lid. You need very little paint.
- *Tape the fabric* to a smooth, flat surface so it doesn't move when stamping.
- *Ink the stamp* by tapping it lightly on the pad several times. Don't press too hard or you will get too much ink on it. To use a make-up wedge, tap the smallest side of the wedge on the paint to saturate it. Work the paint into the sponge. Using a light touch, dab the paint onto the stamp surface. Cover all of the artwork but do not allow excess paint to collect in the crevices or on the stamp foundation.
- *Press the stamp firmly* to the fabric. Take your time and press evenly on all parts of the stamp. Lift the stamp straight up. Practice will tell you how much ink it takes to get a good image.
- *If the image isn't right*, a second stamping might be necessary. Lay a piece of scrap fabric next to your final project and stamp it first, several times if necessary. Then stamp the actual block.
- *Touch up* an incomplete line with a *Pigma Pen* .01 if the color matches.

With the right stamp, ink, and practice, your inkings will look as good as those on antique quilts. Remember that stamped images on antique quilts were not always perfect. Sometimes the ink was too thick and sometimes too fine.

A modern stamped signature.

FREEHAND WRITING

Inking freehand is a wonderful way to sign quilts because it is fast and requires very little preparation or equipment. The fragile pen replicates the delicate inkings on the finest signature quilts of the nineteenth century, and the signature is yours, signed by the maker. It is just as much fun to duplicate the fine inking on old quilts as it is to imitate their fine workmanship.

The Size of the Writing

The original inkings on quilts signed in the 1850's are minute. The inking below is a detail from a block of the *Snowflake* quilt, dated 1850 (the quilt is on page 19). Notice how minute the inking is. Today we are free to write in any size we want, any-where we want, on a quilt. We may imitate the delicate inkings of the nineteenth century or be bold with large pen points.

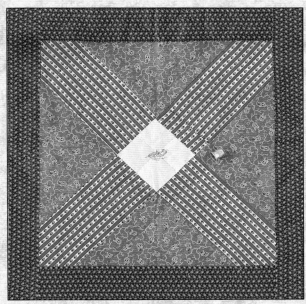

A block from the **Snowflake** quilt. The thimble shows how small nineteenth century inking could be.

Pigma .01 inking on **Starburst** block.

The Pens

Today we have the means to write beauti-fully and with confidence on signature quilts. The first and most important consideration is the pen we use. There are many pens on the market, and more are becoming available all the time. We should continually experiment with new pens, asking some simple questions:

1. How permanent is the pen through multiple washings?
2. How permanent is the pen in sunlight over time ?
3. How much does it bleed as I write?
4. Does it contain toxins that will rot the fabric over time?

These questions are not easily answered. The pens are not always designed with fabric in mind. Yet, through experimentation and evaluation, we can adapt the tools available today to our purposes.

For writing on fabric, our current favorite is the **Pigma Micron**™ for tiny inkings and the **Identipen**™ for large inkings. We use the Pigma point .01 for most writing on quilt blocks. It has a fragile, felt-tipped point and slow ink flow, so the first rule in using it is to *write with a light touch and more slowly than you would on paper.* If you press too heavily, it drags and catches on the weave of the fabric.

The Pigma is permanent on most fabrics (although signed quilts should be kept out of the sun), does not damage fabric, and writes smoothly without bleeding. It comes in several point sizes and eight colors. The point sizes range from .005 (very tiny) to .08 (thick). The size we use most is .01. This fine point replicates the tiny inkings on nine-teenth century quilts, yet it makes a solid, visible line.

When we want to write larger letters in larger spaces, we switch to the point .05 or the Identipen. The Pigma also comes in a brush tip which is wonderful for shading and drawing.

The Identipen has two points on one pen. The small point is about as large as the Pigma .05 and the large point is very large. The pen has a much faster ink flow than the Pigma, yet it doesn't bleed much, and it is ideal for writing in large spaces. The Microperm™ is a fine-pointed pen with the point size of the Pigma .01 and the ink-flow of the Identipen.

Samples of writing with different pen points.

The Pigma is available in eight colors. Black and brown reproduce the look of antique quilts. The ink we see on these old quilts is either black or has faded to a sepia brown, so both colors make antique-looking signatures. For modern embellishing, the other colors are great fun.

The Identipen also comes in eight colors. The brown is a lovely chocolate color rather than the rusty brown of the Pigma, and the other colors are bright and rich.

Navajo Inspirations I inked in colored Pigma .01.

The Fabric

General Considerations

When planning a signature quilt, choosing the fabric on which to write is an important consideration. This can be a difficult problem. At the very least, think about it early in the quilt-planning phase. We have found that the best fabric for most permanent pens is a high quality, closely woven, 100% cotton. Always pre-wash the fabric to get rid of the sizing (which acts as a barrier to ink penetration), and iron so it is smooth when you are ready to ink.

Be aware that fabrics vary; one fabric might be a good quality 100% cotton, but still bleed more than another.

Pigment White on Muslin

The popular white-on-white muslin is not an inkable fabric. The white design is actually painted on, and the ink cannot penetrate through it into the muslin. This makes writing on the fabric difficult. Also, pigment white prints tend to flake away with washing. So, although it is pretty, avoid white-on-white muslins as the fabric for your signature quilts.

Tracing on Fabric

Consider whether you will be tracing on the fabric. Those of us who cannot draw lovely banners and pictures but want them on our quilts have found that tracing them is an easy and effective method of decorating quilts. We will discuss tracing methods later, but if you think you might want to trace, be sure your fabric is light enough in color to see through. Some fabrics can be seen through easily; for others, you need a light box. Choose a fabric which gives you (and the friends who may sign your quilt) the option to trace.

Test the Ink and Fabric Together

Experiment with inking **before** beginning to sew your quilt blocks. Follow these steps:

1. *Choose several fabrics* suitable for background fabrics.
2. *Prewash the fabrics.*
3. *Cut small pieces* of each fabric.
4. *Write something* on the pieces. Notice if they bleed as you ink. Since you usually write and draw more slowly on fabric than on paper, there may be some bleeding. Keep this to a minimum.
5. *Set the ink* if necessary. The Pigma pen needs no special setting. For other pens, follow the manufacturer's directions. We have found that waiting twenty-four hours before test-washing helps all inks. Wash the samples as you would a fine quilt, gently and quickly in cold water with a mild or quilt detergent.
6. *Examine the fabric swatches* to see which agreed with the pen of your choice. This experiment should help to narrow down your fabric choices.

Stabilize the Fabric for Writing

When writing on fabric, it's important to keep it from sliding. Placed directly over paper or on a light box (both of which are slippery), the fabric will slide and compromise your control. There are several ways to stabilize fabric to make writing easier.

1. *Layer two fabrics.* For most projects, we recommend the simple method of laying the good fabric over another piece of muslin, which may or may not be taped down, as needed. For short inkings such as a simple signature, this is anchor enough. Susan uses this method for almost all of her inkings.

2. *Tape or pin the fabric to smooth surfaces.* If you trace over a piece of paper or a light box, tape or pin the fabric to the paper. Trace only what you need, remove the fabric as soon as possible, and lay it over a second piece of fabric to stabilize it while filling in details.

3. *Iron the fabric onto freezer paper.* If you are going to give pieces of fabric to friends to be signed, iron them onto freezer paper, with the wrong side of the fabric to the shiny side of the paper. This gives the inexperienced signer a smooth surface on which to write.

4. *Provide guidelines for inexperienced signers.* This can be done in either of two ways:

   a. Draw lines with a thick-pointed pen on the dull side of the freezer paper. Iron the fabric onto the freezer paper so the lines appear where you want the person to sign. They will show through the fabric and provide guidelines.

   b. Use a striped fabric for signing. Look for an inconspicuous stripe on a light-colored fabric. This is what Susan did when she sent fabric to her daughter's friends for *Leslie's Graduation* on page 27.

A striped fabric was used in **Leslie's Graduation Quilt.**

EMBELLISHING HANDWRITING

Just as many women in the nineteenth century took lessons in fine handwriting, you may wish to take calligraphy lessons. But most of us who want to sign quilts only once in a while can use simple little tricks to embellish our handwriting and produce the illusion of calligraphy. Throughout our lives, we have been taught to simplify our handwriting, so the idea of going wild with curves, squiggles, and flourishes sometimes goes against the grain. But decorative swirls can turn an ordinary signature into a spectacular one. They are easy to learn and may be applied to any kind of printing or script.

We recommend using your own handwriting when writing on quilts, but there is no reason not to make it fancy. The techniques we discuss work well whether you print or write. In either case, we recommend that you write the letters first and then go back to add the flourishes.

PEPPER'S PRINTING PLUS

Since everyone can print legibly with practice, Pepper likes to use a method she calls *Printing Plus.* For those of you who worry about the beauty of your handwriting, *Printing Plus* is a wonderful solution. Use 1/8″ graph paper to make the task easier. Follow these simple steps to practice printing:

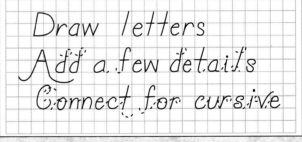

Pepper's "Printing Plus."

1. Try your name, a date, and a short saying such as *Remember Me* or *Friendship's Offering.* For capital letters, use four of the squares (a whole 1/4″). For lower case letters, use the 1/8″ squares and leave one square between each word.

   The 1/8″ size letters will not suit all the signature patches you may want to sign. It is just for practice. Graph paper marked in 1/4″ squares is also available, if you want to enlarge your printing.

2. Add tails. When you like the general look and placement of the letters, begin to decorate them as in the examples provided. Concentrate most of your efforts on the capital letters. These add-ons are to complement the letters, not to obscure them, so a little experimenting goes a long way! When you feel confident with adding details, try connecting the letters. Your "writing" will look like copy-book cursive.

3. Trace the letters. Once you have practiced and decorated your printing, and it looks exactly as you want, slip the paper model underneath the fabric signature patch and trace the letters. Trace lightly. Then go back to darken and re-embellish the letters at your leisure. Take your time and relax. While your mistakes are certainly correctable on the paper model, a messy block on a friend's signature quilt is another matter!

SUSAN'S LETTERING TECHNIQUES

Before writing on an important fabric patch, practice cursive writing just as you did printing. Practice the following techniques on paper first, if you wish, and then on fabric. Susan recommends working on fabric right away to get the feel of the pen on fabric. When practicing the handwriting techniques that follow, remember: *write slowly and lightly.*

The Extended First or Last Letter

1. Write the names, dates, and sayings you want on fabric.
2. Simply extend the first or last letter under the entire word, phrase, or line. The line may be straight or curved, made with a ruler or freehand:

3. Attach decorative squiggles or leaves at the tail of the line:

The Gaudy Tail

Exaggeration in both size and curl is the goal in making gaudy tails. The simplest antique calligraphy device was to make the letters themselves decorative. Look at the examples below:

Normal   Curly   Gaudy

The tail can hang from any letter in the word. "Y", which already has a tail, can be turned into a gaudy tail.

The tail can wrap around the entire word, or two tails can form a frame for the word.

To try Gaudy Tails, practice in this way:

1. Practice drawing large loops on fabric with the pen. Remember that you cannot write as quickly on fabric as on paper, so become adept at swirling slowly.
2. Write some words, leaving a lot of space around each one.
3. Add gaudy tails to the words. Remember: they can never be too large or swirly. Adding tails to already-written words is easy to do on fabric because fabric is forgiving and you can fill in gaps.

The Freehand Flourish

This versatile decorative element is often seen in antique autograph albums, and is useful anywhere you need to fill space. It is frequently seen under a name or date, or between two pieces of information.

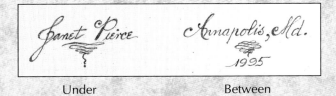

Under   Between

On a separate sheet of paper or on fabric, practice the flowing, loose stroke as described in the stages below until you feel comfortable.

1. Begin by drawing large flourishes to get the motion. Then practice smaller flourishes which will be more useful on quilt blocks.

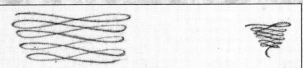

Large   Small

2. Practice making lines parallel and flowing.

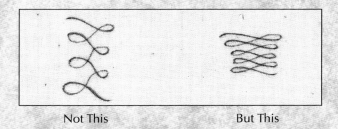

Not This   But This

3. Practice getting smaller.
4. Practice going from small to large to small.

TRACING DRAWINGS

Those of us who cannot draw our own beautiful banners or pictures may still have them on our quilts simply by tracing. Any picture you see in a copyright-free book may be traced, and these drawings can act as the jumping-off points for your own quilt embellishments. Susan has designed several books of traceable designs especially for quilters. (See *Sources* for more information.) Tracing complicated designs is easy if you follow these simple steps:

1. Simplify the picture to be traced. Examine it and decide what the essential elements are. Eliminate extraneous lines and shading, keeping only the main outlines which will help you copy the drawing.

Drawing to be traced.

2. Thicken the main lines you have chosen for tracing. Use a thick-point pen. You may simply go over the important outlines on the picture, or place a sheet of paper over the picture and trace these main lines onto it. The latter method is less confusing on complicated designs because it eliminates all extraneous lines.

3. Lay the fabric over the darkened outline. Trace the lines onto the fabric with the fabric pen, lightly and in continuous lines. Avoid short, sketchy lines. You can always darken them later.
4. Remove the fabric and place it over a single layer of fabric to anchor it.
5. Add details freehand with lines and shading. Use the edge of the pen for shading and use a light touch. Shading takes practice. Use the Pigma pen held on its side to achieve the delicate, sketchy look you are aiming for, or use the Pigma Brush which shades beautifully.

First traced outline (step 3). Shading begun (step 5).

TRACING WORDS AND PHRASES

This process works well for large writing areas but not for small, because even with a light box, tiny letters are difficult to trace. We recommend that when signing in a small space, you simply sign freehand, embellishing as you like with the techniques suggested previously. When the lettering is large and very visible on the quilt, the tracing method works well.

An inked block from **Depression Baskets.**

The phrase above, *When this you see, Remember Me,* was first composed on a computer. It is easy to typeset any phrase to be traced in any script and print it out. If you do not have access to a computer and printer, go to a copy center. They will be happy to compose several phrases, messages, names, dates, any words you want. To prepare to trace, follow this simple procedure:

1. Choose the size and shape of the area in which you will write.
2. Choose only simple, short phrases to trace. It is usually too tedious to trace long phrases. They are better written freehand.
3. Print the phrases on a computer in a script of your choice.
4. Reduce or enlarge the phrases to the size you need, using a copy machine.
5. Practice tracing and centering the phrases, using a light box. Practice first on paper and then on fabric.

6. If the letters in your chosen script get thick and thin, consider the thick areas as spaces to be filled in later. For example: ℱ. Trace only the outline, ℱ and fill in freehand later.

7. When you feel comfortable with the tracing process, lay the actual fabric over the phrase. Trace. Then fill in letters if necessary.

SOLUTIONS FOR SPECIAL SITUATIONS

How To Keep Signature Spaces from "Jumping Out"

We made the pair of quilts on pages 48 and 49 to be displayed at Quilt Expo 1994 in Karlsruhe, Germany. They illustrate the challenges you may encounter when putting signable spaces into quilt blocks: how to fill large spaces, and what to do when these light-colored spaces look like holes in the quilt. The two quilts, based on the *Sarah's Star* block, are the same size with the same layout and border, but vary in color and in the alternating blocks. Because we wanted to write on the quilts, we chose alternating blocks with large, open spaces.

The alternating block in Susan's quilt, *Starburst,* is simply an opened-up version of *Sarah's Star.* By using the outer section but replacing the inner stars with one large square, she provided room in which to write. The alternating block in Pepper's quilt, *Blue Ribbons,* is called *Friendship Rosette,* and the center block was designed to contain a large writing space.

How to Fill Large Spaces

Large spaces require large decorations. Susan chose large inkings for the blocks on *Starburst.* They were traced using the method described on the previous page. Two of the designs, the eagle and the center oval, were found in copyright-free books, and the others are based on antique pen and ink drawings in Susan's collection. Pepper chose stencils she designed, and combined them with inking. On both quilts, the decorations are proportionate to the spaces, a good rule to follow in your signature squares.

How to Keep Light-Colored Fabrics from Becoming Visual Holes

Signature fabrics must be light in color so that the writing on them shows, but they could become visual holes in a dark quilt. For example, in *Starburst,* any open, light fabric would stand out against the bright, strong colors in the rest of the quilt. Plain white or muslin looked drab and, from a distance, created empty holes in the quilt. The multi-colored stripe filled the bill admirably, being light enough to allow the inking to show but providing a bit of color and movement. In addition, the lines of the stripe provided wonderful guidelines for writing in straight lines. (Susan frequently uses a stripe in the signing area, especially when she is asking non-experienced signers to write.) By repeating the light stripe in the border, she kept the four large, light squares from jumping out at the viewer. The light fabric became part of the total design.

A block from **Starburst.**

In *Blue Ribbons* (page 49), Pepper had less of a hole-in-the-quilt problem because there were already flashes of light fabric in several of the star blocks which repeated the signature fabrics. She used two different light fabrics for variety, and put the darker of the two in the large center space. The four corner signature spaces echo the shape of the large center and are lighter in color. Both the camel and the white are repeated elsewhere in the quilt and integrated into the dark-light design.

Starburst by Susan McKelvey, Millersville, Maryland, 1994. 40 x 40 inches. Collection of the quiltmaker.

Blue Ribbons by Pepper Cory, Lansing, Michigan, 1994. Quilted by Gail Hill, Holt, Michigan. 41 x 41 inches.
Collection of the quiltmaker.

The problem of light writing spaces jumping out of a quilt occurs most often on dark quilts. Look at *Amish Baskets* on page 58. Try to imagine it with muslin in the writing spaces. The four small triangles would be inappropriate in this vibrant, dark quilt. You would not ordinarily think of the turquoise fabric as suitable for writing, but it is light enough to see through with a light box and blends beautifully with the Amish colors.

For exciting signature fabrics, experiment with unusual fabrics and colors in solids, stripes and pale prints. Go beyond the traditional muslin, and use colors which blend with your quilt.

ADDING PHOTOGRAPHS

Photographs are a wonderful addition to signature quilts. They fit in perfectly with the tradition of sentimentality, adding pictorial emphasis to the penned names and phrases of remembrance. The technique of incorporating photographs is a simple one. Any block which has a space large enough may be adapted to hold photographs.

There are many ways to reproduce photographs on fabric, in black and white, and color. See *Sources* for the titles of several books on techniques and the names of businesses which specialize in photo-transfer.

Susan's quilt, *Sunrise, Sunset* is a good example of how to successfully incorporate photographs into a signature quilt. By eliminating the tiny leaves in the center of the *Petals and Sprigs* block, Susan created a perfect circle in which to insert a photograph. She placed the photographs of her children in the center of the blocks where the writing would ordinarily go, and wrote instead around the outside of the flower petals. The combination of writing, photographs, and special fabric (the organdy corners are from Susan's wedding dress) makes this quilt a true heirloom signature quilt.

Sunrise, Sunset by Susan McKelvey, Millersville, Maryland, 1989. 36 x 36 inches.
Collection of the quiltmaker.

The Techniques

Color Strategies for Signature Quilts

Color selection is, and should remain, a personal choice. We all have our favorite colors, and these are reflected in the quilts we make. Many people plan their quilt color schemes around the decor of their homes. But home decorating trends change with fashion, and it is unwise to let wallpaper or carpet dictate your quiltmaking style. In order to enjoy your signature quilt for many years in a variety of settings, the easiest approach to quilt color combinations is simply to use the colors you love.

Signature quilts, more than any other kind of quilt, reflect the characters of their makers. When a signature quilt begins with donated blocks, the resulting quilt is a natural combination of the block-makers' color preferences and those of the recipient who assembles the quilt. Other signature quilts display carefully coordinated color harmonies because they are the works of single makers who planned and controlled all of the steps in the quiltmaking process. Whichever kind of signature quilt you make, here are some helpful suggestions. Samples are on p. 52.

VARIETY ADDS SPICE

Variety may be added to a quilt through the use of pattern, fabric, and design. But variety in color is something quilters often overlook. You may choose to repeat your favorite color combinations, or to seek inspiration from traditionally successful harmonies. *Think color* when considering how a fabric will look in a quilt. Your ability to choose striking color schemes will increase dramatically.

Vary the Values

Include a variety of values (lights, mediums, and darks) in your quilt. This adds sparkle, depth, and richness. Using many values is a good way to add variety without adding too many colors, espe-cially if you are being cautious about a lot of color, or you just want a tightly controlled color scheme. If a certain pattern limits your color choices, as in a red and green appliqué design, then instead of repeating the same fabric in every block, introduce different red and green fabrics of varying values.

Vary the Prints

Include a variety of fabrics, both solids and prints. Solids and solid prints (those prints which appear solid when viewed from a distance) provide a soothing resting place for the eye in a print-filled quilt. Prints come in every size and style. Use many of them within one quilt. Do not be afraid to combine florals both large and small, geometrics, stripes, plaids, directionals and tossed prints. They add life to the quilt.

Vary the Background Fabrics

Vary the background fabrics for different blocks or sections of a quilt. What makes a fabric suit-able for the background is its color, not the size or busyness of its pattern. Soft, quiet, grayed colors such as beiges and gray-blues are effective back-ground choices with brighter colors.

Audition Your Fabrics

When auditioning fabrics for inclusion in a signature quilt, pin generous swatches against a white wall and step back at least five feet. Color is a long-distance illusion, and only from a distance do the elements within a print meld into the actual colors you will see in a quilt. After choosing fabrics, cut small pieces of each, paste them on a sheet of paper, and file this color guide with the block patterns and project information.

Vary the values.

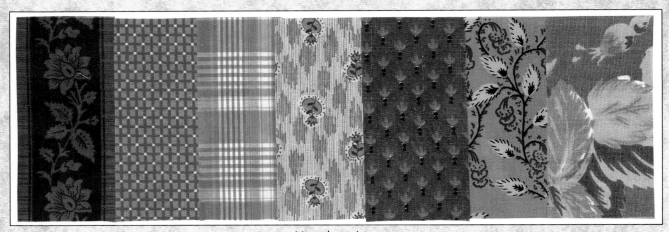

Vary the prints.

Vary the background fabrics.

TWO-COLOR QUILTS FROM THE TURN OF THE CENTURY

A classic two-color combination always works. Many excellent antique signature quilts testify to the enduring appeal of red and white. These were the colors of the Methodist Church, and many quilting groups of this denomination made a great number of red and white quilts. In addition, Red Cross signature quilts, also in red and white, were made to raise money for that organization. The combination of white and any strong color guarantees a graphic quilt design.

Even within a controlled two-color scheme, you may increase visual interest with a variety of fabrics.

Snowball, makers unknown, c. 1890. 70 x 86 inches. Collection of Mary and Tom Sharp, Georgetown, Texas.

MANY-COLORED QUILTS

When many people participate in making a signature quilt, the resulting quilt may contain many colors. The coordinator's task is to put the quilt together so that the blocks blend. In a many-colored signature quilt, it is sometimes useful to balance strong colors with some grayed or soft colors. A signature quilt in all wild, blaring colors does not invite the viewer to come closer and take the time to read the inscriptions. Position the strong colors by manipulating the block arrangement, called the *quilt set*. The possibilities for block arrangements are endless. The quilts in this book will give you many ideas for interesting quilt sets.

COLOR COMBINATIONS INSPIRED BY QUILTS FROM THE PAST

When designing a signature quilt from beginning to end, you only need to please yourself. If you are fond of quilts from a particular historic period, use them as inspirations for your own color choices. Both of us sometimes design quilts which use modern fabrics to create an antique flavor. To illustrate how modern quilts may be inspired by historic color schemes, we have chosen the following gallery of quilts.

City Houses by Pepper Cory, Lansing, Michigan, 1995. 39 x 39 inches. Collection of the quiltmaker.

Heart's Response by Barbara Gabel, Arnold, Maryland, 1994. 40 x 40 inches. Collection of the quiltmaker.

Red, Green and White Quilts from the 1850's

The red, green, and white quilts from this period still serve to inspire today's quilters. Barbara Gable's *Heart's Response*, made in these traditional colors, balances four appliqué blocks set on point in a center diamond arrangement. The narrow red sashing picks up the red of the hearts, while the soft, dark green corners act as background to frame the high contrast center medallion.

Susan's *Three Reels* on page 81 is another quilt which uses the traditional red, green, and white color scheme, but she replaced bright white with soft beige and mellow gold. Framed by the dark green of the sashing and borders, the red blocks stand out against the light background. The large-scale antique gold floral softens the high contrast usually found in a red, green and white quilt.

Family and Friends by Pepper Cory, Lansing, Michigan, 1995. Quilted by Gail Hill, Holt, Michigan. 74 x 86 inches. Collection of the quiltmaker.

Brown and Pink Quilts from the 1860's

The colors in Pepper's *Family and Friends* sampler quilt were based on colors popular in the 1860's, when shades of pink, yellow, and brown were added to the earlier reds and greens. To plan the quilt, Pepper pasted fabric swatches and titled the paste-up *Gone with the Wind*. When her friends saw only the completed blocks of the quilt, they commented, "My, they're rather brown!" Therefore, the cherry red shaded stripe was chosen to separate the blocks and to balance the large beige areas of fancy quilting. Viewers are attracted to the bold red strips that contain the blocks, much as all eyes were focused on Scarlett O'Hara in her gaudy red gown.

The Richardson-McKelvey Family by Susan McKelvey, Millersville, Maryland, 1986. 60 x 74 inches. Collection of the quiltmaker.

Faded Blue, Gray and Brown Quilts from the Turn of the Century

In *The Richardson-McKelvey Family*, Susan's modern fabrics replicate the soft, homespun look of late nineteenth century quilts. In the everyday quilts from the turn of the century, we see a great variety of fabrics and colors: shirting fabrics in geometric prints of blue, gray and black; brown left from earlier times; tiny florals of pinks and reds; and plaids galore. In addition, because these quilts were utility quilts and were washed frequently, many have faded. To achieve this faded look, Susan used a full range of colors and prints, but carefully limited her palette to pale, almost washed-out versions of each color. The result is a quiet quilt, difficult to distinguish from its antique inspirations.

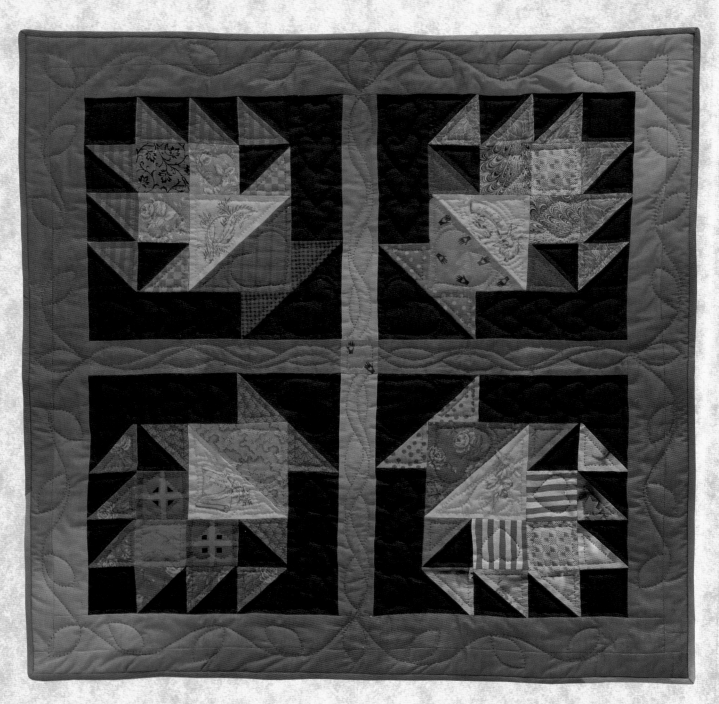

Amish Baskets by Susan McKelvey, Millersville, Maryland, 1994. 32 x 32 inches. Collection of the quiltmaker.

Pennsylvania Amish Quilts from the Early Twentieth Century

Susan's *Amish Baskets* combines the colors used by the Lancaster County, Pennsylvania Amish at the turn of the century: magenta, purple, blue, and turquoise. She chose solid turquoise as the signature fabric instead of muslin, which would have jumped out at the viewer and destroyed the period color scheme. The turquoise is light enough to write on, but dark enough to blend into the dark quilt.

The Techniques

Depression Baskets by Susan McKelvey, Millersville, Maryland, 1994. 54 x 54 inches. Collection of the quiltmaker.

Depression Green Quilts from the 1930's

Quilts of an entirely different color style characterize the 1920's and 1930's. Depression era quilts frequently contain what has become known as *Depression Green*, combined with open areas of muslin and large, cheerful floral prints, often originally feedsacks. Susan's *Depression Baskets* retains the flavor of Depression quilts by including all of these elements. Many of the florals in the quilt are, in fact, feedsack fabrics from the 1930's.

Feedsack Cakestand by Eileen Schamel, Boonesboro, Maryland, 1994. 29 x 29 inches.
Collection of the quiltmaker.

Eileen Schamel's *Feedsack Cakestand* is made entirely of antique 1930's fabrics and makes a perfect miniature period quilt. Again, we see feed- sack fabrics in large, simple florals on a muslin back- ground, with decorative quilting typical of the period in the open spaces.

COLOR CHALLENGES FOR GROUP-MADE QUILTS

When a group undertakes a signature quilt, too often the lowest color denominator rules. For safety, the group chooses the least offensive, blandest color combinations. The result is a nice, but not great, quilt. Try one of these suggestions for choosing an effective color scheme for a group quilt:

- Assign the design and color choices to one person in the group and go with her decision.
- Stick with a classic color scheme such as red and white.
- Choose one common color or fabric and leave the rest of the color choices up to the individual blockmakers.
- Allow total freedom.

Whether you choose a common color or total freedom, you have a coordinating challenge ahead of you when your talented friends hand all of the blocks back to you. First, lay out the blocks — either spread them out on the floor or pin them to a wall — and see which blocks stand out. The ones which contain strong colors are usually the most visible. Rearrange the blocks, mixing the strong ones with the weaker ones, until the composition is balanced. Now you are beginning to think of the quilt as a whole. Often when making a signature quilt with blocks of diverse colors, we get caught up in the parts and overlook the whole.

Coordinating Blocks by Different Quiltmakers

- Add more blocks of a consistent color to help draw the quilt together.
- Frame all the blocks with a narrow border of the same color before designing the set of the quilt. This is rather like framing paintings before decid-ing how to hang them in your house. At the very least, framing each block guarantees that all the blocks are the same size.
- Use multiple borders to echo important colors in the blocks. The borders also serve to contain the quilt's composition.
- If one color or one block stands out too much, find a similar fabric and repeat the color else-where in the quilt.

VISUAL TRICKS FOR SEEING THE WHOLE QUILT

- The first trick is simply to *squint*. This blurs lines and focuses your eyes on color only.
- Try using opera glasses or binoculars, looking through the wrong end, to miniaturize the quilt. Both methods make it easy to see which blocks and colors stand out.
- Let time elapse. If possible, put the quilt-in-progress in an unfrequented place (Susan likes to come upon it around a corner for added surprise). Leave and return often, sneaking up on the quilt in different light over several hours or even days. As you round the corner, you see the quilt anew. Look for what captures your attention. This response usually involves color. Ask yourself whether you want that element to stand out. If yes, you have achieved your goal. If no, how can you balance it? Try moving blocks, surrounding the strong block, or possibly substituting a quieter block. Color is a first glance impression. Make your quilt a first glance experience as often as possible before finally sewing it together.

Quilters love to play with color. Group quilts present special color challenges. Spend as much time as you need, arranging, designing, and experiment-ing. The methods suggested here are designed to help you make a spectacular signature quilt!

Making Signature Quilts in Groups

Signature quilts naturally lend themselves to group participation, not only to divide labor, but also to enjoy the stimulation provided by diverse viewpoints and ideas. People like to work in groups when the reasons for coming together are positive and the results are pleasing. Like the quilting parties of old, these groups are often called *bees*. The oldest and most popular of these groups is the *friendship quilting bee*.

FRIENDSHIP BEES

Friendship bees take many forms, but two models are common. First is the product-oriented group with a particular goal in mind. Perhaps the members want to make a signed friendship quilt, symbolic of their friendship. Or they might be making the guild's raffle quilt for a future quilt show. In either case, there is a definite, stated purpose for the group, which gives it form and meaning.

A less structured, more generalized friendship bee might also become an important part of a quilter's life. This group of friends meets regularly but does not always have a stated goal. In this group, the social activity of meeting is as important as the quiltmaking.

The following descriptions of how these two kinds of groups function may be helpful when you want to start a quilting bee. They are meant only as guidelines, not rigid rules. Every group will develop its own spirit in time, and the group's cohesion will evolve as people interact.

The Product Bee

Since the object of a product-oriented bee is to make quilts, it can have many members. A workable number is twenty. Because of its large size, meeting in a public place such as a school or church is advisable, and the group needs a leader from the outset. If you are the group initiator, that leader is you! If you need members, you may advertise your group by making an announcement at a local quilt guild meeting. You might also put a sign in the local quilt shop. It won't be long before interested quilters contact you for more information.

Set a time, date and place for the first meeting. Ask all of the members to bring calendars and suggestions to this meeting. Begin and end the meeting at a reasonable time. Few people will want to stay in a group which lingers too late, and a school or church location will often determine the length of the meeting.

Individual expectations should be discussed at the beginning. You may be surprised at what people expect from this group. Group members need to realize that some expectations are not applicable in this bee. For example, if your group's purpose is to make a raffle quilt, then choosing a pattern, setting work goals, and making sure each person understands her part in the process is essential. However, the person who expects to learn to piece or quilt will be disappointed if the primary purpose is to make the raffle quilt in a timely manner. All teaching and learning is secondary. While quilters are generous with their expertise, it is unreasonable to expect a quilt-making group to take the place of a class.

After the initial meeting of the product bee, every member needs to make a commitment to the meetings and to producing the work required. While some members cannot come to every meeting, they may remain a viable part of the group if they do their assignments. Other members may need to send blocks through the mail. If people begin to drop out of the group, the goal of completing the quilt may fall by the wayside. Therefore, before joining a product-oriented bee, prospective members should be aware of the commitment involved.

When the product bee is organized and the work is apportioned, the group really begins to take shape. As work on the quilt proceeds, and bee members start to see results, everyone will be inspired to work harder and contribute.

The initiator should produce a telephone list of members and distribute it at the second meeting. At the top of the list, state the time and place of the meetings. Perhaps someone will think of an appropriate name for the bee. Identifying yourselves as a group encourages commitment to the objectives of the group.

The Social Bee

After a while, it becomes obvious who in the group has time to attend the meetings, who actually quilts, and who interacts well within the group.

Western Star by the members of the Sunbonnet Sues in Canoes, Lansing, Michigan: Betty Bergeon, Gayle Cain, Enola Clegg, Daisy DeHaven, Edna Eckert, Jan Gagliano, Dusty DeHaven Hailey, Barbara Hawkins, Gail Hill, Mary Hutchins, Jane Johnson, Agnes Ketchey, Carol Seamon and Sue Stephenson, 1995. Arranged by Pepper Cory. 70 x 96 inches.

Those who do not want to continue after the project is completed will drop out, leaving the remaining members to form a social bee. The pressure of a deadline is gone, and these quilters stay together because they get along well and want to quilt together on a regular basis.

The social bee is usually smaller than the product bee. The meetings no longer require large, public meeting spaces. Most social bees can meet in members' homes. The social quilting bee has become simply a group of friends who quilt together.

The *Western Star* on page 63 is a signature quilt made by a social quilting bee, and its development illustrates the process just discussed. After a group of friends traveled to the International Quilt Festival in Houston, Texas, Pepper suggested they use the *Star of the West* block to make a quilt commemorating their trip. Because the quilters in this group are experts, there were no problems with sizing the blocks when the finished products were returned. The real challenge lay in combining the blocks because of their diversity of colors and prints.

The stair-step set was chosen because it encourages the viewer to look more closely at the individual blocks without directly comparing them. A more conventional set would have emphasized the blocks' differences. In addition, the small squares of soft denim blue are the repetitive elements which hold the composition together. The blue squares were originally a white background print of western scenes, a perfect theme, but the glaring white fought with the stars. In order to use the fabric, Pepper over-dyed the squares denim blue, so that the small squares receded and quietly did their job of linking stars together.

The striped train-and-mountain fabric creates an interesting inner border which the star blocks occasionally interrupt. This fabric was carefully mitered at the corners to maintain the continuous stripe illusion. Identical star blocks against a dramatic black background (upper right and lower left) balance the strong diagonal movement of the star blocks. To contain the stars, a thin, bright pink strip was sewn before the final framing border of red.

Quilting Groups and Friendship

Because American society is so mobile, families often become separated by great distances, and friendships become all the more important. One of the most difficult aspects of moving is finding new friends in new places.

For the quilter, the local quilt guild provides an instant connection to women with common interests. Quilt and fabric shops know where the local quilt guild meets; they can tell new customers about the meetings, and can put them in touch with guild members. Often the people who work in the shops are members.

Quilt magazines willingly run inquiries to help quilters connect with others; some have *Pen Pal* sections, and there are even quilt groups communicating on-line via computers.

More than any other craft today, quilting attracts and keeps dedicated people and brings together women of all ages, races, education, and careers. It is easy to lay aside differences when quilting is the major topic of conversation. Today quilting is truly the tie that binds, and nothing better exemplifies this commitment than the signature quilt.

Two signed blocks from **Cracker**, a wall hanging by Gail Hill, Holt, Michigan, 1995.

A Gallery of Signature Inspirations

For the Animals by Pepper Cory, Lansing, Michigan, 1994. 21 x 21 inches. Collection of the quiltmaker.

A Time Remembered by Rolinda Collinson, Friendship, Maryland, 1994. 26 x 26 inches. Collection of the quiltmaker.

From **Holiday Houses**. Block by
Jane Johnson, p. 28.

Northwind block, from **Hours of the Day**,
by Susan McKelvey, p. 35.

Rising Sun block by Jan Gagliano.
From **Fast Friends**, p. 72.

From **Embroidered Friendship Quilt**, p. 25.

Gail Hill's block from **Western Star**, p. 63.

From **Memories of Mom** by Nina Major Lord.

The Techniques

From **The Primitive Hall Quilt Top**, p. 20.

From **Shakertown Quilt,** by Pepper Cory, p. 39.

From **Checkerboard**, p. 23.

Roman Stripe block from **Family & Friends**
by Pepper Cory, p. 56.

House block by Gail Hill.
From **Holiday Houses**, p. 28.

Bride's Brilliant block from
Jan Gagliano's **Fast Friends,** p. 72.

Navajo Inspirations I by Linda Baker, Arnold, Maryland, 1995. 36 x 56 inches. Collection of the quiltmaker.

Here, There and Everywhere by Alexandra Capadalis Dupré, Long Beach, New York, 1994. 42 x 42 inches. Collection of the quiltmaker.

In Honor and Memory of the Needlewomen in My Family by Eleanor Eckman, Lutherville, Maryland, 1994. 27 x 27 inches. Collection of the quiltmaker.

A Bit of Immortality by Lynn A. Irwin, Sparks, Maryland, 1995. 30 x 30 inches. Collection of the quiltmaker.

The Techniques

Book Three
The
Collection

Finally, we present The Signature Block Collection, a fifty-block compilation of beautiful patterns old and new, adapted for writing. Included are templates for forty pieced blocks, ten appliqué blocks and four projects to help you begin. We hope that you will use these blocks in signature quilts of your own to create a special legacy of kinship and memory.

Fast Friends by Jan Gagliano, Haslett, Michigan, 1994. 81 x 94 inches. Collection of the quiltmaker.

Choosing Signature Quilt Blocks

TRADITIONAL DESIGNS

Makers of signature quilts of the past knew that many blocks could be adapted for signing. A study of any selection of signed quilts shows that quilters used a variety of blocks, both pieced and appliquéd, in one-block quilts or combined in album quilts. Several blocks became so popular as signature blocks that they are practically synonymous with the genre.

The best-known of these blocks is the *Chimney Sweep*. "By about 1850...the *Chimney Sweep* had become a universal favorite for the autograph quilt."[59] It became so popular that it was commonly identified as *The Album Patch*, and is still known by that name. It was also called the *Friendship Block*. *Chimney Sweep* quilts were made throughout the country, "from Vermont to Oregon."[60] Although easy to piece, the *Chimney Sweep* looks complex, with many pieces, so a single block looks intricate despite its simplicity. This pattern lends itself to using many fabrics or a few, making it a good block for using scraps. (Many signature quilts, especially early ones, were scrap quilts.) It looks beautiful whether set on square or on point in the quilt.

Another block often seen on signature quilts is the *Snowflake*. It was used so often that it too acquired various names, including the *Album Block*, *Autograph Cross*, and *Album Cross*.[61]

An extremely popular signature block, especially in Pennsylvania, was *The Rolling Stone*. The earliest *Rolling Stone* quilt, found in Montgomery County, Pennsylvania, was dated 1851. Many more are documented as having been made in that county between 1851 and 1892.[62]

The *Reel* was so popular that it appears in some variation in almost every album friendship quilt. In Pennsylvania, it was popular in "the Lehigh Valley [and] in the eastern half of the state."[63] This simple appliqué block makes an ideal signature block with four places in which to write. It can be varied in countless ways, and mixes easily with other blocks,

both pieced and appliquéd. Refer to the visual index (beginning on p. 138) to see these block designs.

ADAPTING TRADITIONAL BLOCKS

There are thousands of quilt blocks, which means that there are thousands of signature blocks, because you may sign anywhere on any block: in any open space or corner, tucked around an appliqué design, or anywhere on the background. Signature quilts have been signed this way throughout quilt history.

In any open space or corner

Tucked around an appliqué design

Anywhere on the background

In addition, almost any quilt block may be adapted to become a signature block. Just substitute a signable fabric for any piece in the block, with space in which to sign. In many of the designs chosen, adapted and designed for this book, we have tried to open up new, unusual spaces for signing. Examine the block to see where a signed space would be effective.

Many classic signature blocks have limited space set aside for signature patches, but even these traditional patterns may be adapted to provide more room for writing.

One easily-adapted block is the *Freedom* block. Young men received signature quilts made from this block when they left home or finished apprenticeships. Like other favorite signature blocks, the *Freedom* block could be set in a quilt either square or on the diagonal. In the traditional version of this block, only the center square is signed, but depending on the placement of the fabrics, other signature spaces are possible. The illustrations below show the white or light spaces suitable for signing.

Freedom blocks.

Chimney Sweep has many possible signature patches. The first block is the traditional arrangement, but as you can see, there are several others.

 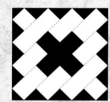

Chimney Sweep blocks.

There are many blocks, rarely seen in traditional signature quilts, which would make beautiful signature blocks. One of these is *Kansas Beauty*, an intriguing pattern which swirls around a center square.

Kansas Beauty blocks.

If a group of inexperienced quiltmakers is making a signature quilt, the complexity of the pattern may be a concern. It is better to begin with a simple block like *Attic Windows* or *Roman Stripe*, both of which make good signature blocks. Each is easy to make. By dividing a 12″ square into nine equal divisions (4″ units), each block yields nine signature patches.

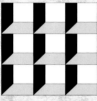 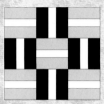

Attic Windows   *Roman Stripe*

Cross and Crown was a favorite signature block in quilts made by church quilting bees of the nineteenth century. This block has many other names, including *Bear's Paw* and *Duck's Foot in the Mud*. The Quakers in Pennsylvania, who made many signature quilts, used it often and called it *The Hand of Friendship*. While the early *Cross and Crown* blocks were signed only in the center square, the adapted blocks can accommodate four or even five signatures.

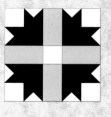 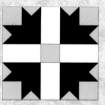

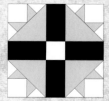

Cross and Crown blocks.

DESIGNING NEW BLOCKS

Occasionally you want a signature block containing a large area for signatures. Rather than a traditional block, perhaps a new block, *Bride's Brilliant*, will do. Inspired by the configuration of the top of a brilliant-cut diamond, this pattern has a large octagonal area for signing. There is ample room for a great deal of information, and, depending on your fabric choices, *Bride's Brilliant* can resemble a diamond, a star, or even a flower.

Bride's Brilliant.

Pennants.

If you are making a quilt for a boating enthusiast, *Pennants* is an appropriate choice. The signature patches look like the yachting flags called *burgees*. Imagine this pattern in a quilt made in the striking nautical colors of red, white, and blue!

Quilters never tire of the *House* block. The door, the window, and the sidewalk pieces are all possibilities for signature patches. The appeal of this folk art motif is undeniable, and each block maker might personalize her block to represent her own home. Groups making *House* blocks for a friend who is moving have been known to sign their names and addresses on their blocks, a not so subtle reminder to the recipient to stay in touch.

House.

We encourage you to look at all quilt blocks as possible signature blocks. The possibilities are endless. *The Signature Block Collection* contains fifty signature blocks – traditional, adapted, and original – to inspire you and your friends to design your own signature quilts and become part of the tradition begun so long ago.

Itchy Feet by Lynn Phillips, Abingdon, Maryland, 1995. 42 x 42 inches. Collection of the quiltmaker.

Daylight Serenade by Ruth Ann Klos, Fork, Maryland, 1994. 30 x 30 inches. Collection of the quiltmaker.

The One-Block Medallion

❧

DAYLIGHT SERENADE
BLOCK: PETALS AND SPRIGS

*A*ny single block may become the center medallion of a small quilt. Just add one or more borders, either simple or elaborate. We have chosen the block *Petals and Sprigs* because it is a beautiful block design with plenty of room in which to write. Ruth Ann Klos selected this pattern to make her lovely one-block medallion quilt called *Daylight Serenade*.

Useful Hints for Dramatic One-Block Medallion Quilts

1. Choose any block you like. An elaborate block is good.
2. Ruth Ann set her block on point, a placement which enlarges the size of the wall hanging.
3. Notice that the inked design fills the center space.
4. The use of a dark fabric for the four corner triangles provides high contast of value and makes the light muslin square stand out.
5. A busy, colorful printed fabric fills the four large, open spaces nicely and carries the colors used in the center outward.

6. Repeating the white background from the center medallion on the border opens up the space and lends the quilt size.
7. Ruth Ann repeated the petal and leaf sprig as a scallop border. This echo device in both color and shape is particularly effective.
8. The prairie points create a showy but simple outer border. Notice that this narrow border repeats the strongest color from the medallion, the red. It is a good idea to repeat a color from the main part of the quilt in the border. This echoes the strongest color in a small space such as the binding or, in this case, the small prairie points, showing just enough of the color.
9. Close grid quilting behind the main design makes the design stand out.
10. Elaborate quilting enhances the wall hanging.
11. Embellishments such as the ruched flowers with pearl centers enhance and personalize the block.

Christmas Greetings by Pepper Cory, Lansing, Michigan, 1994. 24 x 32 inches. Collection of Susan McKelvey.

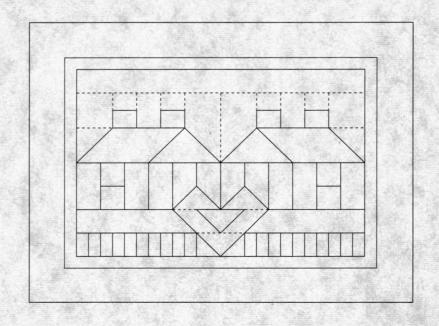

The Collection

The Two-Block Quilt

CHRISTMAS GREETINGS
BLOCK: HOUSE

*T*his wall hanging, *Christmas Greetings*, was a holiday gift from Pepper to Susan. The symbol of the twin houses is appropriate for a person-to-person signature quilt. The houses are linked by a common sky, a signed heart, and a picket fence. These elements suggest that even though the people may be far apart, they are linked through friendship.

The *House* block is made twice. In order to obtain a right and left house, reverse the templates when cutting the pieces for the second house.

The illustration below the quilt shows a heart-shaped patch linking the houses together. This piece is composed of four triangles (template E, page 89), plus the right and left "sidewalk" pieces. At the bottom of the heart there are two small right triangles (template J, page 90) at each side of the picket fence.

The picket fence is made from small rectangles, 1″ x 2″. Add 1/4″ on all sides for the seam allowance. If you would like the traditional white picket fence, make half the pickets light (cut 10), and half dark (cut 10), for a total of twenty pickets.

The extra strip of sky fabric across the tops of the houses provides room for the placement of a star, which is appliquéd over the seam joining the two blocks. The sky strip is 2″ x 24″. Again, add 1/4″ to all sides for the seam allowance.

The inner border is 1″ wide, and the outer border is 3″ wide, plus 1/4″ seam allowance on all sides. The finished *Christmas Greetings* wall hanging measures 24″ x 32″. To hang, make a rod pocket 4″ wide, and blind stitch it to the back of the piece just below the binding. Or you might like to make three tabs, sewing them to the top of the hanging, placing one tab in the center and one at each of the two ends. Place a dowel through the tabs and hang.

Notice that on page 78 the dashed lines in the illustration are seams between pieces of the same fabric since they are not readily visible in the photograph.

Three Reels by Susan McKelvey, Millersville, Maryland, 1994.
27 x 64 inches. Collection of the quiltmaker.

THREE REELS
BLOCKS: THE REEL, REEL AND LEAF, OAK
LEAF AND REEL

Although most quilts are square or rectangular, the long, narrow shape of three blocks in a row makes a useful wall hanging or table runner. It is perfect to place above a bed or on a hall table, where you want width but not necessarily height.

Any three blocks may be used, all the same or different. Susan chose to show three variations on one traditional pattern, *The Reel*. She centered the simplest block, *The Reel*, between the two more elaborate variations, *Reel and Leaf* on top and *Oak Leaf and Reel* on bottom. She chose the traditional color scheme from antique *Reel* blocks, red and green on a white background.

Procedure for Making a Three-Block Quilt

1. Choose any blocks you like. Consider how they go together and whether they will balance each other. Experiment with these configurations:
   • two elaborate and one simple.
   • two pieced and one appliquéd (or vice versa).
   • parallel shapes.
   • parallel direction of the block designs.
2. Select a color scheme to tie the three blocks together.
3. Make the blocks.

4. Sign the blocks.
5. Decide on the layout of the three blocks, considering balance as in #1.
6. Decide whether you will add sashing, as Susan did. If yes, sew it on. For a dramatic, stylized quilt, use a high color-contrast sashing, which acts as a strong outline around the blocks and makes them stand out from the background. For a softer contrast, use a color similar to the block background. For an even softer look, eliminate sashing entirely.
7. Add the corner background triangles. If you use the same color as the background of the blocks, the blocks will appear to be floating on the background. If you choose a slightly different color and value from the background, as Susan did, this choice echoes the center background as well as emphasizing the blocks as separate entities. By using no sashing and a high contrast print in the triangles (as in Project 1), the blocks will stand out.
8. For the border, repeat some color or fabric from the blocks. Susan chose green rather than red because a large red border would have been too strong. The dark green quiets the quilt.

Two for Two by Pepper Cory, Lansing, Michigan, and Susan McKelvey, Millersville, Maryland, 1995. 34 x 34 inches. Collection of the quiltmakers.

The Collection

The Four-Block Quilt

❧

TWO FOR TWO
BLOCKS: ACORN MEDALLION, CHIMNEY
SWEEP, MEMORY, OAK LEAF AND REEL

The wall hanging *Two for Two* is a combination of blocks made by Pepper and Susan.

The appliqué blocks, *Oak Leaf and Reel* (upper right) and *Acorn Medallion* (lower left), were initially larger than the pieced blocks. Susan recommends cutting your background square at least 2″ larger than the 12″ finished size. When you have finished appliquéing, trim the block to the 12-1/2″ size, or the pieced block size.

The pieced *Memory* block (upper left) and the traditional *Chimney Sweep* (lower right) were made using the templates as they appear in the *Block Collection* of this book.

Before being sewn together, all the blocks were sized to 12-1/2″ square.

When combining blocks made by different quiltmakers, coordinating the colors is a concern. Since both Susan and Pepper love antique quilts and often buy reproduction fabrics, coordinating their efforts was not a problem. They decided that the appliqué blocks would be on light backgrounds and that the pieced blocks would similarly have light fabrics around their outside edges. The choice of the dark blue and green for the sashing and corner squares was clear once the blocks were placed together as a group.

Rather than stripped sashing composed of even increments, the sashing with narrower bands of blue around the green creates a more interesting frame for the blocks. The dimensions for the stripped sashing are: blue 3/4″ (cut 1-1/4″), green 2″ (cut 2-1/2″), and again blue 3/4″ (cut 1-1/4″). The dark teal squares between the blocks are 3-1/2″ (cut 4″).

The quilting is very simple. In the appliqué blocks, the quilting outlines the shapes. In the pieced *Memory* block, the quilting cuts across the block in straight lines toward the corners. In *Chimney Sweep*, the quilting outlines the pieces within the block. However, the quilting does not run across any of the signature patches in the blocks because that would be visually distracting. The binding is the same deep teal as the corner squares. Since most walls are light colored, a dark binding ensures the best definition of the quilt for the viewer.

Working With The Collection

On the following pages you will find forty pieced and ten appliquéd blocks, all suitable for signing. Many of the blocks share templates. To make it easier for you to find the correct templates, we have divided the fifty blocks into six sections. Each section is preceded by a visual key which displays the blocks in that section. Template designations are listed below each block on this page. Block drawings on the template pages illustrate where the templates are in each block.

The finished size of all blocks is 12″ x 12″. A seam allowance of 1/4″ is indicated on the pieced block templates. Because this is a large collection, we have marked the templates with letters, double letters and a combination of letters and numbers. Refer to the block illustration to make sure you are using the correct templates.

We use some templates on both sides, for example K and K rev. (reversed). When you see a template marked *rev.*, use that template and then turn it over to use as the reverse template. The lower case *rev.* always indicates a reverse template.

Arrows on the templates indicate the direction for placing templates on the grain of the fabric. Occasionally you will find templates that are used for more than one block. When this occurs, check the arrow on the template and adjust the grain line to suit the pattern. For example, in most blocks a right triangle is cut with the perpendicular sides on the straight grain, and the hypotenuse on the bias. The same triangle template in another block may show the hypotenuse parallel to the edge. In this case, it is wiser to cut with the longest side on the grain to prevent the finished block from stretching.

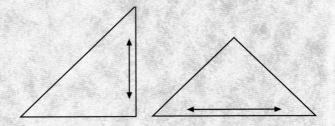

If you want to be creative with fabric images, and you are aware of the pitfalls of bias cutting and sewing, then you may change the grain line designations to suit the design of the fabric. A block that has many bias edges may be secured by stay-stitching around the outside of the block, about 1/8″ from the edge. This keeps the block from stretching before being joined to other blocks.

We have provided one-quarter of each appliqué block design. Be sure to notice where appliqué templates are placed on a fold line. The pieces are designed to fit a twelve inch finished square. Appliqué pieces are given without seam allowances.

Suggestions For Block Construction

MAKING THE PIECED BLOCKS

1. Prepare all fabrics by washing them in warm water, drying them until just damp, and ironing them smooth. Before washing, clip a small triangle from the corners of each length of fabric. This prevents those long unraveled threads that tangle with other fabrics and wrap themselves around the machine's agitator.

2. If you are hand-piecing and prefer to sew along marked lines, trace the patterns without the 1/4″ seam lines. Machine piecers should trace the templates along the outside lines. You may also cut the patterns without templates if you are sure of their dimensions. Use a rotary cutter (put in a new blade before starting), a cutting mat, and a 3″ x 18″ ruler. A larger ruler, while useful for cutting long strips, just gets in the way when cutting a small number of pieces.

3. When tracing around patterns on dark fabrics, use a chalk wheel marker. This makes a delicate line that you can see for cutting but that dusts away afterwards. On light fabrics, use a thin hard-lead (#3) mechanical pencil.

4. For both hand and machine-piecing, cut out the pieces for one block and make a sample block before cutting all of your fabric. This will test the accuracy of the pattern (a must when distributing a pattern to a group!) and alert you to any sewing problems.

5. In most blocks, sew the smaller pieces together first. Whether machine or hand-piecing, do not use quilting thread for sewing. Instead, use a good quality cotton or poly/cotton thread, and match the color to the predominant color in the block, or choose a neutral color.

6. Pin pieces together whether you hand or machine piece. Thin straight pins with small heads are the best pins for this task because most machines can run over one or two without problems, and hand-piecers will find their thread does not get wrapped around these thin pins.

7. If you are machine sewing, do not trust that your sewing machine foot is an exact 1/4″ wide and will guarantee accurate 1/4″ seams. If necessary, place a masking tape piecing guide 1/4″ to the right of where the needle touches the plate of the machine. This way, as you feed the pieces through the machine, you keep their sides against the tape edge, and your machine piecing will be more accurate.

8. If you are hand-piecing, do not use the same size needle you use for hand quilting. If you do, you are taking too much time to hand piece and probably hastening cramping and pain in your hands. Instead, examine the needle you use for hand-quilting. It is likely to be a size 9, 10, or 12 *Between*. Find the same size in a *Sharps* length needle, the same diameter but longer length. When you use a Sharps to hand piece, the needle will feel as familiar as the same size Between, but you can gather more stitches on the needle before pulling through. The speed and regularity of your hand piecing will increase with this minor change in needle length.

9. Keep in mind that blocks with many pieces tend to draw up more (get smaller) than blocks with fewer pieces. Take special care to sew accurately when combining complex and simple blocks in the same quilt. If you have sewn the blocks as accurately as possible, pressing gives them a final chance to lie flat and come out a common size.

10. Some sewers like to press seams as they sew the block, while others wait until the block is done. In either case, always give the block a final pressing to bring it to its proper size. Whenever possible, press the seams toward the darker of the fabrics. As a last touch, hold the iron above the block, steaming it front and back. Mark the block's dimensions on the ironing board cover with a permanent marker. Then press the newly sewn block, limp from steaming, over the guidelines until dry.

MAKING THE APPLIQUÉ BLOCKS

The appliqué patterns in our Signature Block Collection are mostly large, simple shapes, making them easy appliqué projects for beginners. The floral medallions have been designed with space in the center for writing. You may mix or add corner floral designs to any basic medallion shapes such as the *Reel* to create many variations on each medallion.

Susan likes to use freezer paper to transfer the blocks from the pages. The directions below describe this method.

To Transfer the Large, Single-Piece Patterns to Fabric

1. Cut a piece of freezer paper 12″ or larger.
2. Fold it into fourths, and then into eighths.
3. Unfold it, lay one section over the pattern, shiny side down, and trace the pattern on the dull side with a dark heavy marker. A light box is useful at this stage.
4. Refold the paper with the marked part visible. Pin it with one or more straight pins to keep the folds lined up.
5. Cut as you would a paper snowflake, using sharp scissors. This way, even if the original traced shape is slightly different from the pattern, the resulting four sections of your design will be identical.
6. Cut a piece of fabric at least 2″ larger than the pattern you have chosen.
7. Mark the center of the block by folding it in fourths and finger-creasing the center.
8. Iron the freezer paper pattern onto the front of the fabric, matching centers.
9. Mark the seamline (just outside the fold line next to the edge of the freezer paper) with a marker which shows on the fabric. Consider the Pigma .01 on medium-dark fabric where neither chalk nor pencil lines show. It makes a thin line which is easily lost when turned under, it doesn't bleed or run on cotton, and it is visible.
10. Cut the design out while the freezer paper is still on the fabric, leaving a 1/8″ to 1/4″ seam allowance outside the marked paper edge. Remove the freezer paper or leave it on until you sew.
11. Cut the fabric for the background at least two inches larger than the finished block dimension.
12. Mark the sections of the block by folding it in fourths on both the diagonal and the straight of grain, and press the lines.
13. To place the large medallion on the background square, center the medallion over the background. Line up the points, fold, and pin. A light box is useful here.

To Transfer Small Pattern Pieces to Fabric

1. Lay a piece of freezer paper over the pattern drawing, shiny side down, and trace the shape on the dull side with a dark marker. A light box is useful at this stage.
2. Cut out the freezer paper pattern piece.
3. Iron it onto the right side of the appropriate fabric.
4. Mark the seam line.
5. To mark more than one piece of fabric with the same freezer paper pattern, peel the freezer paper off and move to another fabric. Continue to peel and mark as needed. Or, cut a freezer paper pattern for each shape.

Pieced Blocks Based on a Nine-Patch
(Templates A-W)

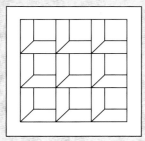

Attic Windows
A, B

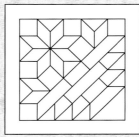

Friendship Basket
D, F, J, K, L, M, O, W,
CS1

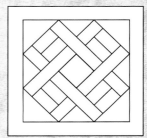

Friendship Links
E, F, H, V, W

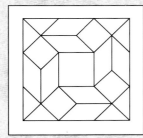

Kansas Beauty
C, E, H, I

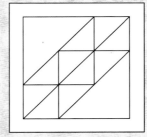

Northwind
F, P

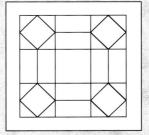

Rolling Stone
C, G, H, J

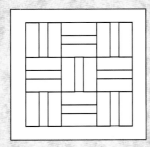

Roman Stripe
R, S

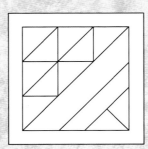

Tried and True
F, T, Q, U

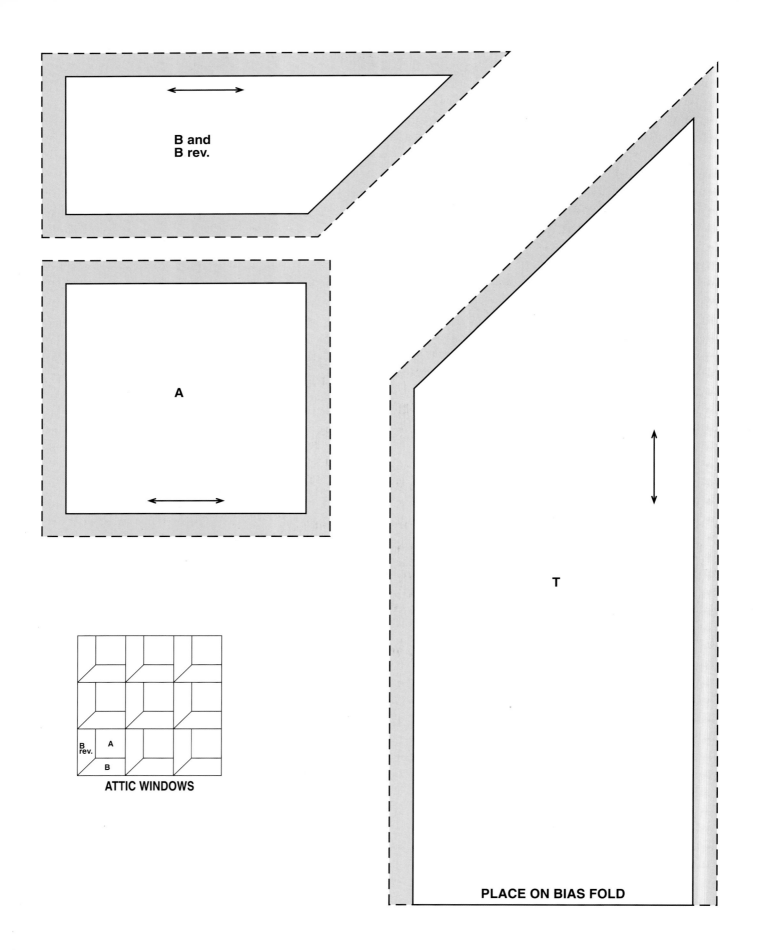

B and
B rev.

A

ATTIC WINDOWS

B
rev.

A

B

T

PLACE ON BIAS FOLD

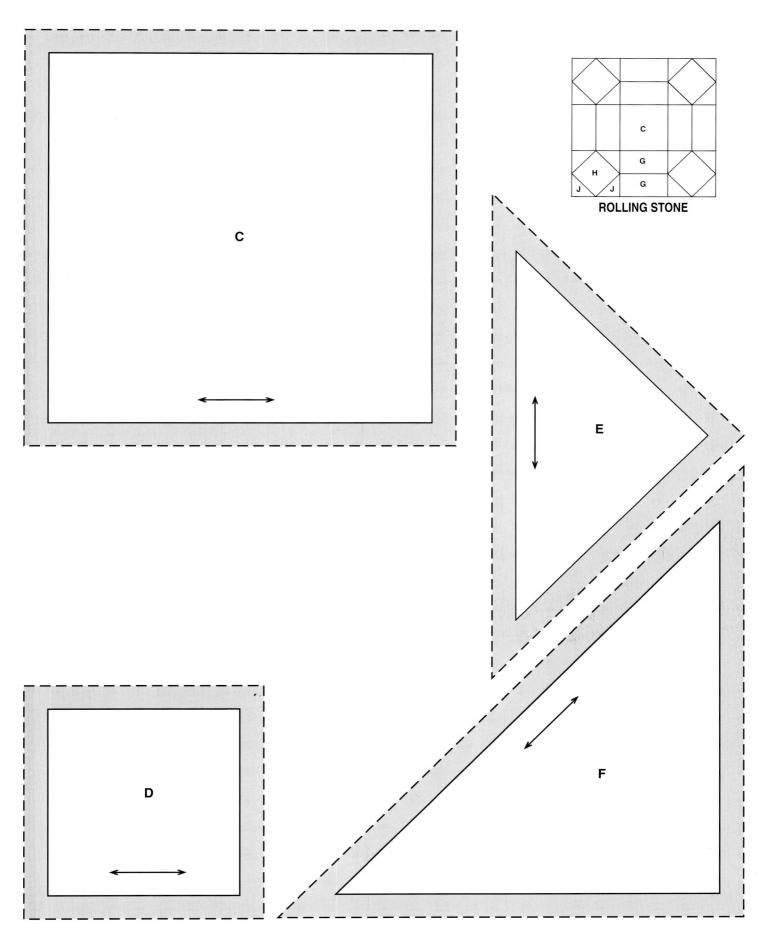

ROLLING STONE

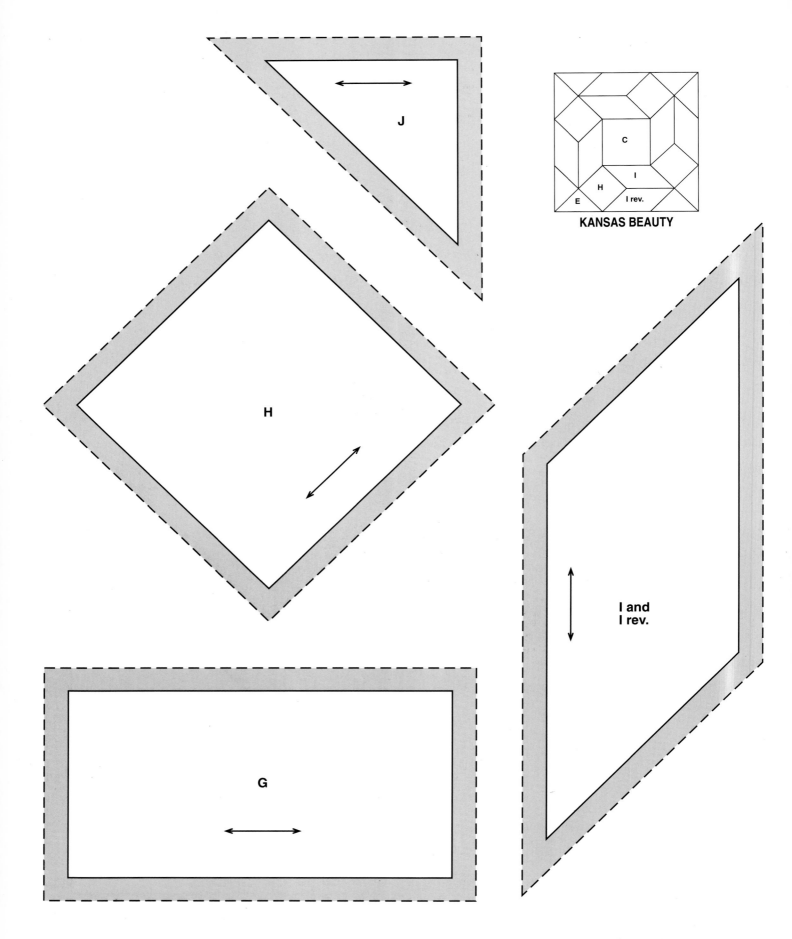

J

H

I and
I rev.

G

C

I

H

E

I rev.

KANSAS BEAUTY

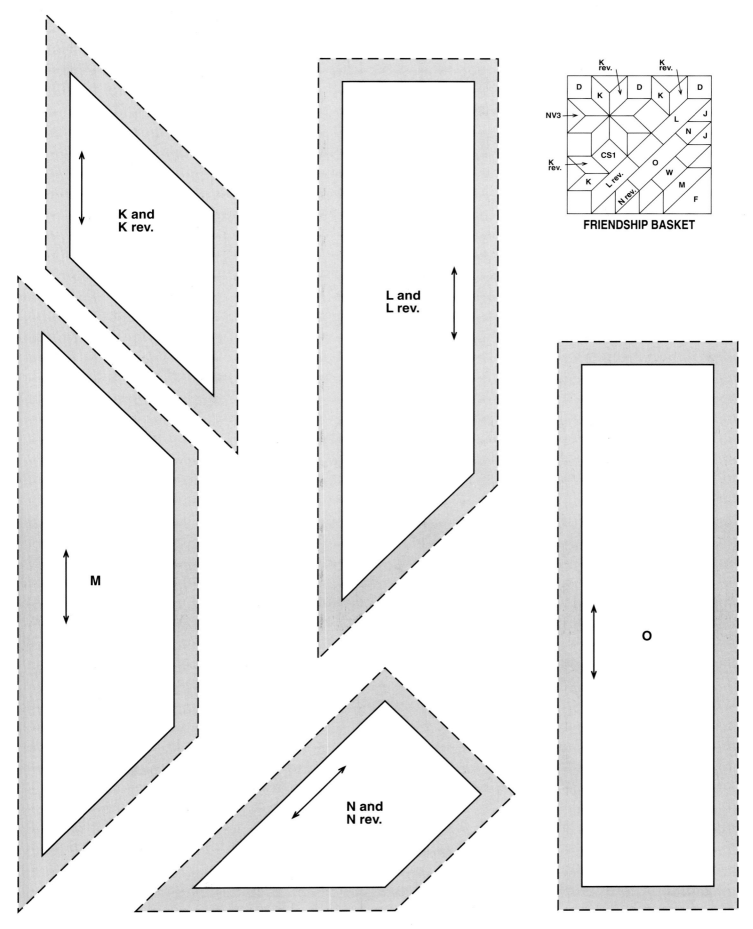

**K and
K rev.**

**L and
L rev.**

M

**N and
N rev.**

O

FRIENDSHIP BASKET

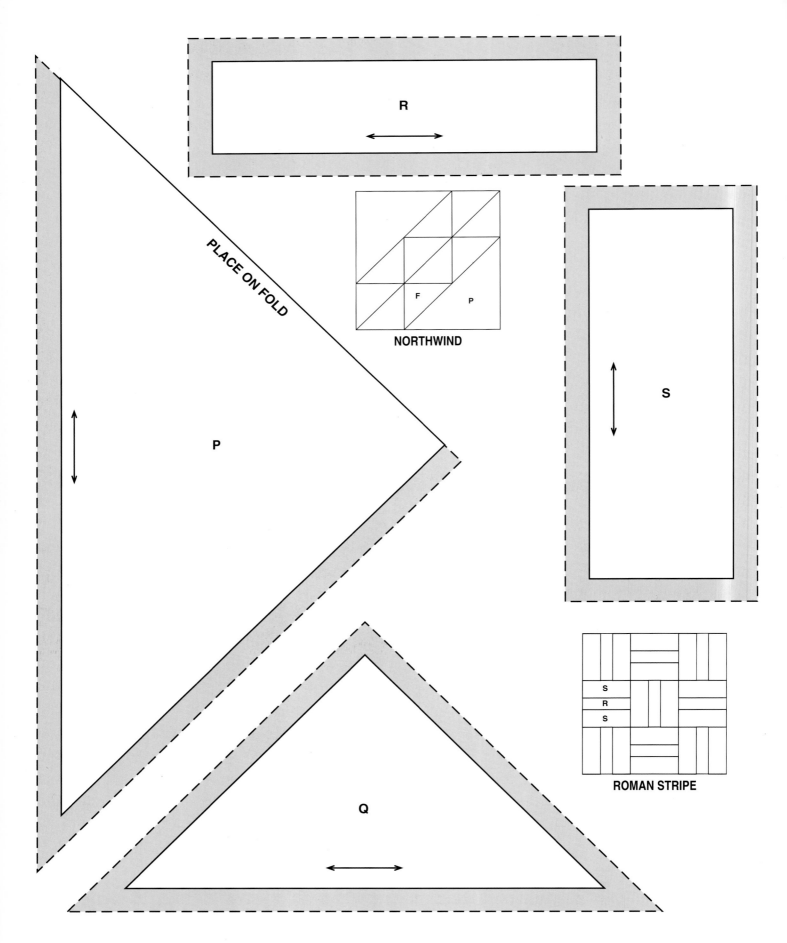

R

PLACE ON FOLD

P

NORTHWIND

F   P

S

ROMAN STRIPE

S
R
S

Q

The Collection

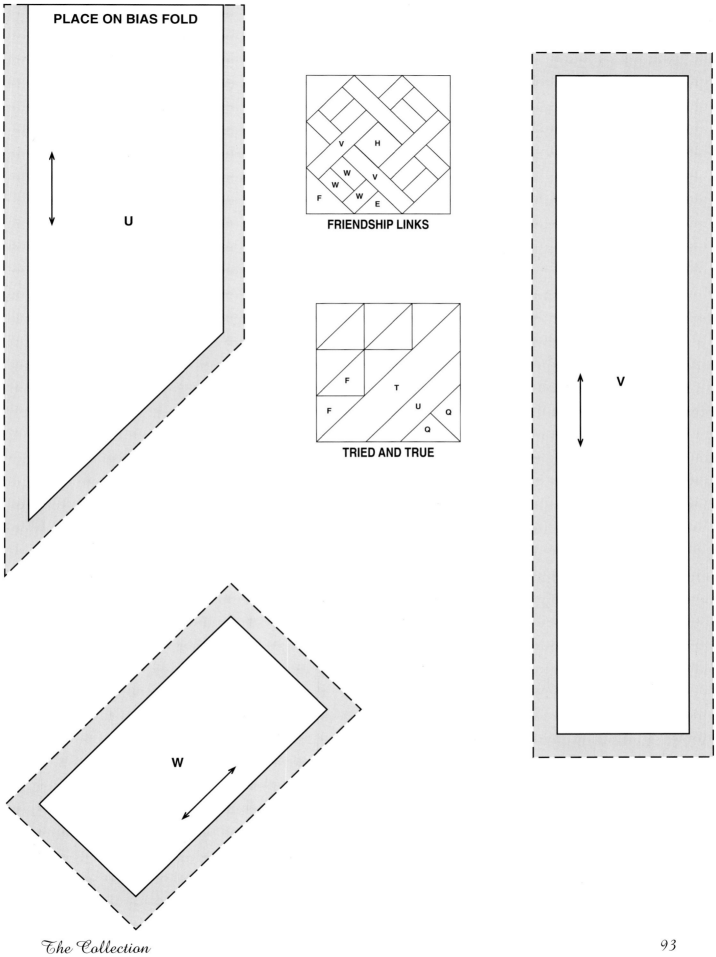

PLACE ON BIAS FOLD

U

FRIENDSHIP LINKS

V H
W V
W
F W E

TRIED AND TRUE

F T
F U Q
Q

V

W

Pieced Blocks Based on a Four-Patch
(Templates AA-NN)

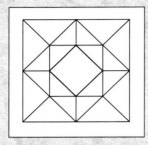

Baltic Puzzle
BB, CC, EE

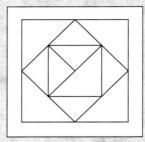

Betsey Wright's Block
CC, DD

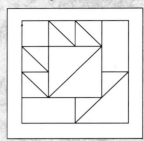

Cactus Pot
AA, BB, DD, HH

Centennial
AA, CC, EE, FF, GG

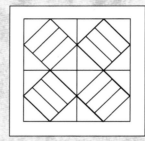

Cracker
BB, II

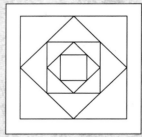

Economy Patch
AA, BB, CC, DD, FF

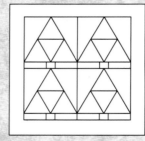

Family Trees
KK, LL, MM, NN

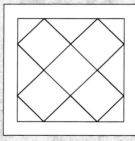

Freedom
BB, CC, EE

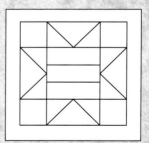

Signature Star
AA, BB, CC, JJ

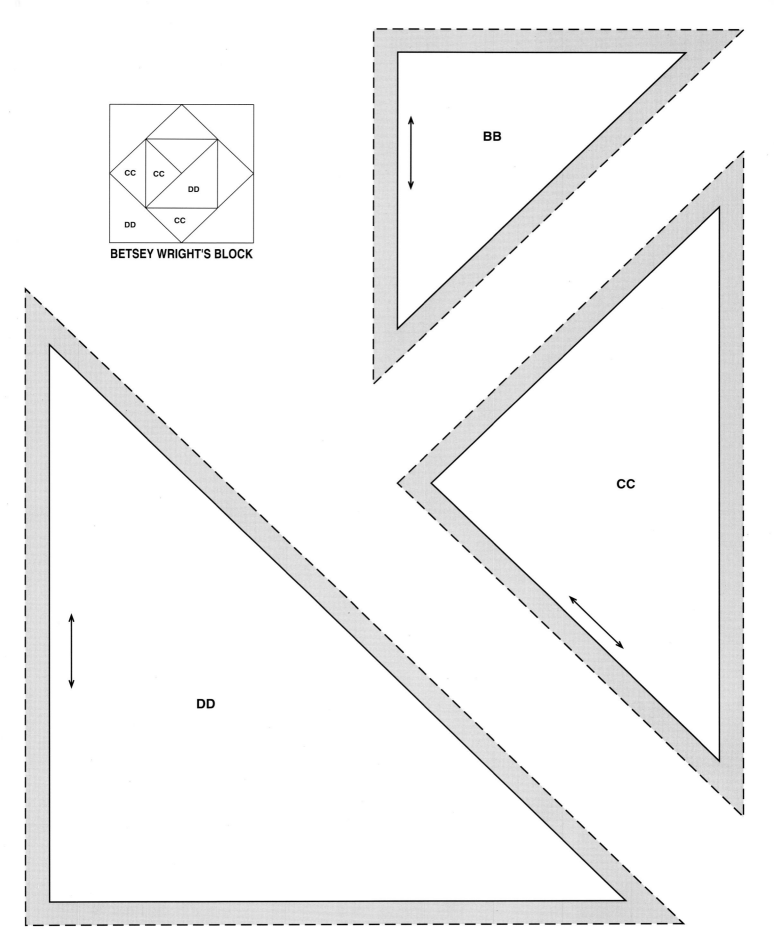

BETSEY WRIGHT'S BLOCK

CC CC
DD
DD CC

BB

CC

DD

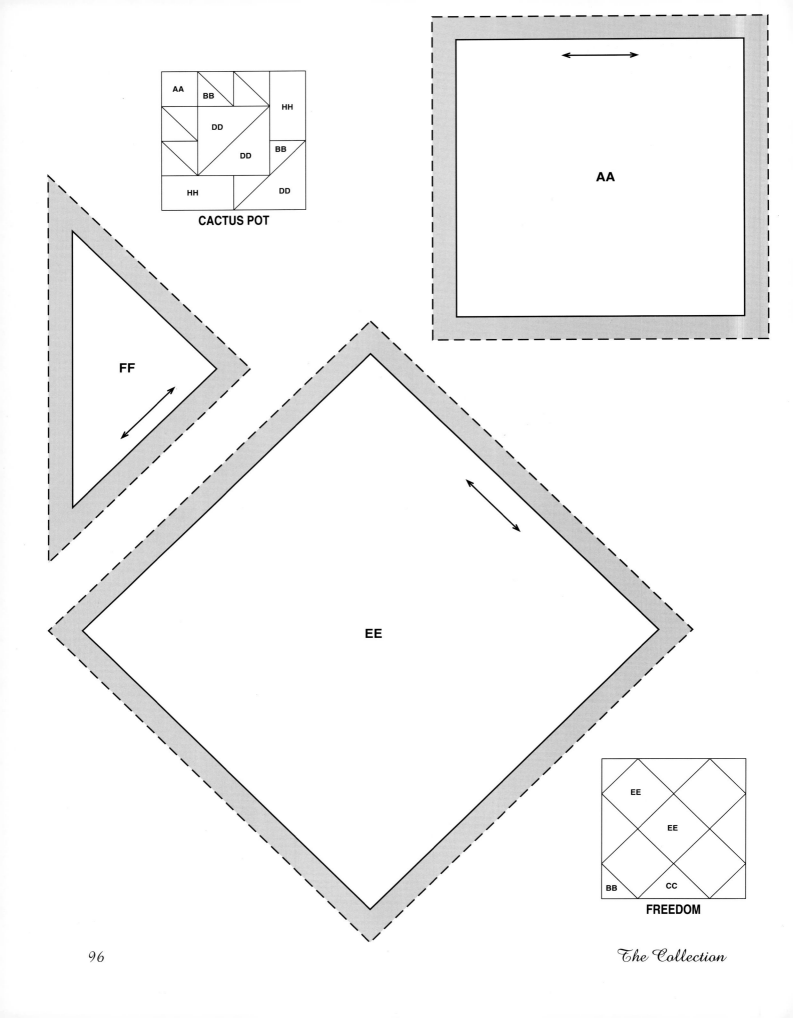

CACTUS POT

AA

FF

EE

FREEDOM

The Collection

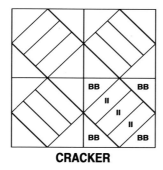

CRACKER

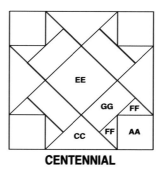

CENTENNIAL

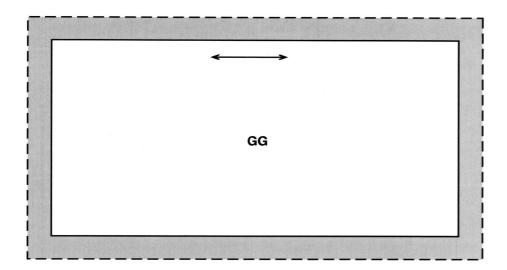

GG

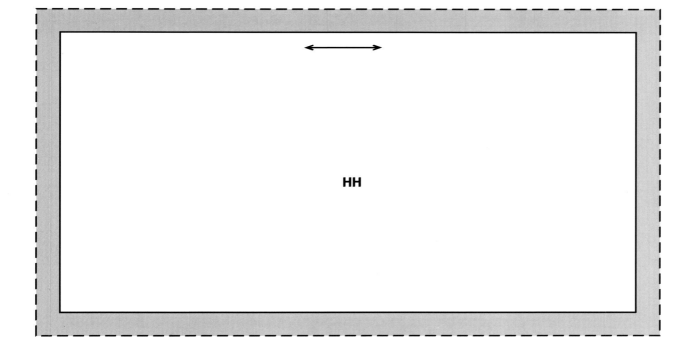

HH

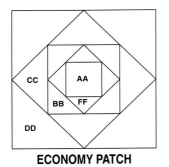

ECONOMY PATCH

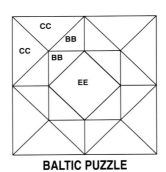

BALTIC PUZZLE

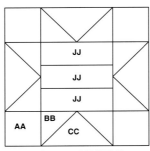

SIGNATURE STAR

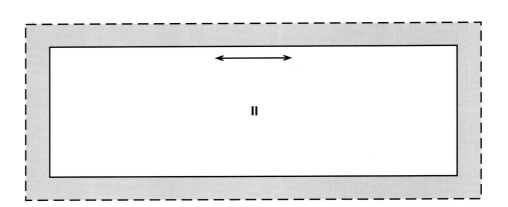

II

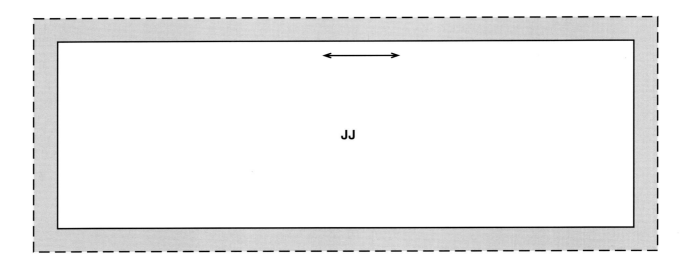

JJ

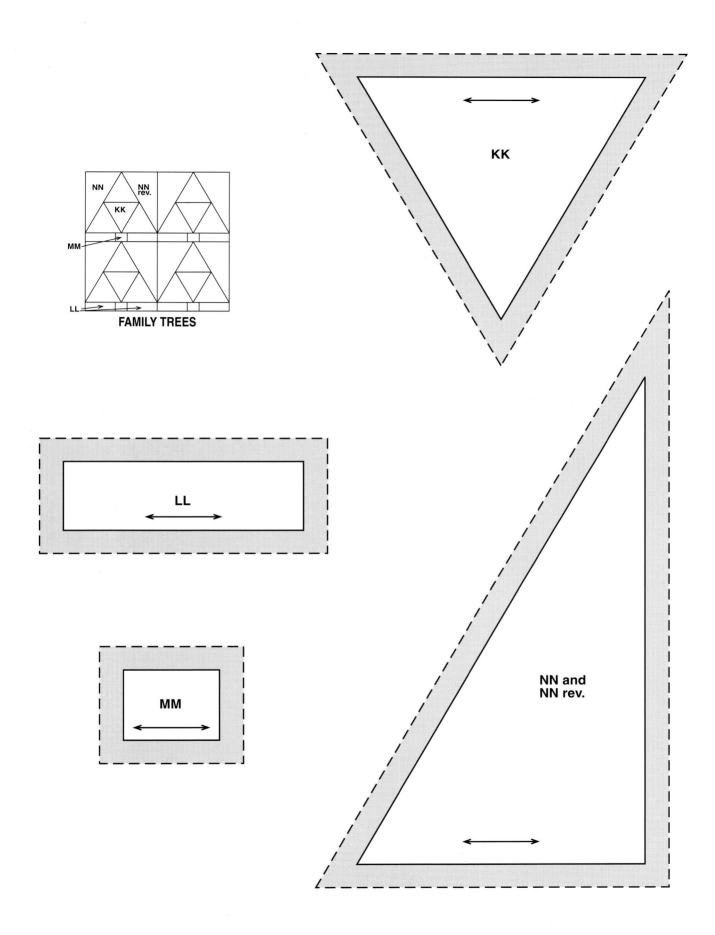

FAMILY TREES

KK

LL

MM

NN and
NN rev.

Pieced Blocks Based on a Five-Patch
(Templates OO-ZZ)

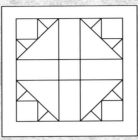

Cross and Crown
OO, QQ, UU, WW

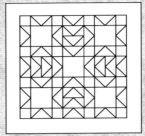

Five Stars
NN, OO, QQ, TT

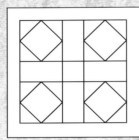

Garden of Eden
OO, PP, WW, XX

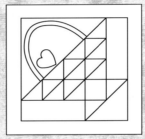

Grandmother's Basket
OO, PP, SS, UU, VV,
YY, ZZ

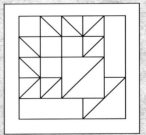

Grape Basket
OO, PP, SS, UU

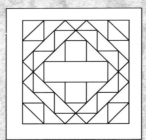

Memory Block
OO, PP, QQ, SS

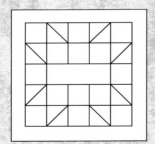

Old Album
OO, PP, SS

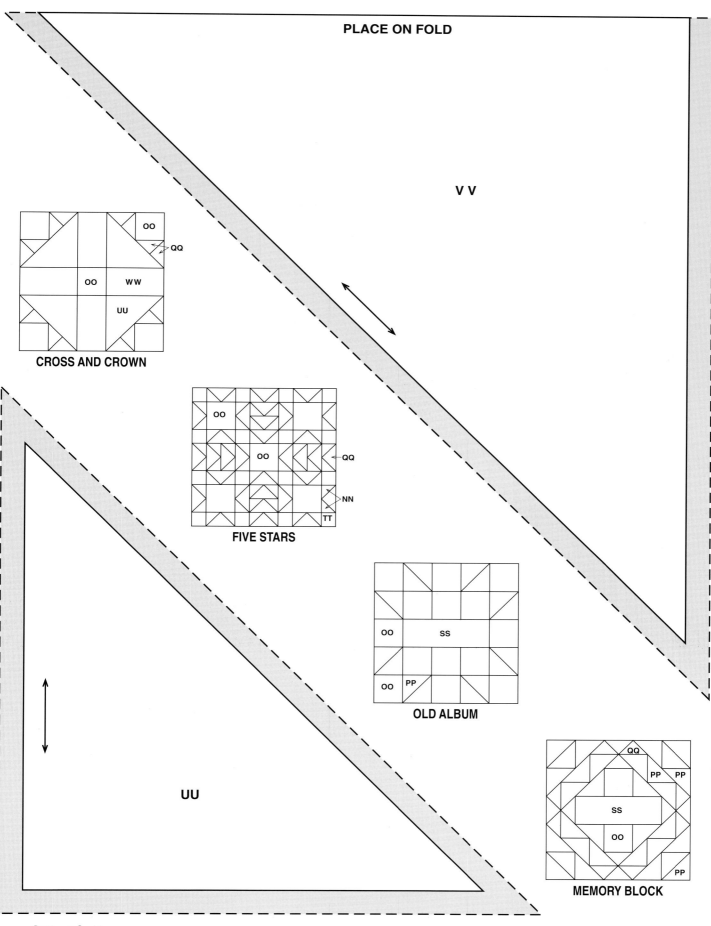

PLACE ON FOLD

V V

OO
QQ

OO   W W
UU

CROSS AND CROWN

OO

OO   QQ

NN
TT

FIVE STARS

OO   SS

OO   PP

OLD ALBUM

UU

QQ
PP   PP

SS

OO

PP

MEMORY BLOCK

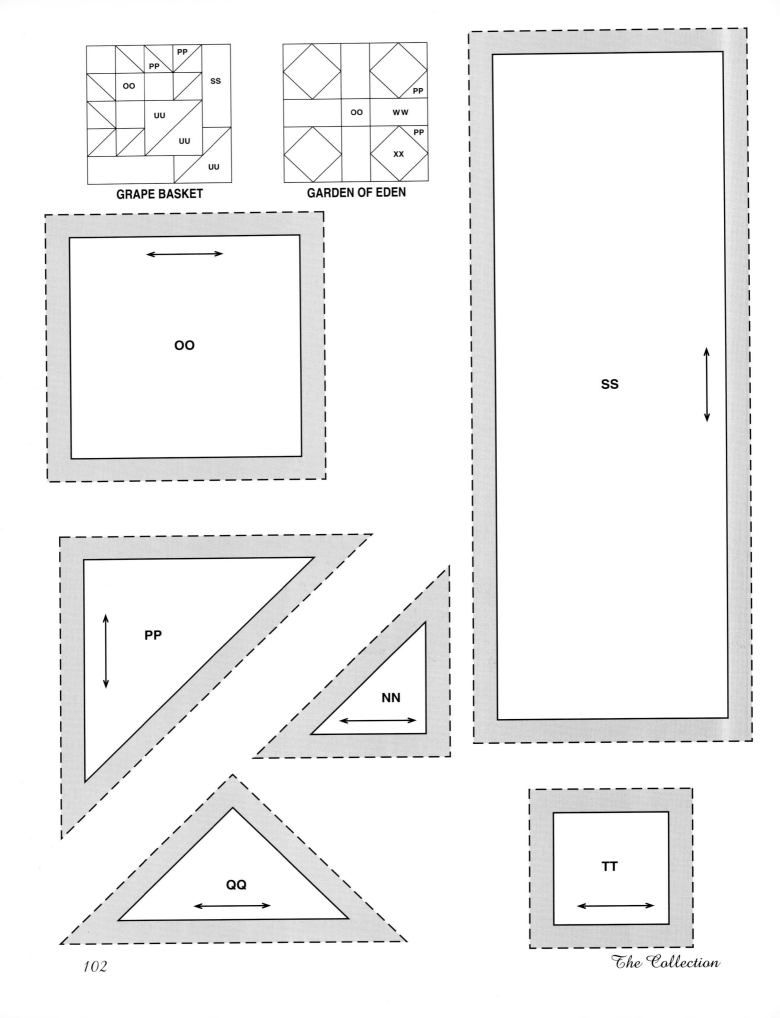

GRAPE BASKET

GARDEN OF EDEN

OO

SS

PP

NN

QQ

TT

The Collection

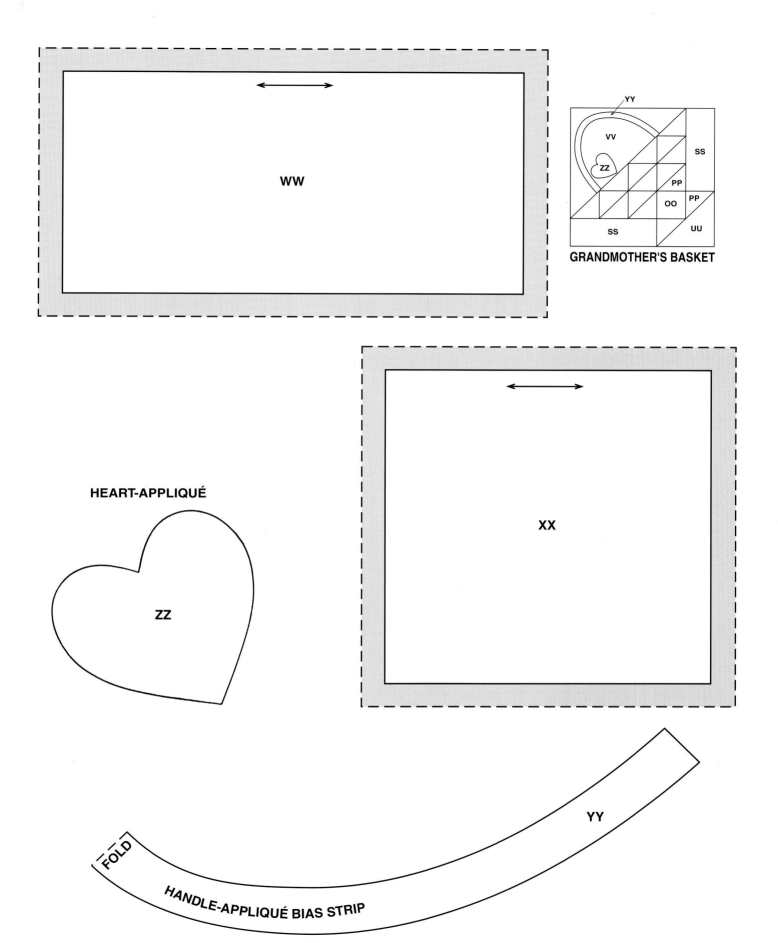

WW

GRANDMOTHER'S BASKET

YY

VV

ZZ

SS

PP

OO

PP

SS

UU

HEART-APPLIQUÉ

ZZ

XX

YY

FOLD

HANDLE-APPLIQUÉ BIAS STRIP

Pieced Blocks with Curved Seams
(Templates CV1-CV26)

Bride's Brilliant
CV1, CV5-CV9

Friendship Knot
CV21-CV26

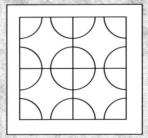

Mill Wheel
CV19, CV20

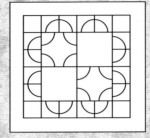

Opening Valentines
CV16-CV18, C, D

Rising Sun
CV1, CV10-CV15

Star of the West
CV1-CV4

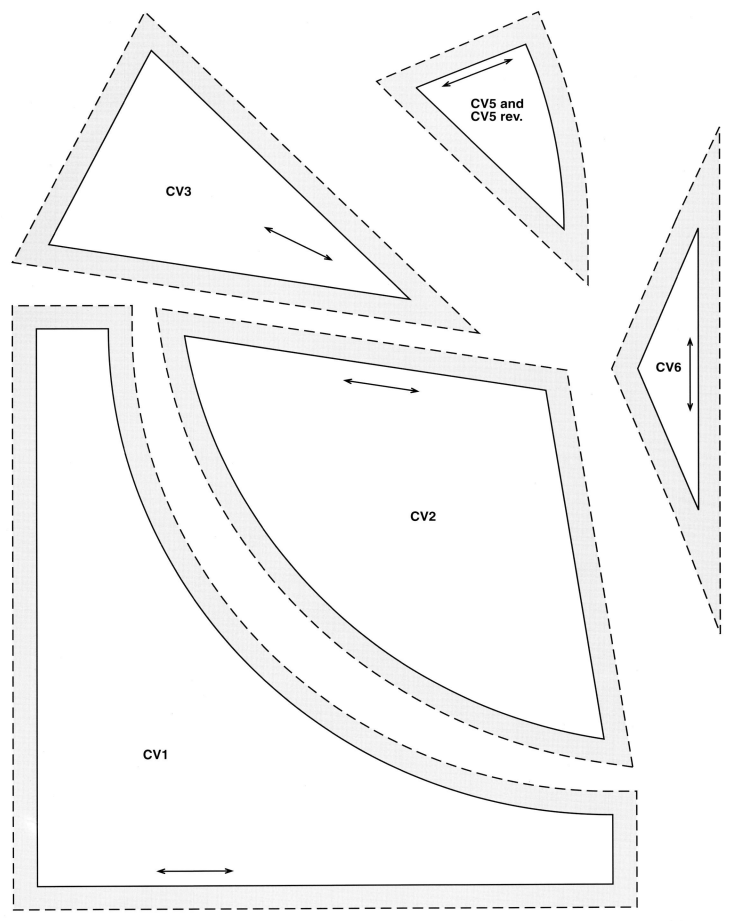

CV5 and
CV5 rev.

CV3

CV6

CV2

CV1

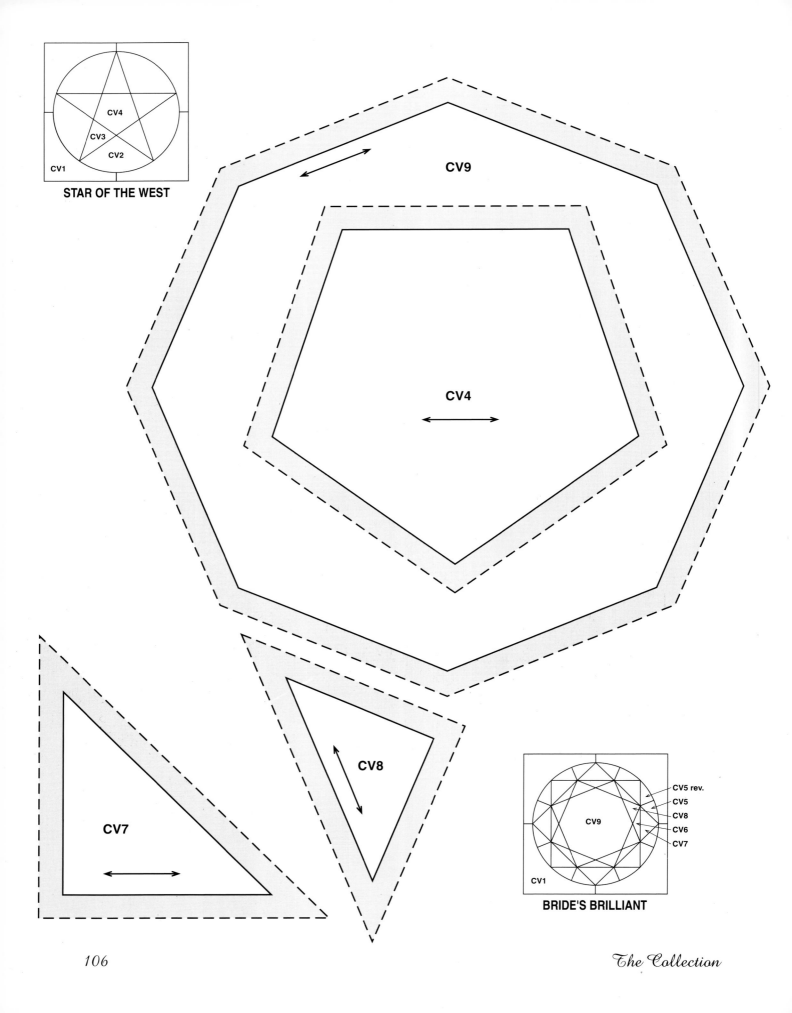

STAR OF THE WEST

CV4

CV3

CV2

CV1

CV9

CV4

CV8

CV7

CV5 rev.

CV5

CV8

CV6

CV7

CV9

CV1

BRIDE'S BRILLIANT

The Collection

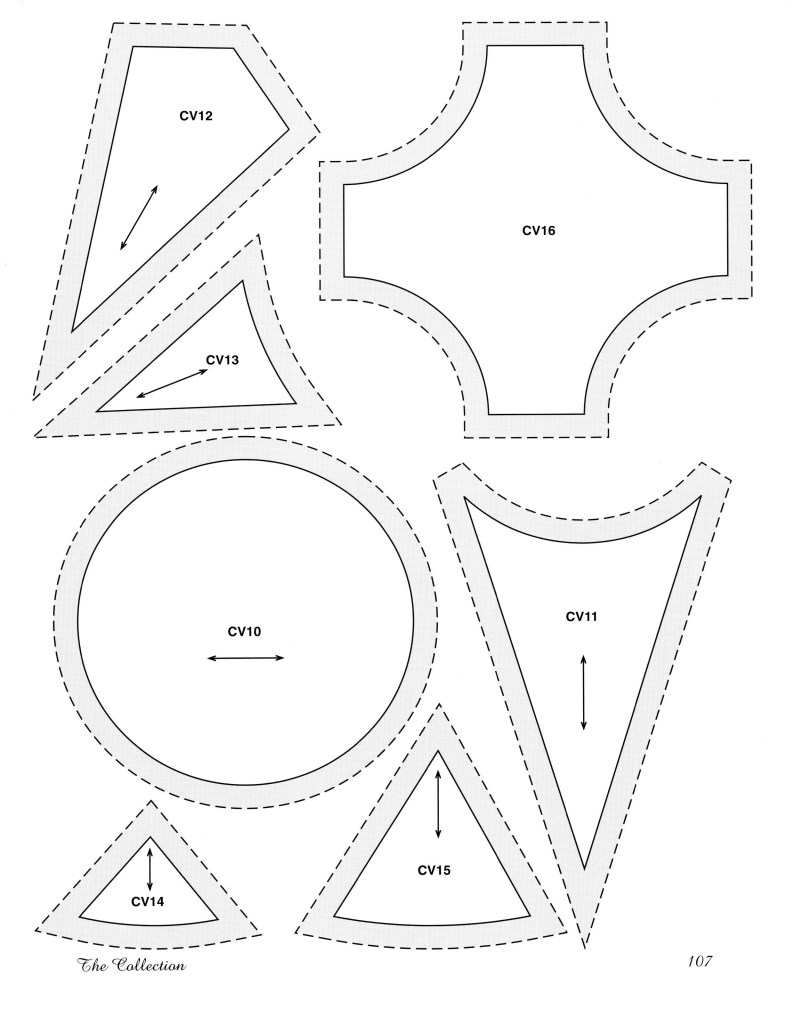

CV12

CV16

CV13

CV10

CV11

CV14

CV15

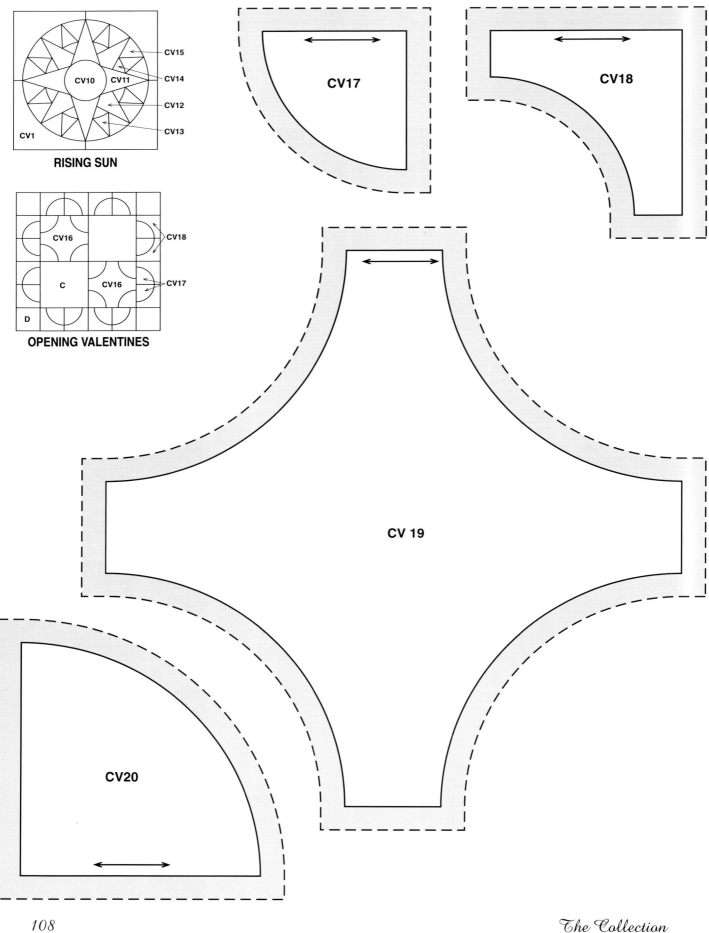

RISING SUN

CV15
CV14
CV12
CV13
CV10
CV11
CV1

OPENING VALENTINES

CV16
CV18
C
CV16
CV17
D

CV17

CV18

CV 19

CV20

The Collection

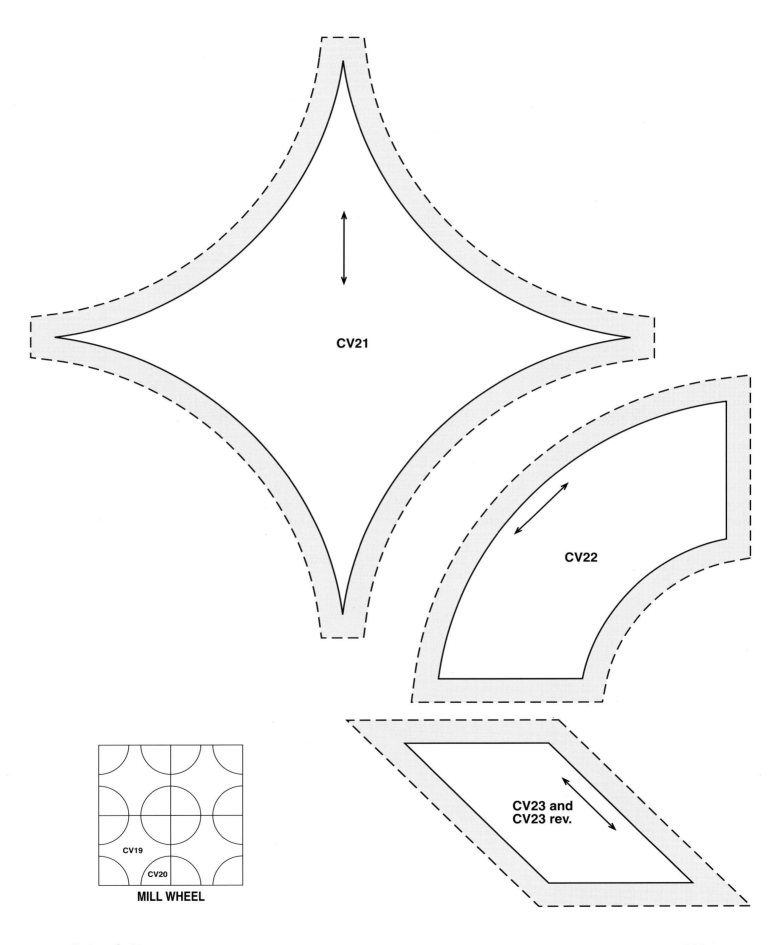

CV21

CV22

CV23 and
CV23 rev.

CV19

CV20

MILL WHEEL

The Collection

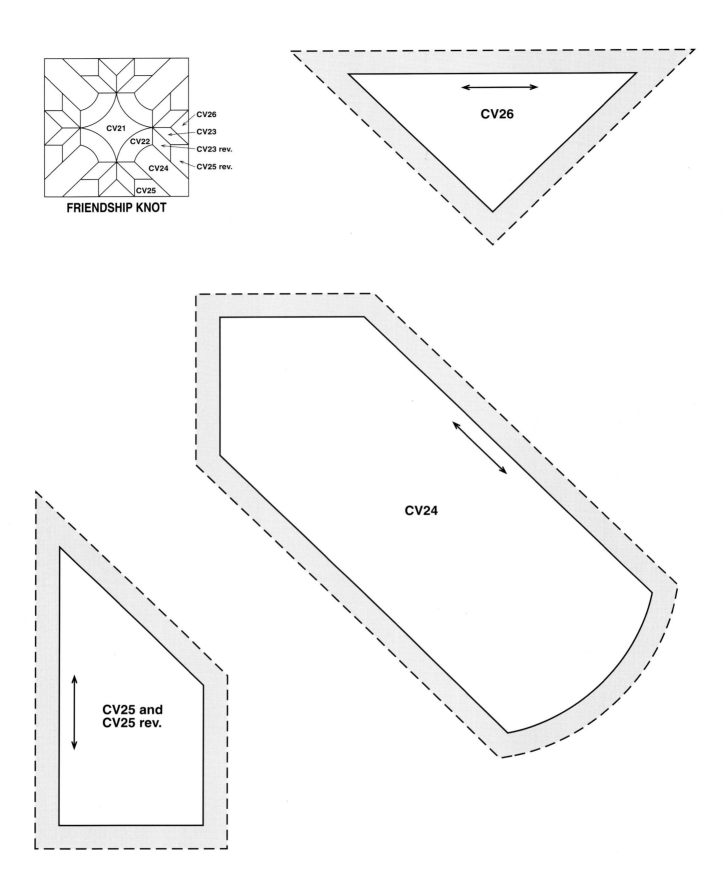

FRIENDSHIP KNOT

CV26

CV24

CV25 and
CV25 rev.

CV21

CV22

CV26
CV23
CV23 rev.
CV25 rev.

CV24

CV25

Other Pieced Blocks

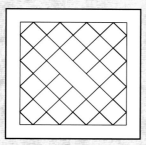

Chimney Sweep (CS)
CS1, CS2, CS3, FF

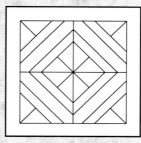

Founders' Block (FB)
FB1, FB2, FB3

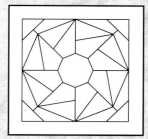

Friendship Circle (FC)
FC1-FC5

Friendship Rosette (FR)
FR1- FR7, J

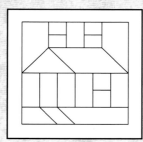

House (HS)
HS1-HS7, D, G, CC

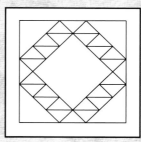

Navajo (NV)
NV1-NV3

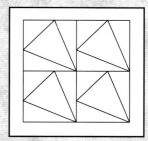

Pennants (PN)
PN1-PN3

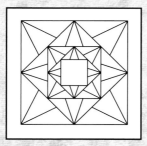

Sarah's Star (SS)
SS1-SS8, AA

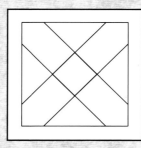

Snowflake (SF)
SF1-SF3

Star in the Cabin (ST)
ST1-ST4

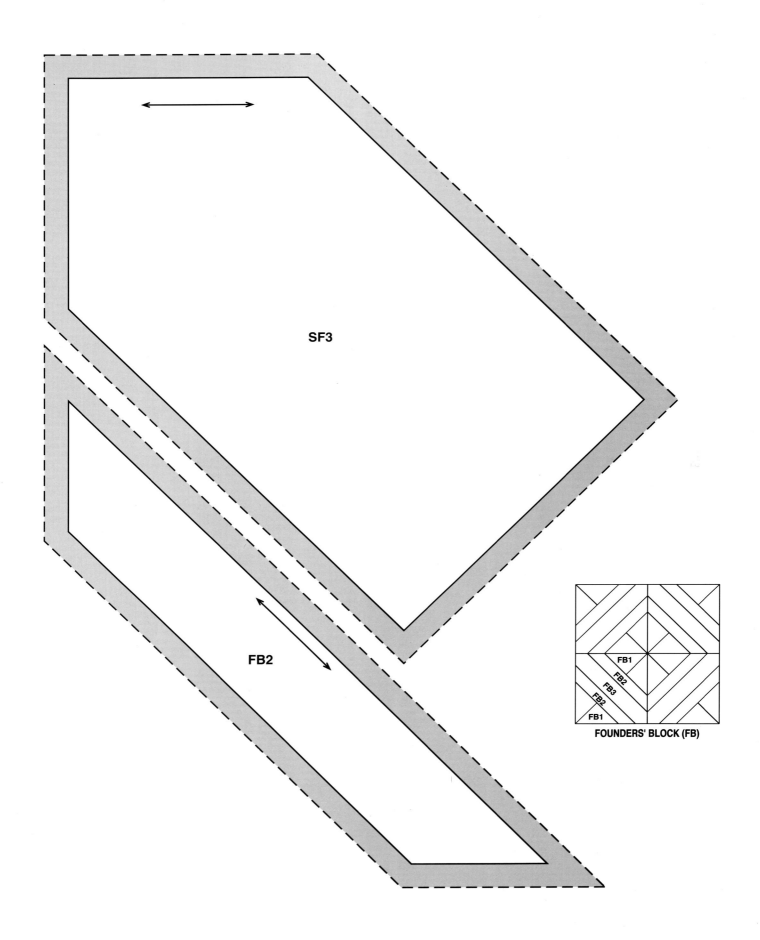

SF3

FB2

FB1
FB2
FB3
FB2
FB1

FOUNDERS' BLOCK (FB)

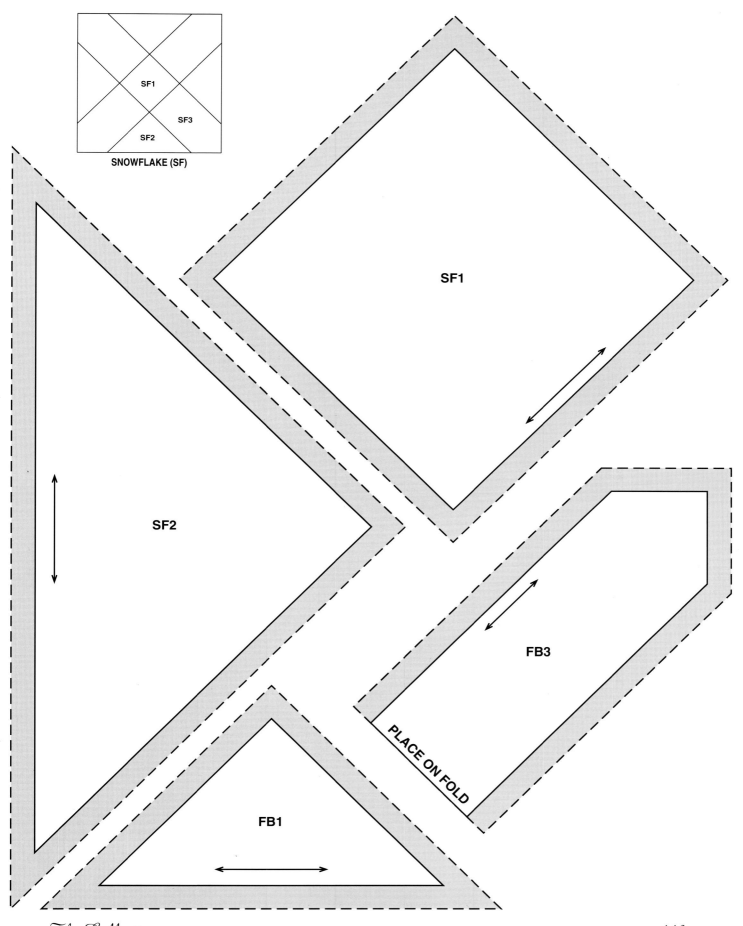

SNOWFLAKE (SF)

SF1

SF2

SF3

FB1

FB3

PLACE ON FOLD

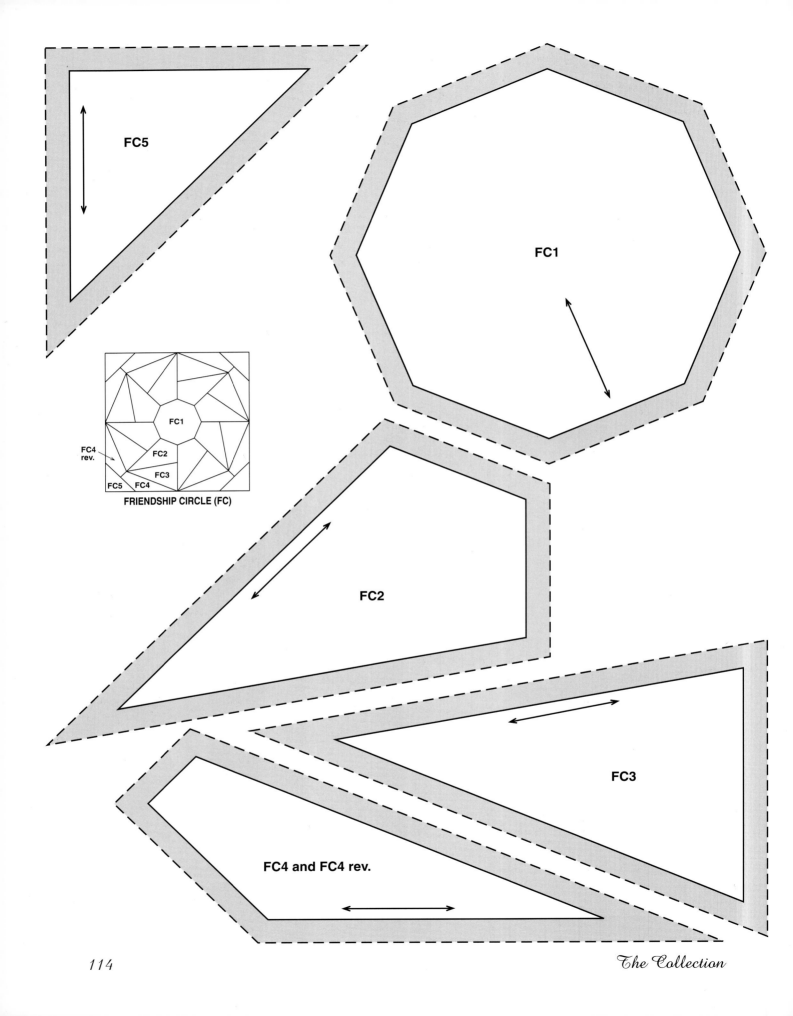

FC5

FC1

FC1

FC4
rev.

FC2

FC3

FC5   FC4

FRIENDSHIP CIRCLE (FC)

FC2

FC3

FC4 and FC4 rev.

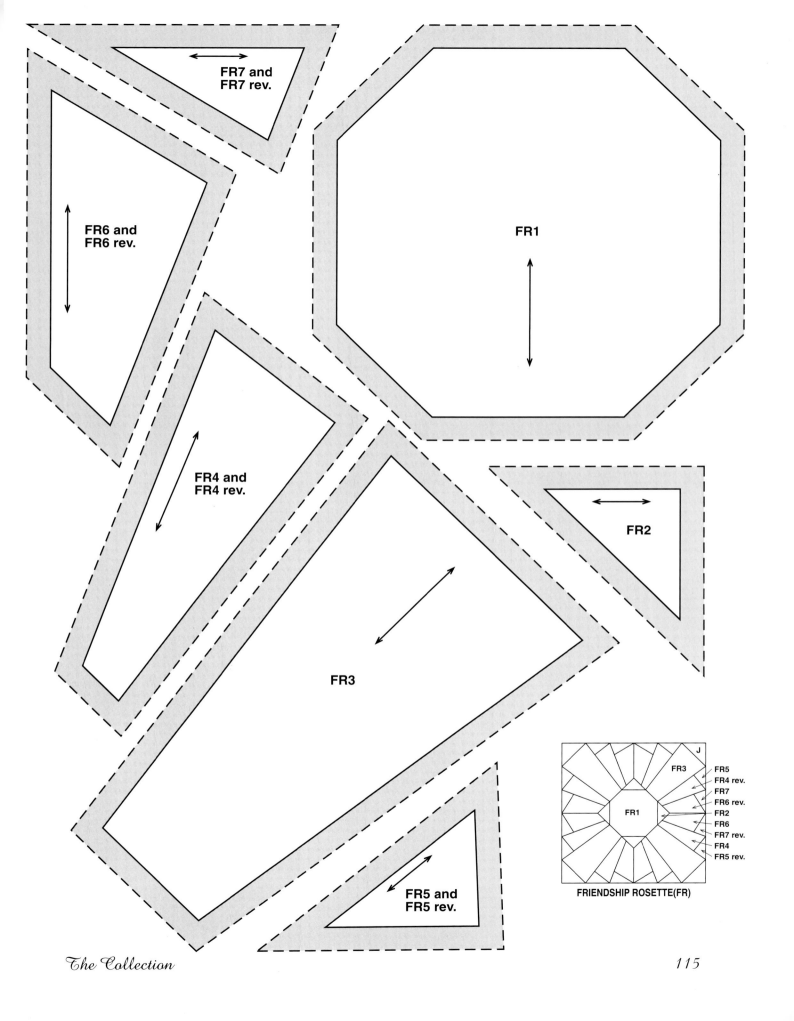

FR7 and
FR7 rev.

FR6 and
FR6 rev.

FR1

FR4 and
FR4 rev.

FR2

FR3

FR5 and
FR5 rev.

FR3
FR5
FR4 rev.
FR7
FR6 rev.
FR1
FR2
FR6
FR7 rev.
FR4
FR5 rev.
J

FRIENDSHIP ROSETTE(FR)

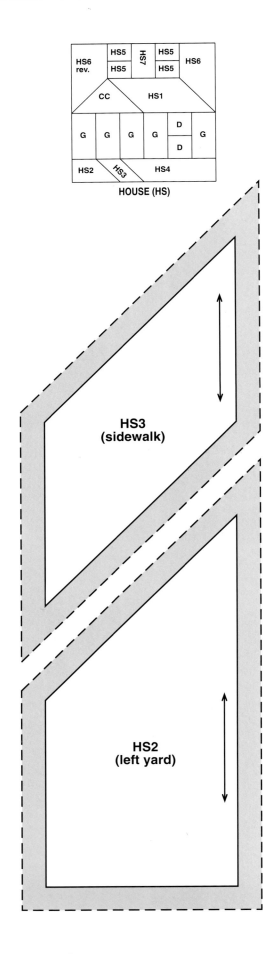

HS3
(sidewalk)

HS2
(left yard)

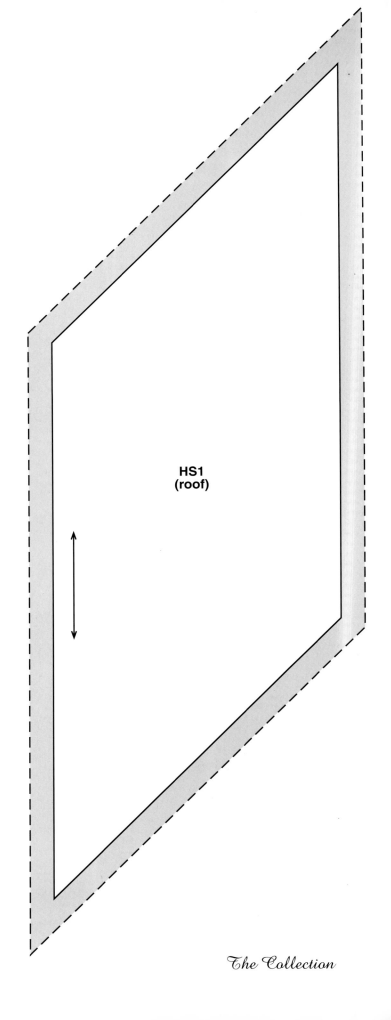

HS1
(roof)

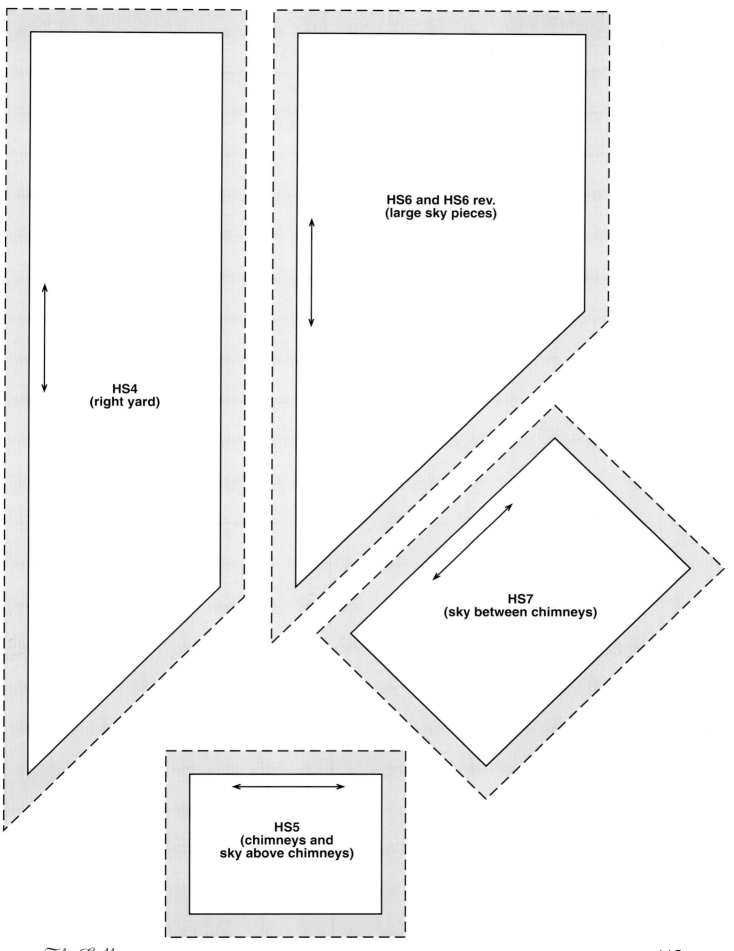

HS6 and HS6 rev.
(large sky pieces)

HS4
(right yard)

HS7
(sky between chimneys)

HS5
(chimneys and
sky above chimneys)

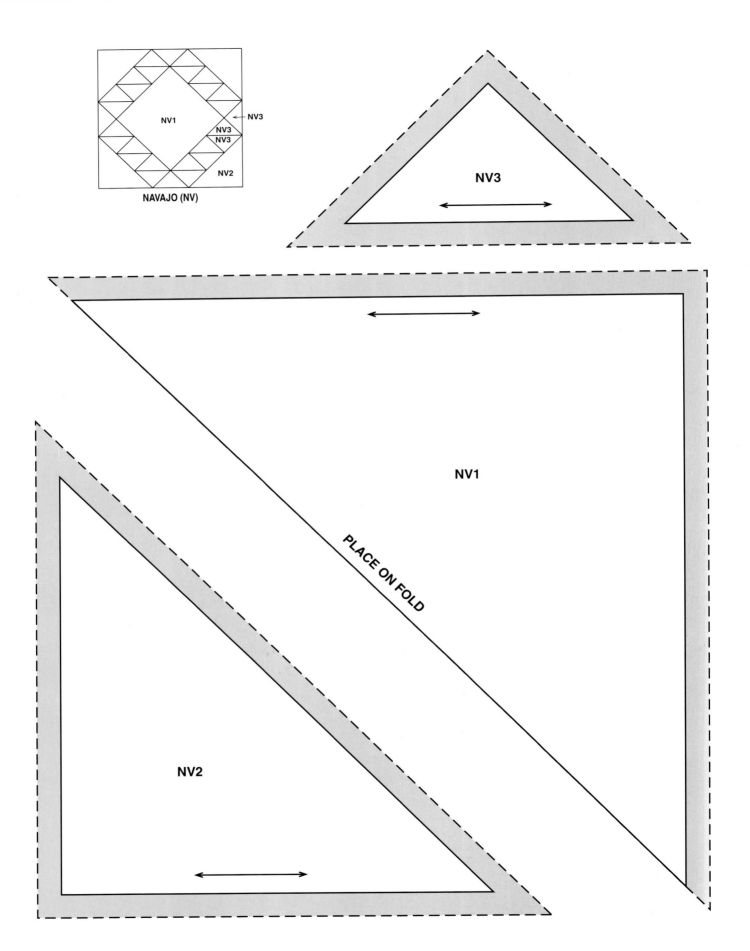

NV1

NV2

NV3

NAVAJO (NV)

NV3

NV3

NV3

PLACE ON FOLD

The Collection

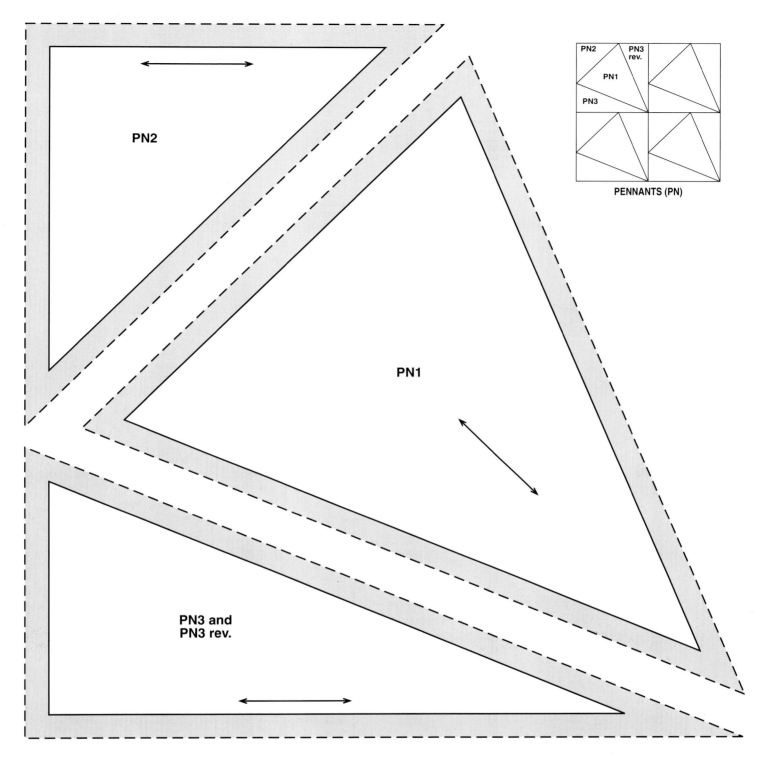

PN2

PN1

PN3 and
PN3 rev.

PN2 PN3 rev.

PN1

PN3

PENNANTS (PN)

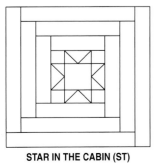

STAR IN THE CABIN (ST)

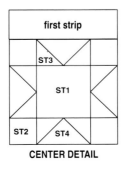

first strip

ST3

ST1

ST2 ST4

CENTER DETAIL

"Log" sizes for
STAR IN THE CABIN
1-1/4˝ x 4-1/2˝ (cut 1)
1-1/4˝ x 5-3/4˝ (cut 2)
1-1/4˝ x 7˝   (cut 2)
1-1/4˝ x 8-1/4˝ (cut 2)
1-1/4˝ x 9-1/2˝ (cut 2)
1-1/4˝ x 10-3/4˝ (cut 2)
1-1/4˝ x 12˝   (cut 1)

*Measurements are finished size
pieces. When cutting, add 1/4˝
seam allowance to all sides.*

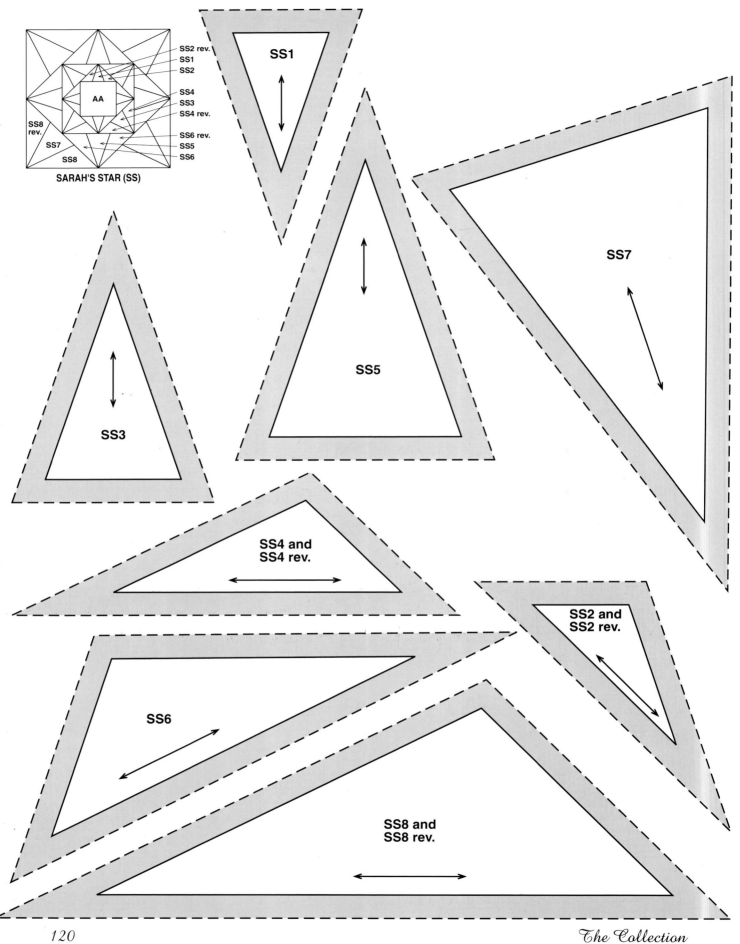

SARAH'S STAR (SS)

SS2 rev.
SS1
SS2
SS4
SS3
SS4 rev.
SS6 rev.
SS5
SS6

AA

SS8 rev.
SS7
SS8

SS1

SS7

SS3

SS5

SS4 and
SS4 rev.

SS2 and
SS2 rev.

SS6

SS8 and
SS8 rev.

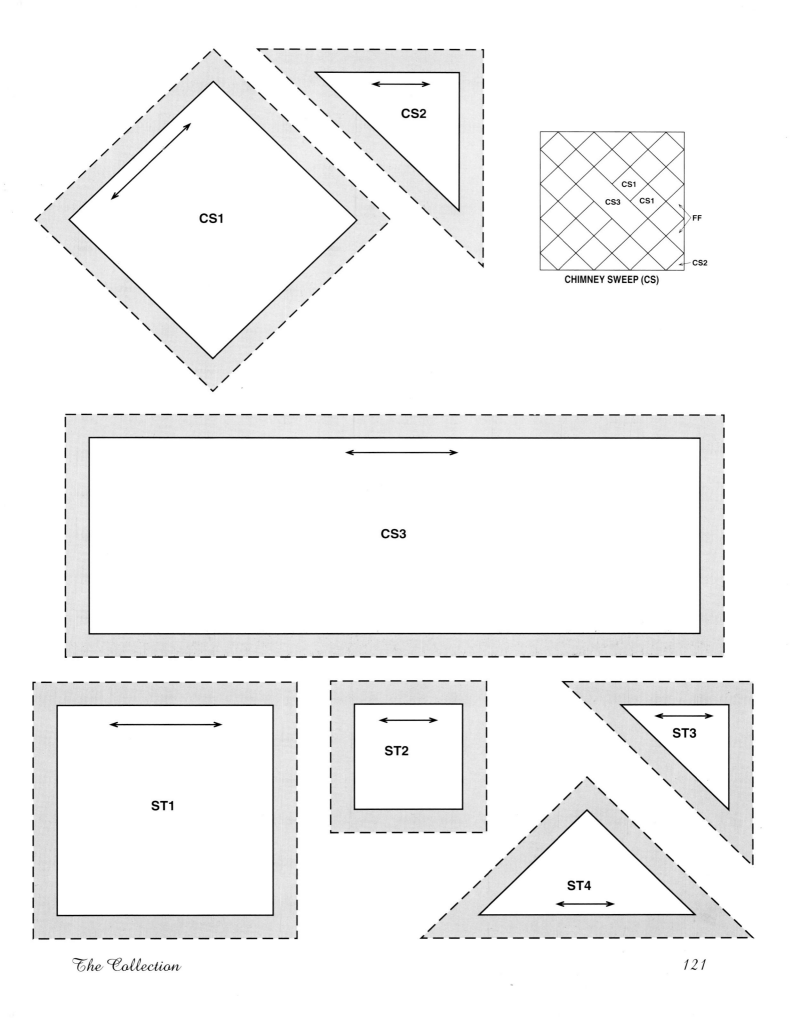

CS2

CS1

CHIMNEY SWEEP (CS)

CS1

CS3   CS1

FF

CS2

CS3

ST1

ST2

ST3

ST4

Appliqué Blocks

Acorn Medallion

Full-Blown Tulip

Heart Medallion

Lily Medallion

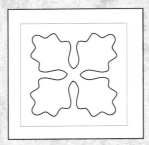

Oak Leaf

Oak Leaf & Reel

Petals & Sprigs

The Reel

Reel & Leaf

Tulip Medallion

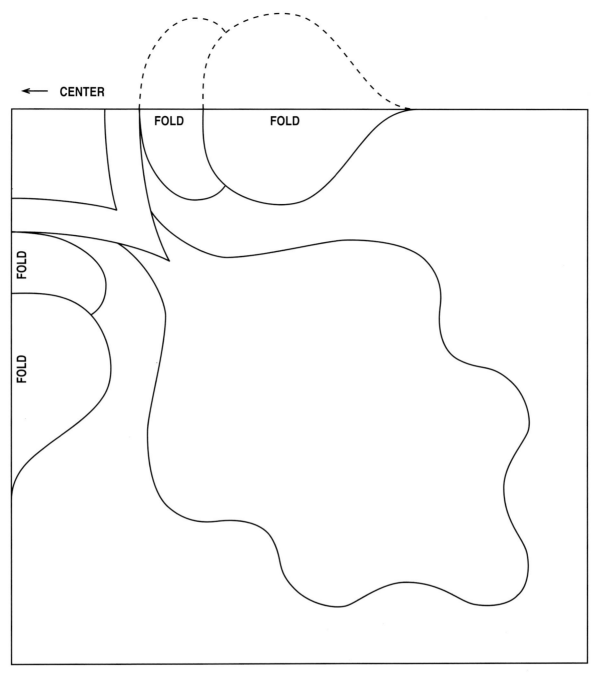

← CENTER

FOLD   FOLD

FOLD

FOLD

FOLD

OUTSIDE EDGE OF BLOCK

ACORN MEDALLION

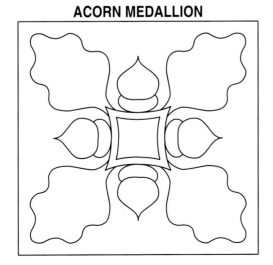

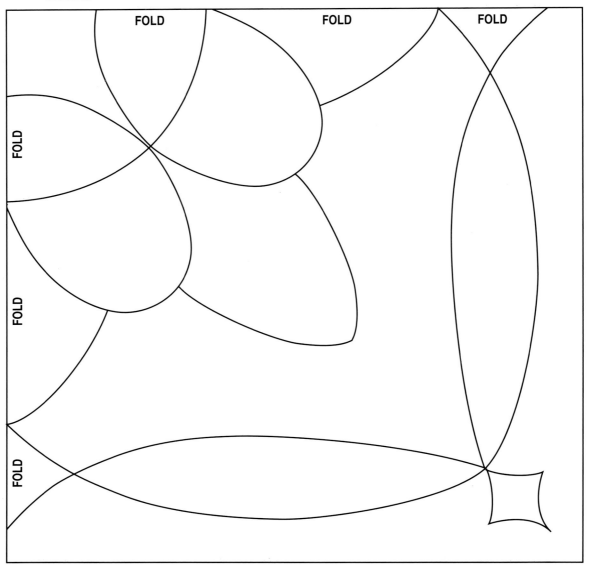

← CENTER

FOLD   FOLD   FOLD

FOLD

FOLD

FOLD

OUTSIDE EDGE OF BLOCK

FULL BLOWN TULIP

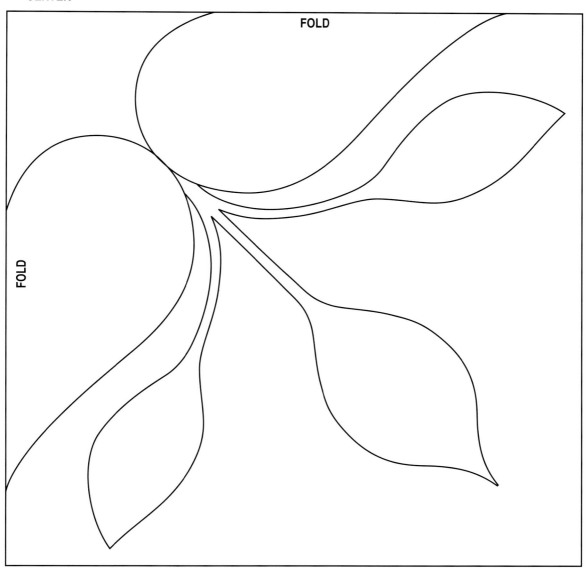

← CENTER

FOLD

FOLD

OUTSIDE EDGE OF BLOCK

HEART MEDALLION

←CENTER

FOLD

FOLD

OUTSIDE EDGE OF BLOCK

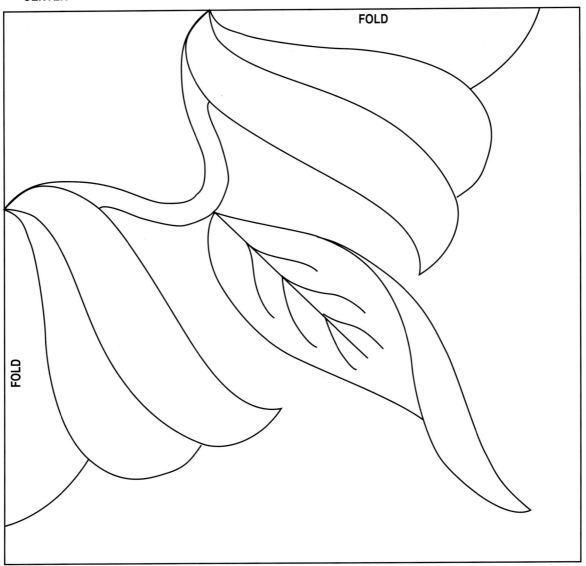

LILY MEDALLION

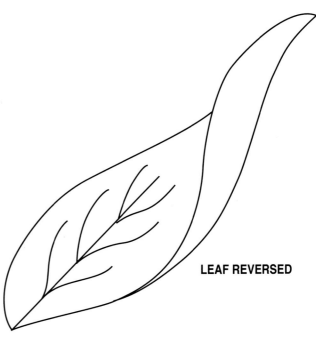

LEAF REVERSED

← CENTER

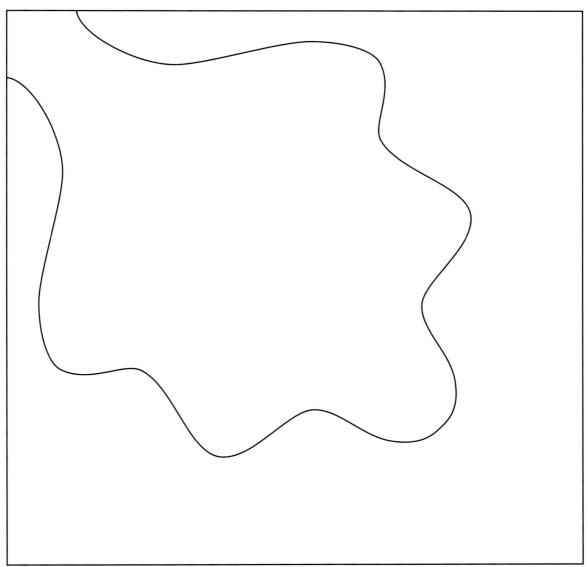

OUTSIDE EDGE OF BLOCK

OAK LEAF

←CENTER

FOLD

FOLD

FOLD

FOLD

FOLD

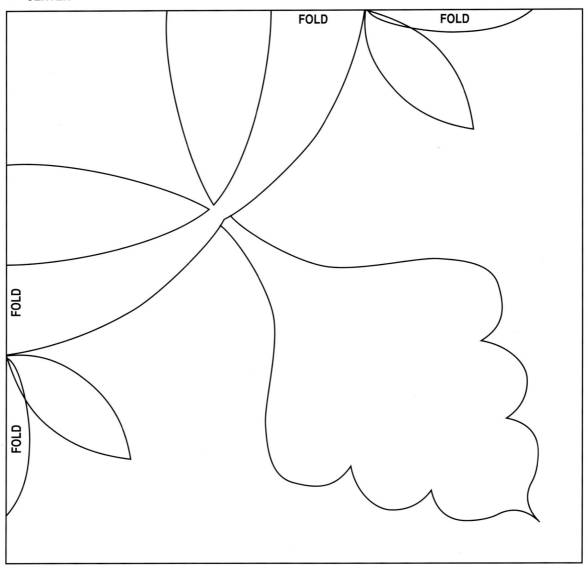

OUTSIDE EDGE OF BLOCK

OAK LEAF AND REEL

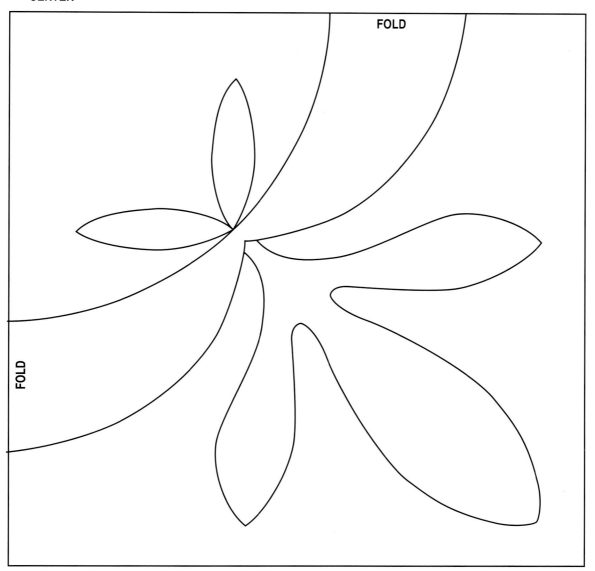

← CENTER

FOLD

FOLD

OUTSIDE EDGE OF BLOCK

PETALS & SPRIGS

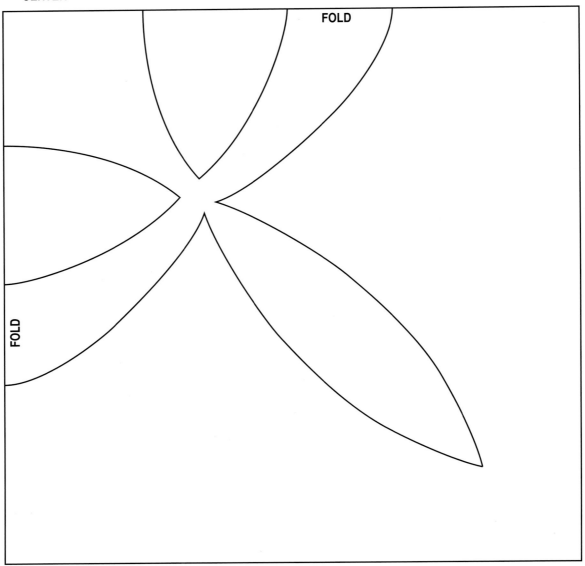

←— CENTER

FOLD

FOLD

OUTSIDE EDGE OF BLOCK

THE REEL

← CENTER

FOLD

FOLD

OUTSIDE EDGE OF BLOCK

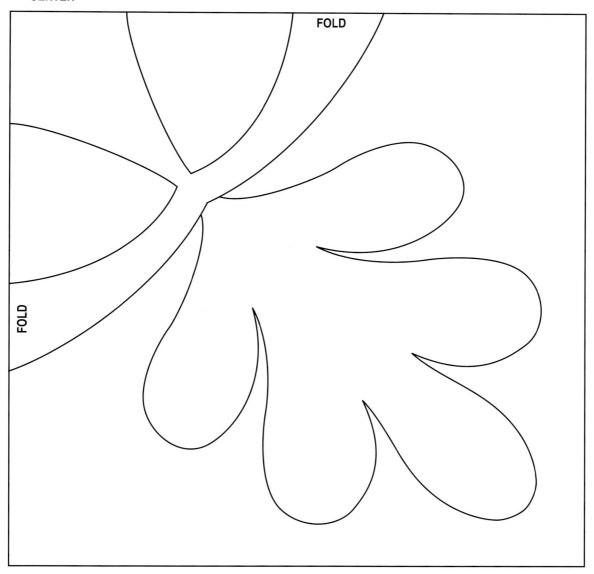

REEL & LEAF

← CENTER

FOLD

FOLD

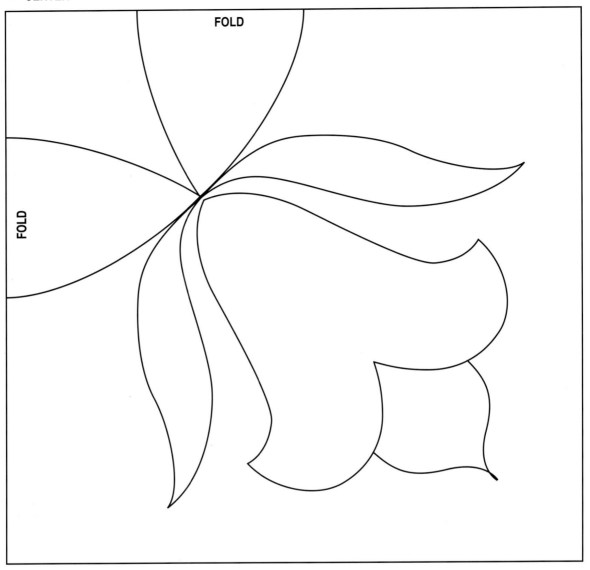

OUTSIDE EDGE OF BLOCK

TULIP MEDALLION

The Collection

Afterward

We anticipate the approach of the twenty-first century with a mixture of high hopes and trepidation. Caught in a whirlwind of change more rapid than any ever experienced, we struggle to determine what of the new is worth accepting and what of the old is worth keeping.

As quilters, we are certain of one thing: quilting is worth preserving, both as an art and a social activity. Today we make quilts for the same reasons our forebears did. We make them for warmth, even though we have the means to purchase manu-factured comforters. We make them for memories, for causes, for celebrations, and to honor our friends.

A signature quilt may accomplish any of these purposes as it evolves into a unique creation. It is a dual document: an expression of its maker's personality and a record of the times in which it was made. As we move together into the next century, we invite you to join us in the continuing tradition of the signature quilt. May the memories you record on your signature quilts become the ties that bind you to the past, present, and future.

Pepper and *Susan*

Dreams of Summer by Hilke K. Reid, Dunkirk, Maryland, 1994.
36 x 36 inches. Collection of the quiltmaker.

Glossary

Calling cards: small cards engraved with the owners' names and frequently embellished with beautiful colored symbols of friendship; a popular 19th century collectible.

Cult of True Womanhood: also called the Cult of Domesticity, the Cult of Sentimentality, and the Cult of Memory. A nineteenth century ideology emphasizing woman's role as center of the home and family and as keeper of tradition.

Friendship quilts: signature quilts made to be given to friends or family members, signed by friends and family members; made of one block repeated throughout the quilt, usually made of pieced blocks.

Friendship Album quilts: signature quilts made to be given to friends or family members, signed by friends and family members; made of many blocks, all different, usually combinations of pieced and appliquéd blocks.

Fund-raising quilts: signature quilts made to raise money for causes of interest to the makers. Usually the right to sign or have a signature on a quilt was sold as part of the fund-raising project, and often additional money was raised by raffling or auctioning the quilt later.

Gift books: usually small books, popular in the mid-nineteenth century, filled with edifying poems and phrases meant to be read and to be copied into autograph books and onto quilts.

Presentation quilts: signature quilts made to be given to important people, often on special occasions, usually made by groups of quilters.

Signature quilts: quilts which contain signed blocks, signed in one of several ways: inking, embroidery, stenciling, stamping.

Spencerian script: roundhand script taught in the nineteenth century; invented by Duntons of Boston and P.R. Spencer, who combined roundhand and angular scripts and made a semi-angular, beautiful, legible script.

Westward Movement: the migration of millions of Americans from the eastern seaboard states to settle the midwest and west; at its height from 1840 - the Civil War.

Sources for Supplies

Ask at your local quilt shop for the books and supplies you need. If they are unavailable, contact these companies:

Copyright Free Books

Dover Clip Art Series, Dover Publications, Inc. Catalogue available upon request from Dover Publications, Inc., 31 East 2nd Street, Mineola, N.Y. 11501.

Graphic Source Clip Art Book Library, Graphic Products Corporation, Wheeling, IL 60090.

Light Boxes

Me Sew Co., 24307 Magic Mountain Pkwy., Suite 195, Valencia, CA 91355, (800) 846-3739.

Seattle Woodworks, Ltd., 13032 Robinhood Lane, Snohomish, WA 98290, (800) 357-9663.

Pens (Pigma™ and Identipen™)

Wallflower Designs by Susan McKelvey, 1161 Goldfinch Lane, Millersville, MD 21108, (410) 923-6895.

Photo Transfer Services

Fabric Fotos, 3601 W. 15th Avenue, Suite 100, Amarillo, TX 79102, (806) 359-8241.

Great American Quilt Factory, Inc., 8970 East Hampden Ave., Denver, CO 80231, (303) 740-6206.

Rubber Stamps and Supplies

Wallflower Designs by Susan McKelvey, 1161 Goldfinch Lane, Millersville, MD 21108, (410) 923-6895.

Jukebox, 14128 Cameron Lane, Santa Ana, CA 92705, (714) 731-2563.

Pelle's, P.O. Box 242, Davenport, CA 95017, (408) 425-4743.

Quilting Stencils, Painting Stencils, Stencil Paints, Brushes and Template Plastic

Quilting Creations by D.J., Inc., P.O. Box 508, Zoar, Ohio 44697.

Traceable Designs for Quilts

Wallflower Designs by Susan McKelvey, 1161 Goldfinch Lane, Millersville, MD 21108, (410) 923-6895.

Footnotes

1. Linda Otto Lipsett, Remember Me: Women and Their Friendship Quilts (San Francisco: The Quilt Digest Press, 1985), p. 28.

2. Jessica F. Nicoll, Quilted for Friends: Delaware Valley Signature Quilts, 1840-1855 (Winterthur: The Winterthur Museum, 1986), p. 5.

3. Jane Bentley Kolter, Forget Me Not (Pittstown: The Main Street Press, 1985), p. 59.

4. Kolter, p. 25.

5. Kolter, p. 16.

6. Starr Ockenga, On Women & Friendship (New York: Stewart, Tabori & Chang, 1993), p. 44.

7. Lipsett, p. 26-27.

8. Kolter, p. 60.

9. Mary Bywater Cross, Treasures in the Trunk: Quilts of the Oregon Trail (Nashville: Rutledge Hill Press, 1993), pp. vii-viii.

10. Nicoll, p. 7.

11. Brackman, Barbara, Clues in the Calico (McLean: EPM Publications, Inc., 1989), p. 20.

12. Brackman, p. 20.

13. Pat Ferrero, Elaine Hedges, and Julie Silber, Hearts and Hands: The Influence of Women & Quilts on American Society (San Francisco: The Quilt Digest Press, 1987), p. 52.

14. Helen Young Frost and Pat Knight Stevenson, Grand Endeavors: Vintage Arizona Quilts and their Makers (Flagstaff: Northland Publishing), pp. 16-17.

15. Ferrero, p. 52.

16. Ferrero, p. 55.

17. Lipsett, p. 16.

18. Ricky Clark, "Fragile Families: Quilts as Kinship Bonds," The Quilt Digest 5 (San Francisco: The Quilt Digest Press, 1987), pp. 6-7.

19. Ferrero, p. 22.

20. Clark, pp. 7-8.

21. Ockenga, pp. 41 and 51.

22. Lipsett, p. 18.

23. Ockenga, p. 100.

24. Ockenga, p. 84.

25. Nicoll, p. 11.

26. Cross, p. ix.

27. Clark, pp. 16-17.

28. Clark, pp. 6-7.

29. Ferrero, p. 82.

30. Ferrero, p. 82.

31. Ferrero, p. 87.

32. Brackman, p. 27.

33. Ferrero, p. 69-72.

34. Abolitionist Baby Quilt, c. 1830's, collection of the Chester County Historical Society.

35. Ferrero, pp. 73-81.

36. Roderick Kiracofe, The American Quilt: A History of Cloth and Comfort 1750-1950 (New York: Clarkson Potter Publishers, 1993), p. 110.

37. Ockenga, p. 44.

38. Kolter, p. 82.

39. Brackman, p. 26.

40. Brackman, p. 33.

41. Lipsett, p. 20.

42. Kolter, p. 81.

43. Kolter, p. 101.

44. Brackman, p. 33.

45. Kolter, p. 116.

46. Nancy and Donald Roan, Lest I Shall Be Forgotten (Green Lane, PA: Goschenhoppen Historians, Inc., 1993), p. 17.

47. Lipsett, p. 17.

48. Lipsett, p. 17.

49. Lipsett, p. 18.

50. Ockenga, p. 151.

51. Ockenga, p. 152.

52. Ockenga, p. 35.

53. Hill, Hill's Manual of Social and Business Forms (Chicago: Hill Standard Book Co., Publishers, @ 1880), p. 40.

54. Ockenga, p. 44.

55. Ockenga, p. 35.

56. Ferrero, p. 33.

57. Kolter, p. 66.

58. Lipsett, pp. 20-21.

59. Kolter, p. 15.

60. Kolter, p. 59.

61. Kiracofe, p. 81.

62. Roan, p. 17.

63. Kolter, pp. 59-60.

A Selected Bibliography

Brackman, Barbara. *Clues in the Calico.* EPM Publications, Inc., McLean, VA, 1989.

Brackman, Barbara. *Encyclopedia of Appliqué.* EPM Publications, Inc., McLean,VA, 1993.

Brackman, Barbara. *Encyclopedia of Pieced Quilt Patterns.* Prairie Flower Publishing, Lawrence, KS, 1984.

Brackman, Barbara, Chinn, Jennie A., Davis, Gayle R., Thompson, Terry, Reimer-Farley, Sara, and Hornback, Nancy. *Kansas Quilts & Quilters.* University Press of Kansas, Lawrence, 1993.

Clark, Ricky. "Fragile Families: Quilts as Kinship Bonds." *Quilt Digest 5.* The Quilt Digest Press, San Francisco, 1987.

Cleveland, Richard L. and Donna Blister. *Plain and Fancy.* The Quilt Digest Press, Gualala, CA, 1991.

Cory, Pepper. *Crosspatch.* C & T Publishing, Lafayette, CA, 1989.

Cory, Pepper. *Happy Trails.* C & T Publishing, Lafayette, CA, 1991.

Cross, Mary Bywater. *Treasures in the Trunk: Quilts of the Oregon Trail.* Rutledge Hill Press, Nashville, 1993.

Elbert, E. Duane, and Kamm, Rachael. *History from the Heart.* Rutledge Hill Press, Nashville, 1993.

Ferraro, Pat, Hedges, Elaine, and Silber, Julie. *Hearts & Hands.* The Quilt Digest Press, San Francisco, 1987.

Frost, Helen Young, and Knight-Stevenson, Pam. *Grand Endeavors: Vintage Arizona Quilts and Their Makers.* Northland Publishing, Flagstaff, AZ, 1992.

Goldman, Marilyn and Wiebusch, Marguerite. *Quilts of Indiana.* Indiana University Press, Bloomington, 1991.

Hill. *Hill's Manual of Social and Business Forms.* Hill Standard Book Co., Publishers, Chicago, circa 1880.

Kiracofe, Roderick. *The American Quilt: A History of Cloth and Comfort 1750-1950.* Clarkson Potter Publishers, New York, 1993.

Kolter, Jane Bentley. *Forget Me Not.* The Main Street Press, Pittstown, NJ, 1985.

Lasansky, Jeannette. *Pieced by Mother.* The Oral Traditions Project of the Union County Historical Society, Lewisburg, PA, 1987.

Lipsett, Linda Otto. *Remember Me: Women & Their Friendship Quilts.* The Quilt Digest Press, San Francisco, 1985.

McKelvey, Susan. *A Treasury of Quilt Labels.* C & T Publishing, Lafayette, CA, 1993.

McKelvey, Susan. *Color for Quilters II.* Wallflower Designs, Millersville, MD, 1994.

McKelvey, Susan. *Friendship's Offering.* C & T Publishing, Lafayette, CA, 1987.

McKelvey, Susan. *Scroll & Banners to Trace.* Wallflower Designs, Millersville, MD, 1990.

Miller, Margaret. *Blockbuster Quilts.* That Patchwork Place, Bothell, WA, 1991.

Nicoll, Jessica F. *Quilted for Friends: Delaware Valley Signature Quilts, 1840-1855.* The Winterthur Museum, Winterthur, 1986.

Ockenga, Starr. *On Women & Friendship.* Stewart, Tabori & Chang, New York, 1993.

Roan, Nancy and Donald. *Lest I Shall Be Forgotten.* Goschenhoppen Historians, Inc., Green Lake, PA, 1993.

Simms, Ami. *Creating Scrapbag Quilts.* Mallery Press, Flint, MI, 1993.

_____ *The Kansas City Star Quilt Pattern Collection.* Central Oklahoma Quilters Guild, Oklahoma City, OK, 1989.

_____ *New Jersey Quilts.* American Quilter's Society, Paducah, KY, 1992.

_____ *The Quilt Engagement Calendar 1988.* E.P. Dutton, New York, NY, 1987.

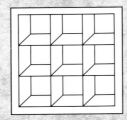
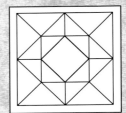
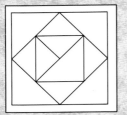
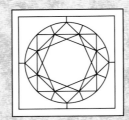
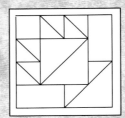

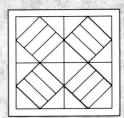
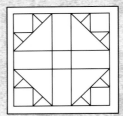
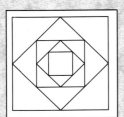
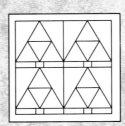
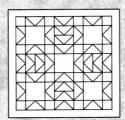

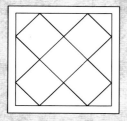

Freedom, p. 96

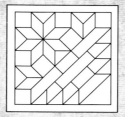

Friendship Basket, p. 91

Friendship Circle, p. 114

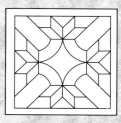

Friendship Knot, p. 110

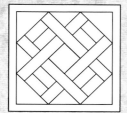

Friendship Links, p. 93

Friendship Rosette, p. 115

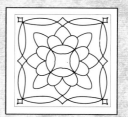

Full-Blown Tulip, p. 124

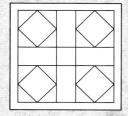

Garden of Eden, p. 102

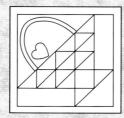

Grandmother's Basket, p. 103

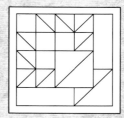

Grape Basket, p. 102

Heart Medallion, p. 125

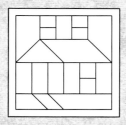

House, p. 116

Kansas Beauty, p. 90

Lily Medallion, p. 126

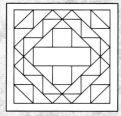

Memory Block, p. 101

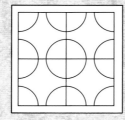

Mill Wheel, p. 109

Navajo, p. 118

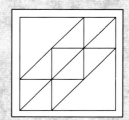

Northwind, p. 92

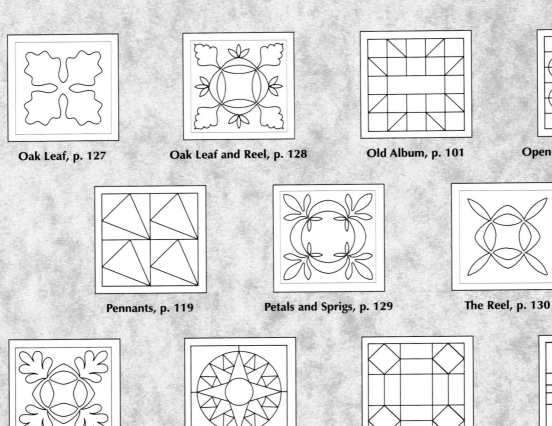

Oak Leaf, p. 127   **Oak Leaf and Reel, p. 128**   **Old Album, p. 101**   **Opening Valentines, p. 108**

Pennants, p. 119   **Petals and Sprigs, p. 129**   **The Reel, p. 130**

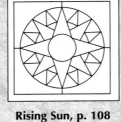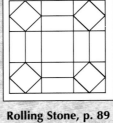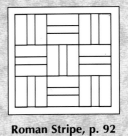

Reel and Leaf, p. 131   **Rising Sun, p. 108**   **Rolling Stone, p. 89**   **Roman Stripe, p. 92**

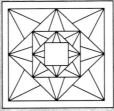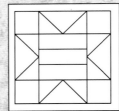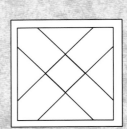

Sarah's Star, p. 120   **Signature Star, p. 98**   **Snowflake, p. 113**

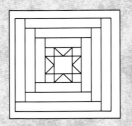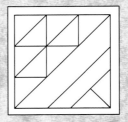

Star in the Cabin, p. 119   **Star of the West, p. 106**   **Tried and True, p. 93**   **Tulip Medallion, p. 132**

About The Quiltmakers

Linda Baker, Arnold, Maryland.
Linda traces her love of quilting to 1980, when she became a founding member of the Annapolis Quilt Guild. She loves piecing and experimenting with color, and several of her quilts have won prizes. Linda's quilts appear in Susan's second book, *Light and Shadows*. Her work has been exhibited in the Tactile Architecture Show at the Decatur House, Washington, D.C.

Rolinda Collinson, Friendship, Maryland.
For Rolinda, the mother of four young children, quilting provides relaxation. Her grandmother, mother and aunt are all quilters, and Rolinda has been quilting since she was a child.

Alexandra Capadalis Dupré, Long Beach, New York.
Although she has a degree in graphic arts, Alex's advice to quilters is simple and direct. "Do what you love and it shows!" Her quilts frequently win awards, including AQS competitions. Her quilted garments have appeared in two Fairfield Fashion Show productions, and her book, *Men's Wear; A Guide to Designing Wearable Art for Men*, will be published in 1996.

Eleanor Eckman, Lutherville, Maryland.
Eleanor's quiltmaking is the legacy of a long family tradition of fine needlework. Her grandmother and great-aunt taught her to use a needle when she was a small child; her mother and aunts carried on the tradition, and her two daughters are both needle artists. Picking up a needle, she says, is her "joy in life, an outlet for creativity, a comfort in time of stress, and perhaps a way to be remembered throughout the years." The Oak Leaf and Reel was made in honor of the needlewomen in her family. Eleanor lives with her husband and their yellow lab, Sandy, and she loves to make appliqué quilts.

Phyllis L. Foust, Baldwin, Maryland.
Phyllis, who loves Baltimore Album and Crazy Quilts, belongs to five quilt guilds because they provide not only friendship but creative energy. She loves taking classes and learning new needlework techniques. Phyllis and her husband enjoy their three children and two grandchildren.

Virginia Fry, Fulton, Maryland.
Virginia has always loved sewing and fabric. At the age of nine, she made her first skirt from feed sacks. She has been quilting for the past twenty-five years, but did not become fully involved until her children were grown. When she is not quilting, Virginia works at Johns Hopkins University.

Barbara Gabel, Arnold, Maryland.
Barbara's interest in quilting began when her mother gave her a Grandmother's Flower Garden quilt top begun by her great-grandmother, and suggested that she finish it. The quilt top lay unfinished until four years ago, when she took a quilting class, and was immediately hooked. Barbara is a science teacher at Arundel Junior High School.

Jan Gagliano, Haslett, Michigan.
Jan confesses that she was a D student in art, but she now thinks her quiltmaking would merit an A for creativity. Never one to follow a pattern exactly, she says that the opportunity for innovation keeps her involved in the quiltmaking process. A member of the Sunbonnet Sues in Canoes, Jan lives with her husband Charlie, whom she calls "my personal patron of the arts."

Barbara Hawkins, Lansing, Michigan.
Barbara fondly recalls a favorite quilt from childhood as her introduction to patchwork and quilting. While attending college, she made a patchwork purse for her mother, but her "smoldering creativity" really caught fire when she joined her local guild six years ago. Barbara is a member of the Sunbonnet Sues in Canoes, which she credits with "immediate support, or at least a reaction" for her quilting projects.

Gail Hill, Holt, Michigan.
A quilter for almost twenty years, Gail admits to a particular weakness for ugly fabrics because "the pretty florals will always be around." She confesses that having children drove her to quiltmaking because she needed to get out of the house. Her quilting group, the Sunbonnet Sues in Canoes, helps her to recognize the humor in quiltmaking. Gail's other hobby is collecting shoulder pads.

Lynn A. Irwin, Sparks, Maryland.

Lynn believes that "the immortality everyone strives for is passed down form generation to generation. It is our link from the past to the future. The process of creating and finishing a project releases our tensions and calms our souls, preparing us for the future at the same time that we reach out to the past. Needlework brings joy and tranquility to my life, and a hope that the beauty of the skill does not die with future generations."

Jodi King, Friendship, Maryland.

An embroiderer since childhood, Jodi discovered quilting in 1990. She has been quilting ever since, adding quilts to her first love, counted cross-stitch.

Ruth Ann Klos, Fork, Maryland.

Ruth Ann took her first quilting class in 1983. She won a blue ribbon for her first quilt, and since that time has won many awards. She now teaches quiltmaking, belongs to four guilds, and continues to take classes as well as to work in her father's business. Ruth Ann says her husband and family "support me in my world of quilting."

Nina Lord, Annapolis, Maryland.

After her aunt taught her to quilt when she was twelve, Nina made several large quilts. She became re-involved in the late seventies when her children were in elementary school, and raffle quilts were good fund-raisiers. Nina is a founding member of the Annapolis Quilt Guild, which she has served in many capacities. A machine piecer and hand quilter, she enjoys quilt challenges and experimenting with color and pattern. One of Nina's quilts appears on the cover of Susan's second book, *Light and Shadows*.

Lynn Phillips, Abingdon, Maryland.

Quilting is only one of many hobbies for Lynn. She has studied art and architecture, and worked as a technical illustrator and graphic artist. Her quiltmaking began in 1986, when she was living in Saudi Arabia and recovering from two broken arms. Lynn is married, and has two cats.

Barbara Rasch, White Hall, Maryland.

Although Barbara quilted for one year, 1979, she didn't become an avid quilter until ten years later, when she joined the Tulip Tree Quilters. Her primary focus is on appliqué work, which she discovered in a class with Mimi Dietrich. Barbara is a member of five quilt groups, both large and small. She is married, with two children living nearby. Her daughter promises that one day she will start a quilt like Mom's.

Nora Reedy, Bel Air, Maryland.

Nora has been quilting for fifteen years and loves appliqué. She is the vice-president of the Flying Geese guild, and also a member of the Baltimore Appliqué Society.

Hilke Reid, Dunkirk, Maryland.

Hilke regards quiltmaking as "the ultimate needlecraft" because it offers balance to a life filled with work and motherhood. She has sewn all her life, learning as a child from packages sent by her grandmother in Germany. After decades of travel and fabric collecting, Hilke discovered quilting in 1991. Scrap quilts are her special passion.

Eileen Schamel, Boonesboro, Maryland.

Eileen has been involved with quilts since childhood, when she learned from her mother, but she didn't make her first quilt, a pieced butterfly, until the 1950's. During the next twenty years, she raised her family and made four quilts. As an antique dealer, she specialized in quilts and 1930's feedsacks. When her daughter insisted that she pick up a twenty-year-old unfinished project, Eileen returned to quilting, which became a passion. She particularly loves miniatures and wall hangings.

Sunbonnet Sues in Canoes, Lansing, Michigan.

The Sues are an informal group of friends united by their mutual love of quilting, their fondness for food, and their need to tell bad jokes. The name of the group originated with a working group which made quilts to commemorate Valerie Fons' canoe odyssey from the North Pole to the South Pole. Meeting every Wednesday night since 1990, the Sues now make quilts for themselves and for special occasions. Past and present members include Betty Bergeon, Gayle Cain, Enola Clegg, Pepper Cory, Daisy DeHaven, Edna Eckert, Valerie Fons, Jan Gagliano, Dusty DeHaven Hailey, Barbara Hawkins, Gail Hill, Mary Hutchins, Jane Johnson, Agnes Ketchey, Carol Seamon and Sue Stephenson.

About The Authors

*P*epper Cory's quilting career began in 1971, with the purchase of an old quilt at a garage sale. After five years of quiltmaking and teaching patchwork, Pepper opened her shop, *Culpepper's Quilts*, the first store to offer quilting supplies and fabrics in Lansing, Michigan.

The interests she developed in Amish quilts, scrap quilts and historical quilts led to the publication of several books, including *Quilting Designs from the Amish, Quilting Designs from Antique Quilts, Crosspatch - Inspirations in Multi-Block Quilts*, and *Happy Trails - Variations on the Classic Drunkard's Path Pattern*. Her column, "The Green Quilter," appears in *Traditional Quiltworks* magazine.

In addition to teaching and writing, Pepper designs quilting tools and quilting stencils for *Quilting Creations by D.J.*, and foundation piecing stencils for *Graphic Impressions*.

Pepper's teaching travels have taken her to twenty-five states, as well as Australia, Belgium, England, Germany and the Netherlands. Pepper practices her profession and her hobby in her quilt studio in the Kalamazoo Center in Lansing, Michigan. She lives with her husband, Rod, who supports her work, but sometimes forces her to take a vacation! Three beloved cats complete Pepper's household.

*S*usan McKelvey took her first quilting class in 1977. Quilting steadily since that time, she has produced numerous works which have appeared in museums, galleries, books, magazines and quilt shows throughout the United States. In 1987, in order to design and produce unusual quilting and writing supplies and patterns, she started her own company, *Wallflower Designs*.

Susan is the author of five books on the subjects of color and writing on and labeling quilts: *Color for Quilters, Light & Shadows, Friendship's Offering, Scrolls & Banners* and *A Treasury of Quilt Labels*. Her fabric designs are produced by Chapel House Fabrics.

Susan's teaching credentials include a B.A. degree in English and Drama at Cornell College, and an M.A. in English and Education at the University of Chicago. She taught English for two years of Peace Corps service in Ethiopia. Since that time, Susan has taught at major conferences throughout the United States and in Germany.

Susan and her husband, Doug, parents of two college age children, live in rural Anne Arundel County, Maryland, with two rescued golden retrievers and two beautiful cats, all of whom think they were born to grace quilts!

Summer's End by Virginia Fry, Fulton, Maryland, 1995. 40 x 40 inches. Collection of the quiltmaker.

FACTIVITY®

JOURNEY AROUND AND INSIDE YOUR AMAZING

BODY

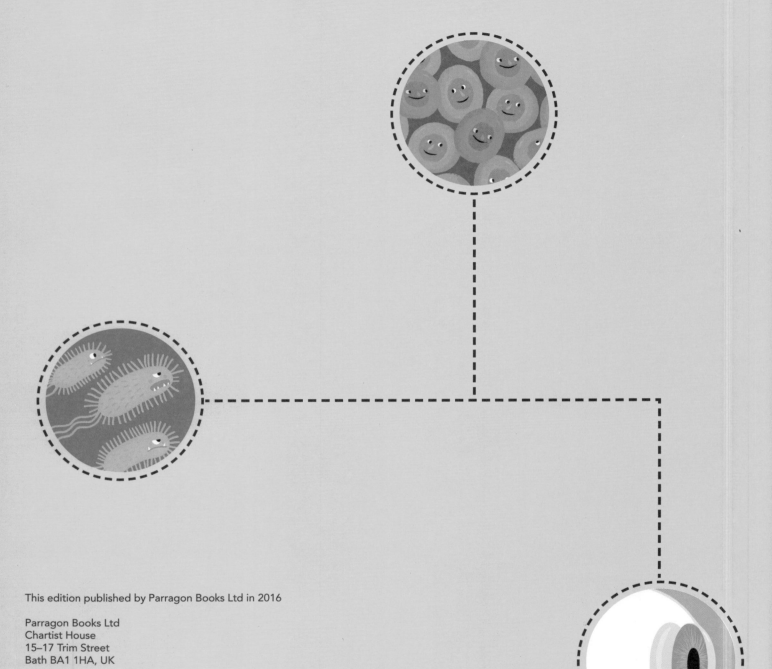

This edition published by Parragon Books Ltd in 2016

Parragon Books Ltd
Chartist House
15–17 Trim Street
Bath BA1 1HA, UK
www.parragon.com

Copyright © Parragon Books Ltd 2014–2016

Written by Anna Claybourne
Illustrated by Mar Ferrero
Consultant: Dr Clare J. Ray

ISBN 978-1-4748-6267-7

Printed in China

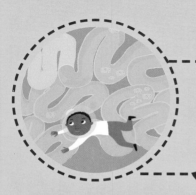

FACTIVITY

JOURNEY AROUND AND INSIDE YOUR AMAZING BODY

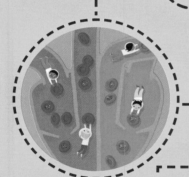

PaRRagon

Bath • New York • Cologne • Melbourne • Delhi
Hong Kong • Shenzhen • Singapore

Contents

Your amazing human body

Your body is an incredible living, breathing, moving, eating, talking, thinking machine. Look closer and you'll discover that your body has many different parts, all working together.

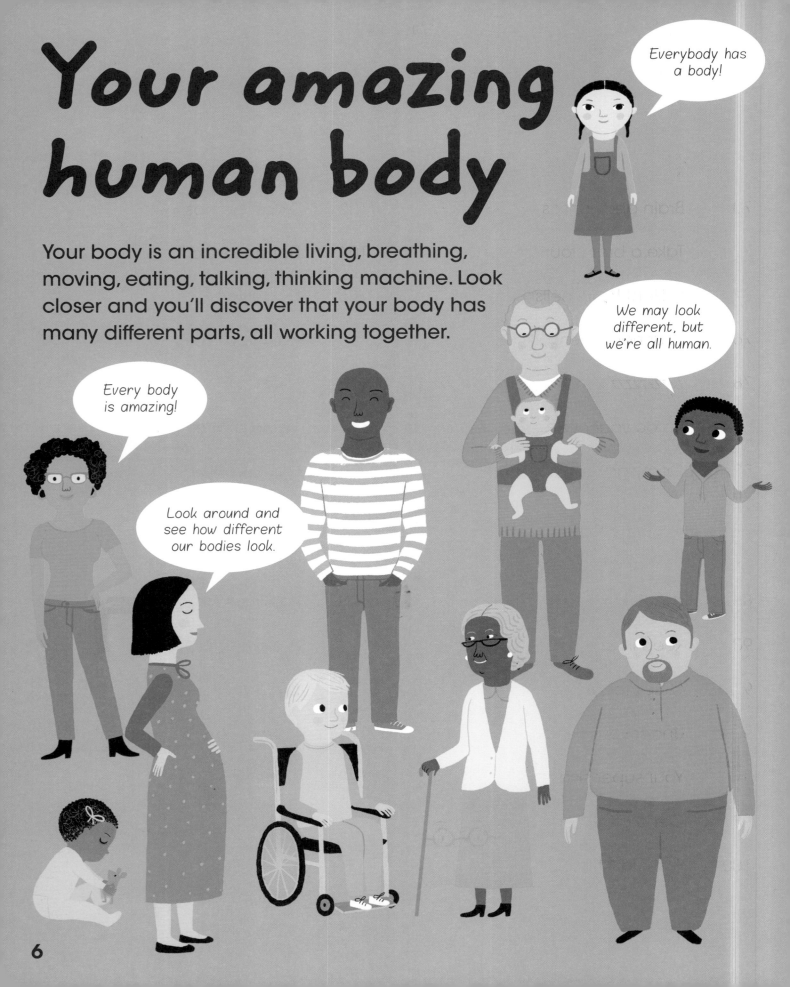

6

HUNDREDS of bones and muscles.

THOUSANDS of miles of tiny tubes.

MILLIONS of hairs.

Just ONE human body has...

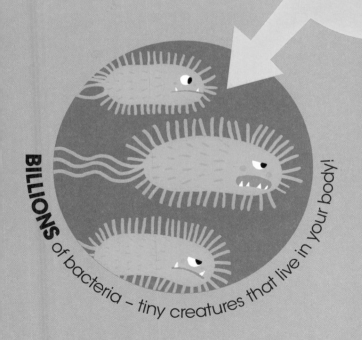

BILLIONS of bacteria – tiny creatures that live in your body!

TRILLIONS of cells – the tiny building blocks that make up living things.

Being human

Living things come in all shapes and sizes, but human beings are unlike most other creatures. We walk upright on two legs, we use our brains to think and our hands to make and do useful things.

The human body is pretty smart when you think about all the things it does.

- Your body grows bigger and bigger until you're an adult.
- It builds new body parts to replace old ones.
- It repairs itself if it gets broken.
- It has special body parts to sense light, sounds, smells, tastes and objects.

My pet dog walks on four legs and has paws instead of hands with fingers and a thumb.

Your body even reads books about itself!

When you look at other animals, you can see what makes humans different.

8

Imagine you had to describe a human being to someone from another planet. Draw yourself and write your report on human beings below.

HUMAN BEING

Size ....

Appearance ....

Colour ....

Body parts ....

Senses ....

Skills ....

....

Body map

This handy body map will help you as you explore the human body.

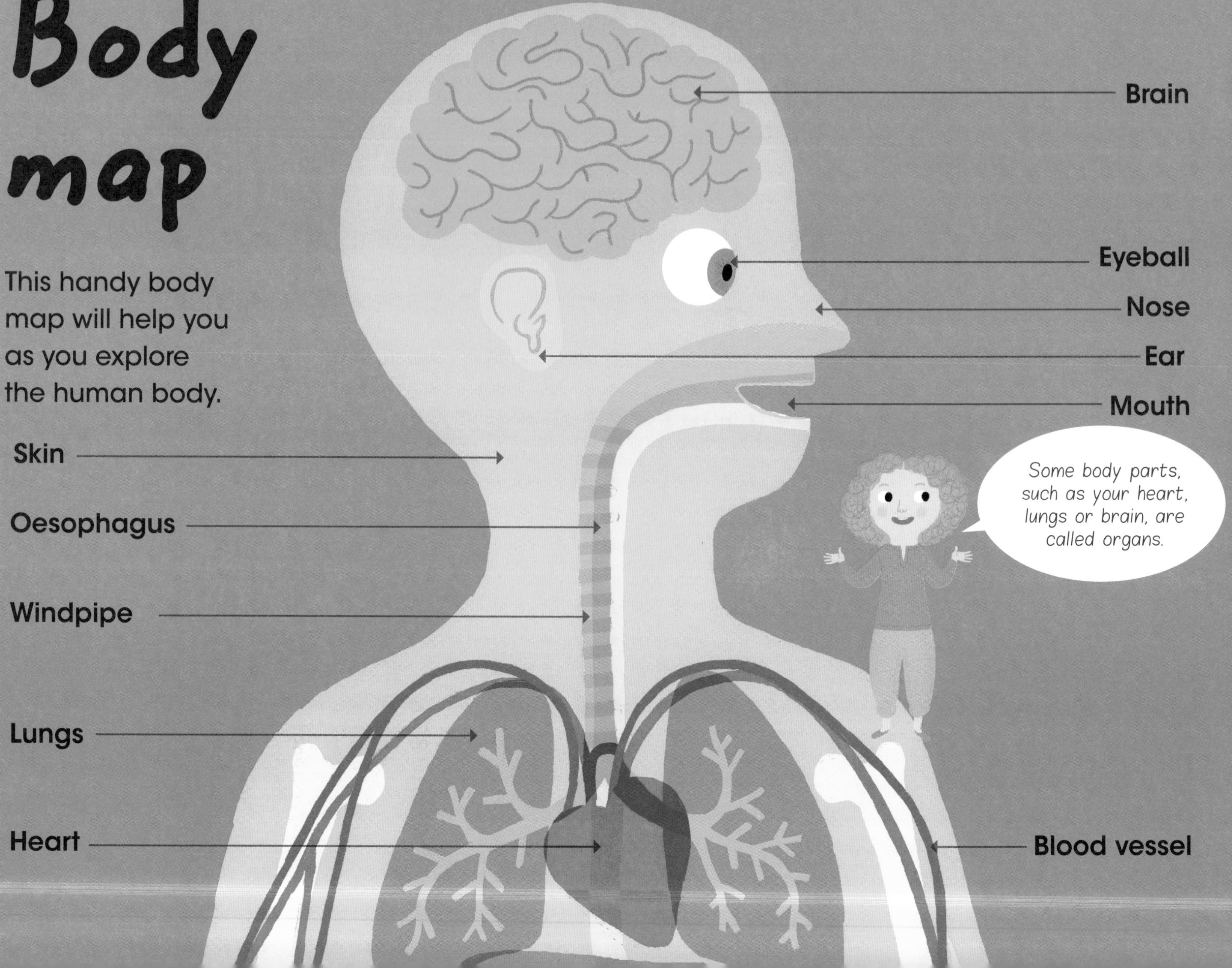

Brain

Eyeball

Nose

Ear

Mouth

Some body parts, such as your heart, lungs or brain, are called organs.

Skin

Oesophagus

Windpipe

Lungs

Heart

Blood vessel

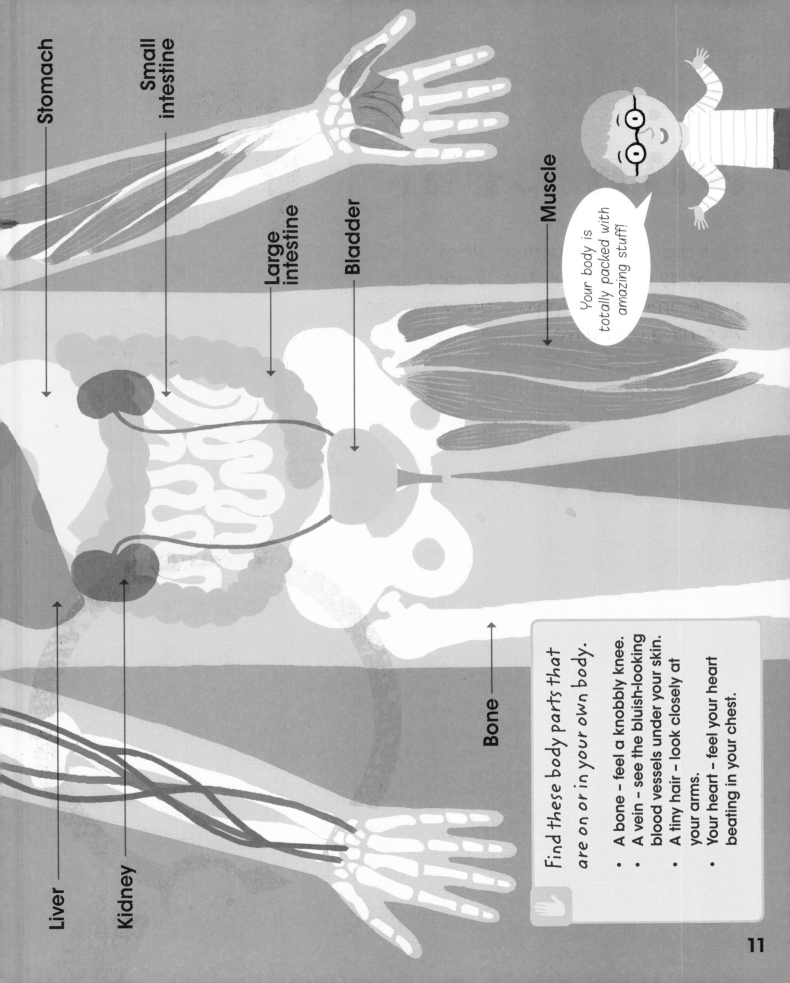

Stomach

Small intestine

Large intestine

Bladder

Muscle

Liver

Kidney

Bone

Your body is totally packed with amazing stuff!

Find these body parts that are on or in your own body.

- A bone – feel a knobbly knee.
- A vein – see the bluish-looking blood vessels under your skin.
- A tiny hair – look closely at your arms.
- Your heart – feel your heart beating in your chest.

11

It all starts with cells

Cells are the tiny building blocks that the body is made of. They work hard all the time, keeping your body moving, breathing and alive.

A microscope can zoom in close enough to see cells.

If you want to see a cell, you'll have to look REALLY closely.

You need to get even closer than this.

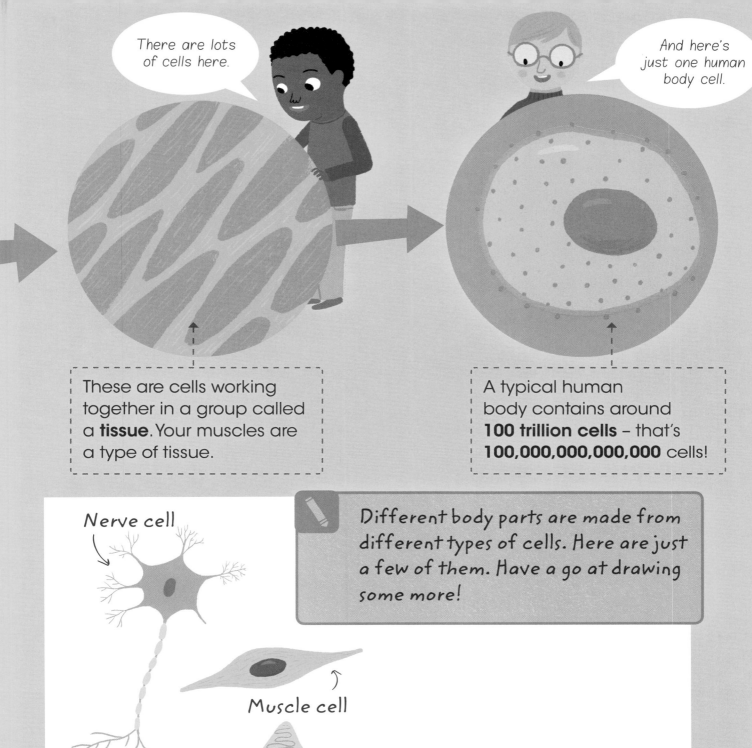

There are lots of cells here.

And here's just one human body cell.

These are cells working together in a group called a **tissue**. Your muscles are a type of tissue.

A typical human body contains around **100 trillion cells** – that's **100,000,000,000,000** cells!

Different body parts are made from different types of cells. Here are just a few of them. Have a go at drawing some more!

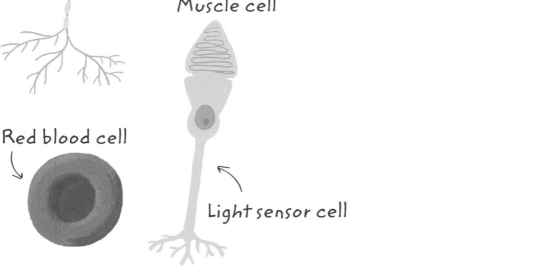

Nerve cell

Muscle cell

Red blood cell

Light sensor cell

13

Bones and muscles

Bones give your body its shape and allow you to move. Your skeleton has more than 200 bones. Muscles are joined to your bones and you use them every time you move.

 Draw what you think you would look like without any bones. Gross!

Without me you'd be a helpless, wobbly blob!

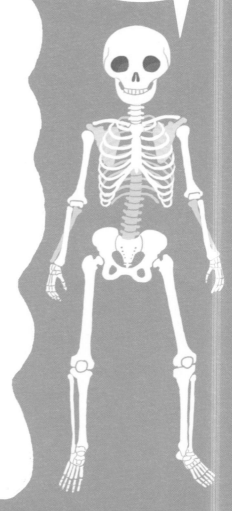

Hey! Are we related?

Bones are your body's framework. Your leg bones are thick and strong to hold your body's weight.

You need knees if you want to run!

Joints are the bendy bits where two bones meet. They make your body flexible, so that you can move about.

Your nifty knee joint

Knee joint

Thigh bone

Muscles pull bones into different positions.

Stretchy **ligaments** fasten one bone to another.

Tendons are like strings tying your muscles to your bones.

Calf bone

Kneecap

Smooth, springy **cartilage** grows at the ends of the bones. It stops the hard ends of the bones rubbing against each other where they meet.

Shinbone

Your skeleton

All your bones join together to make up your skeleton. You can't see your skeleton because it's covered by skin and muscle, so take a quick peek at all those bones below!

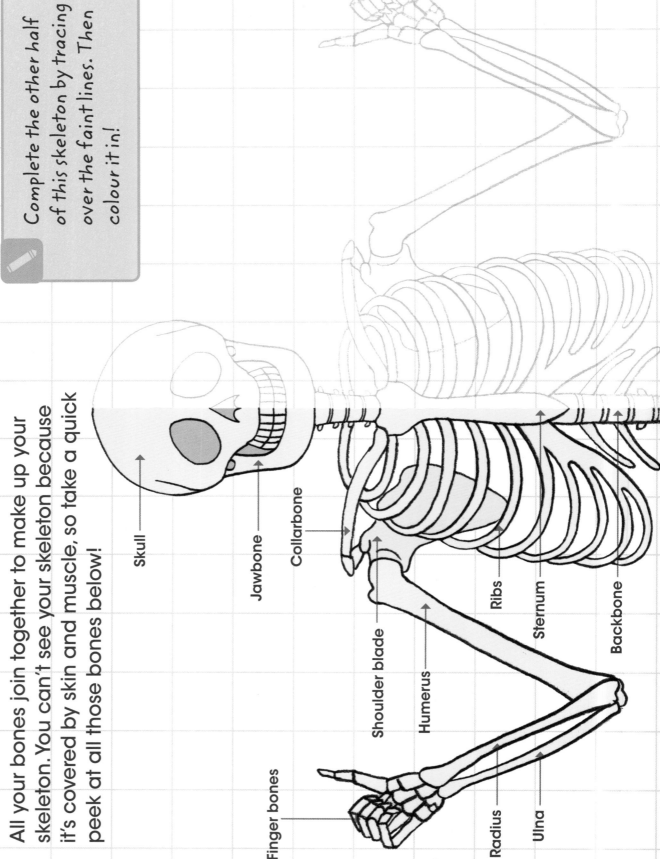

Complete the other half of this skeleton by tracing over the faint lines. Then colour it in!

Skull

Jawbone

Collarbone

Shoulder blade

Humerus

Ribs

Sternum

Backbone

Finger bones

Radius

Ulna

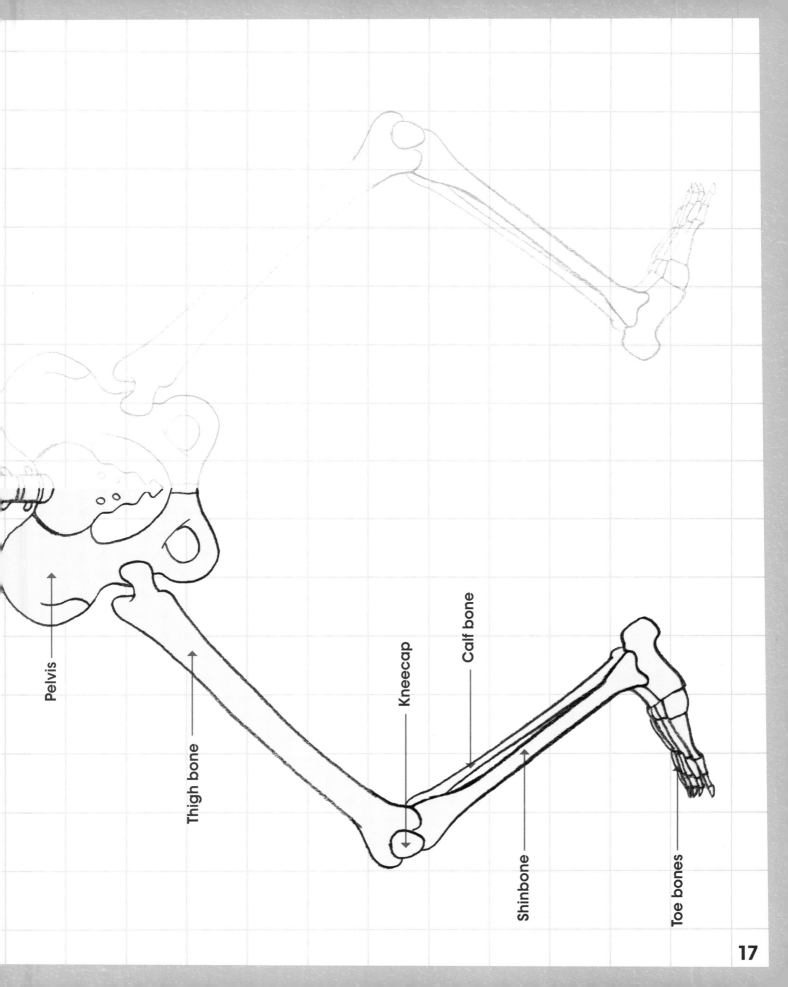

Pelvis

Thigh bone

Kneecap

Calf bone

Shinbone

Toe bones

Look inside a bone

Bones may be hard, but they aren't made of stone! They are alive, like the rest of you. Bones are made up of several layers.

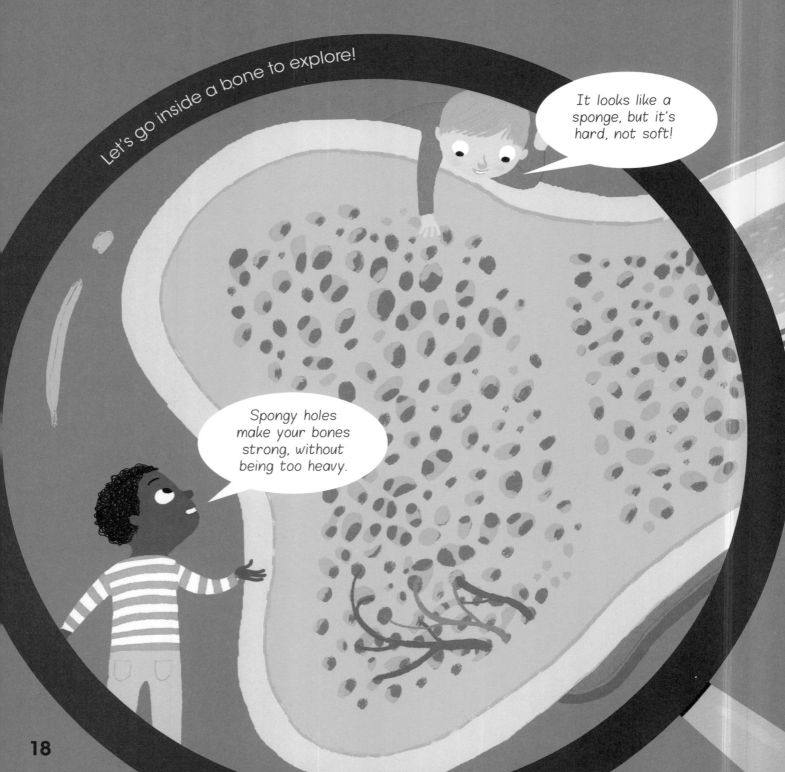

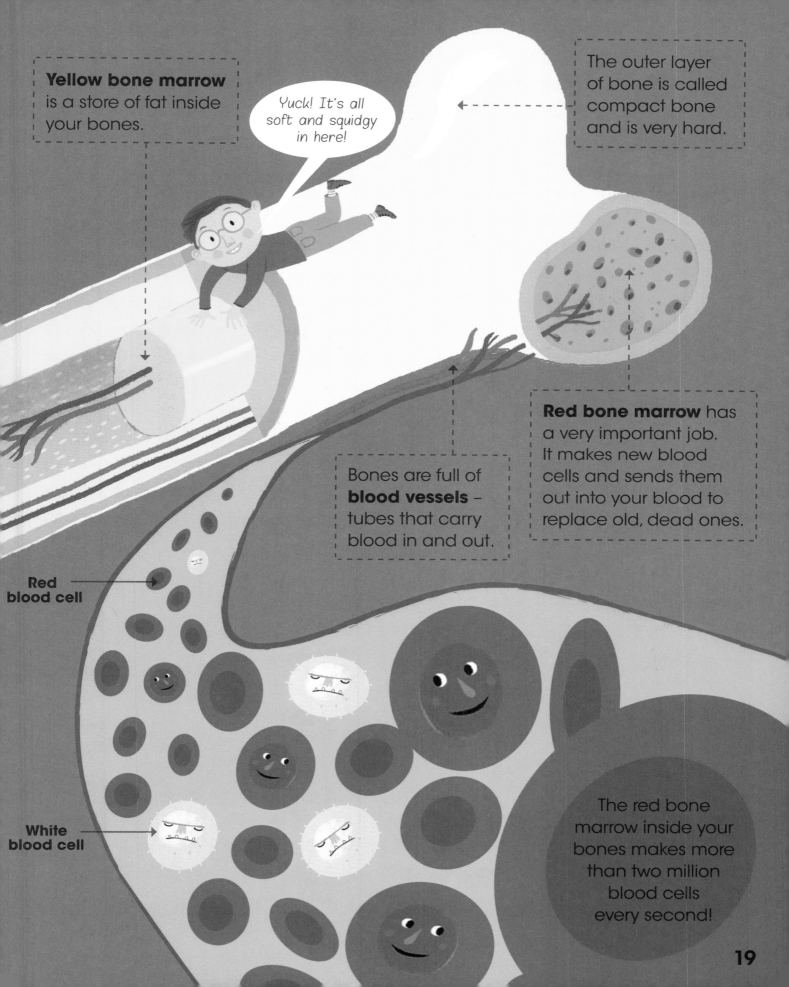

An unlucky break!

Bones are strong, but they can break or crack. If you've ever broken a bone, you'll know it really hurts. Luckily, bones can mend themselves too!

Tough, stringy strands start to fill the gap.

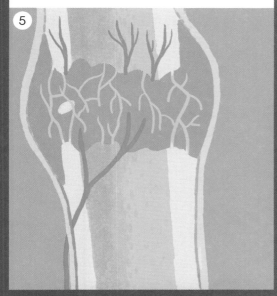

Bone cells build up in the gap, making a solid bone repair.

When it's mended, your arm will be as good as new!

Colour the shapes with an X in them black to create a cool X-ray picture.

Customize a cast

A broken bone is set in a cast to help it heal. It stops the patient moving the broken bone and damaging it further. It also keeps it in the right position so that it will heal straight.

A cast can be totally annoying, but at least you can customize it. Add signatures, doodle some designs, or add cartoon pictures to make this cast the coolest.

Muscle power!

Muscles work by *pulling*. Loads of tiny muscle cells work together to make the muscle shorter. This pulls on the bone to make it move. That's teamwork!

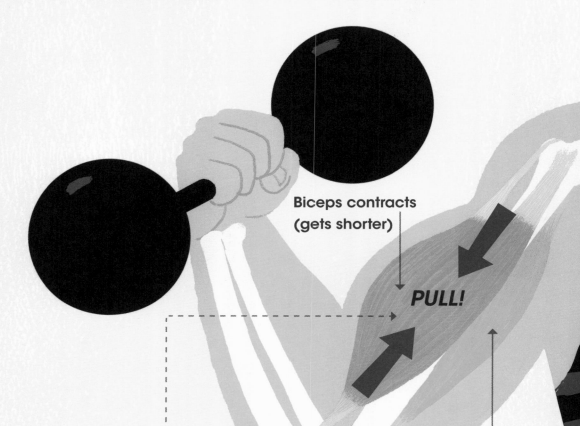

Biceps contracts (gets shorter)

PULL!

Triceps relaxes (gets longer)

The **biceps** is connected to two arm bones, joining them together. When the biceps muscle pulls, the arm bones move towards each other and the arm bends.

But now what? Muscles can only pull. When the biceps isn't pulling on the arm, it relaxes and stops pulling. It can't push your forearm the other way.

24

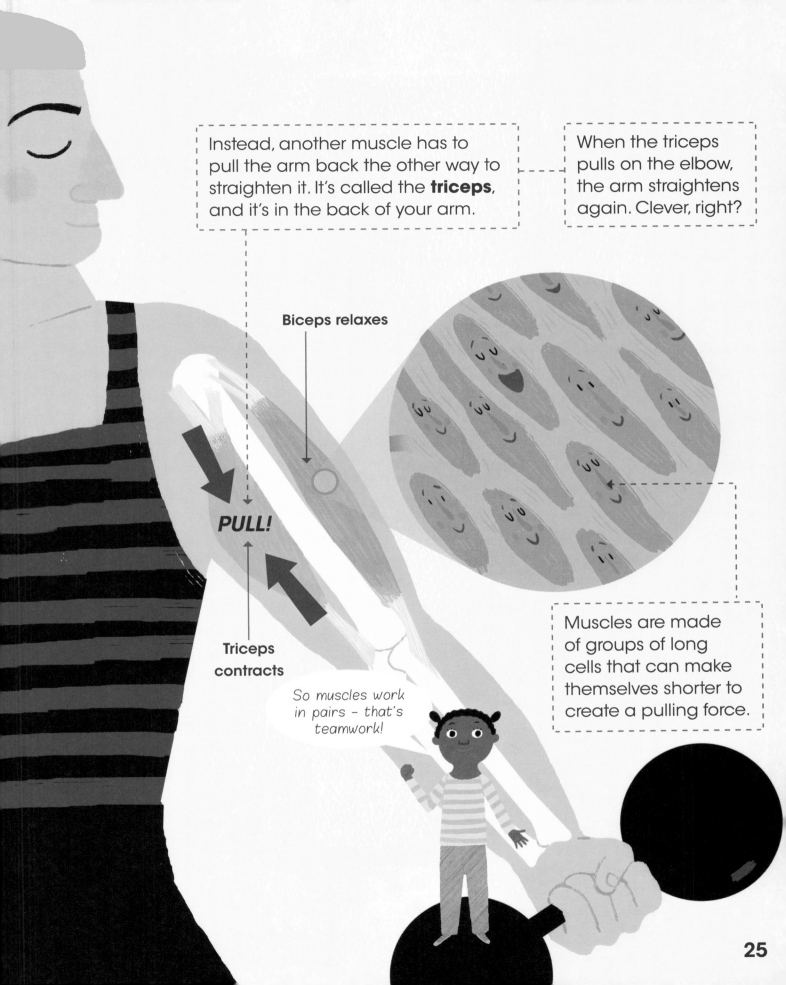

Instead, another muscle has to pull the arm back the other way to straighten it. It's called the **triceps**, and it's in the back of your arm.

When the triceps pulls on the elbow, the arm straightens again. Clever, right?

Biceps relaxes

PULL!

Triceps contracts

So muscles work in pairs – that's teamwork!

Muscles are made of groups of long cells that can make themselves shorter to create a pulling force.

25

Muscle fact zone

Muscles get your body moving, providing the power for everything from breathing and pumping blood around to running – or even just blinking!

1. Muscles are made up of millions of muscle fibres all neatly arranged in rows. Muscles make up about 40 percent of your body weight.

40%

Are you one of the few people who can use muscle power to wiggle their ears?

2. Your skeleton has about 640 different muscles to keep you on the move. You've even got muscles in your ears!

3. Even your eyes have got muscles! They keep your eyes focused and control the amount of light that enters the eye. They also help you to blink.

4. Some muscles are controlled by our thoughts. Others work without us thinking about it. Your heart is made of cardiac muscle that beats automatically, 24 hours a day!

Brrr. Time to create my own heatwave!

5. Shivering uses the heat made by hundreds of muscles expanding and contracting to warm us up when it is cold.

6. The strongest muscles in your body are the muscles that you chew with. They're called the masseters!

? Quick muscle quiz

How many muscles do you think your arm will use to tick the correct answer to this question?

5 ⬭

25 ⬭

250 ⬭

Terrific tendons

Your fingers don't have any muscles, so how can you move them? The answer is tendons – strings that join your fingers to the muscles in your arm that make them move.

 To see how tendons work, build a model hand and make it move! Ask a grown-up to help you.

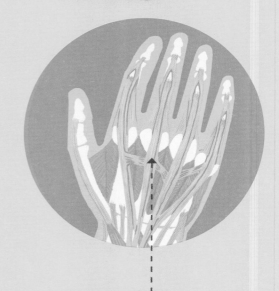

You can feel the **tendons** running along the back of your hand if you bend your fingers and then relax them. They feel a little bit like cords.

You will need:

scissors

marker pen

string

sticky tape

rubber glove

straws

1

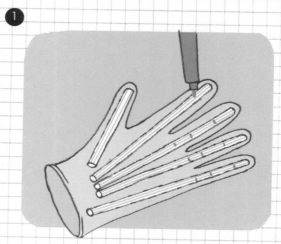

Lay the straws on the glove and mark where the finger and thumb joints would be.

2

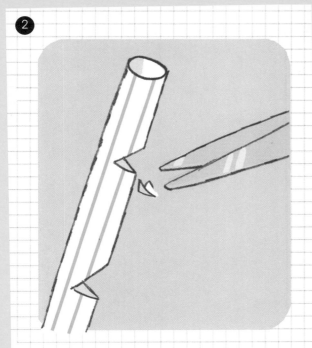

Carefully cut triangle-shaped notches at the lines in the straws to make the joints.

3

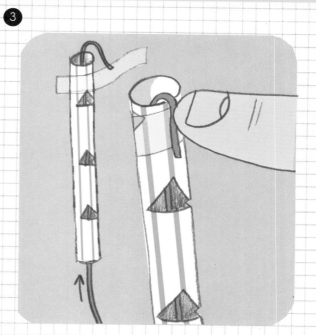

Thread strings through the straws and tape in place at the top.

4

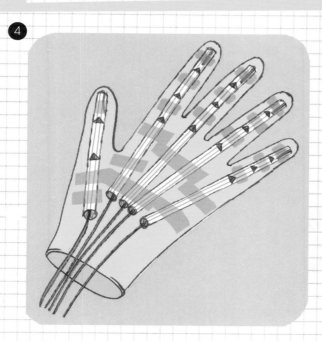

Tape the straws to the glove with the notches face up. (Don't put tape over the notches.)

5

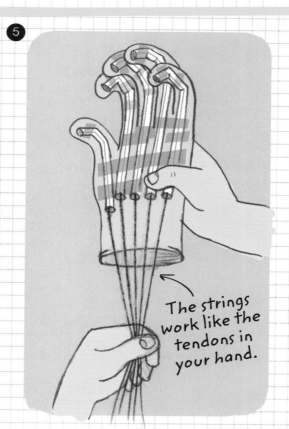

The strings work like the tendons in your hand.

Hold the glove at the wrist and pull the strings! See how the fingers curl up on their own.

Squeezy muscles

Your body also has muscles in its organs and body tubes. Rings of muscles squeeze to move food and blood through your tubes!

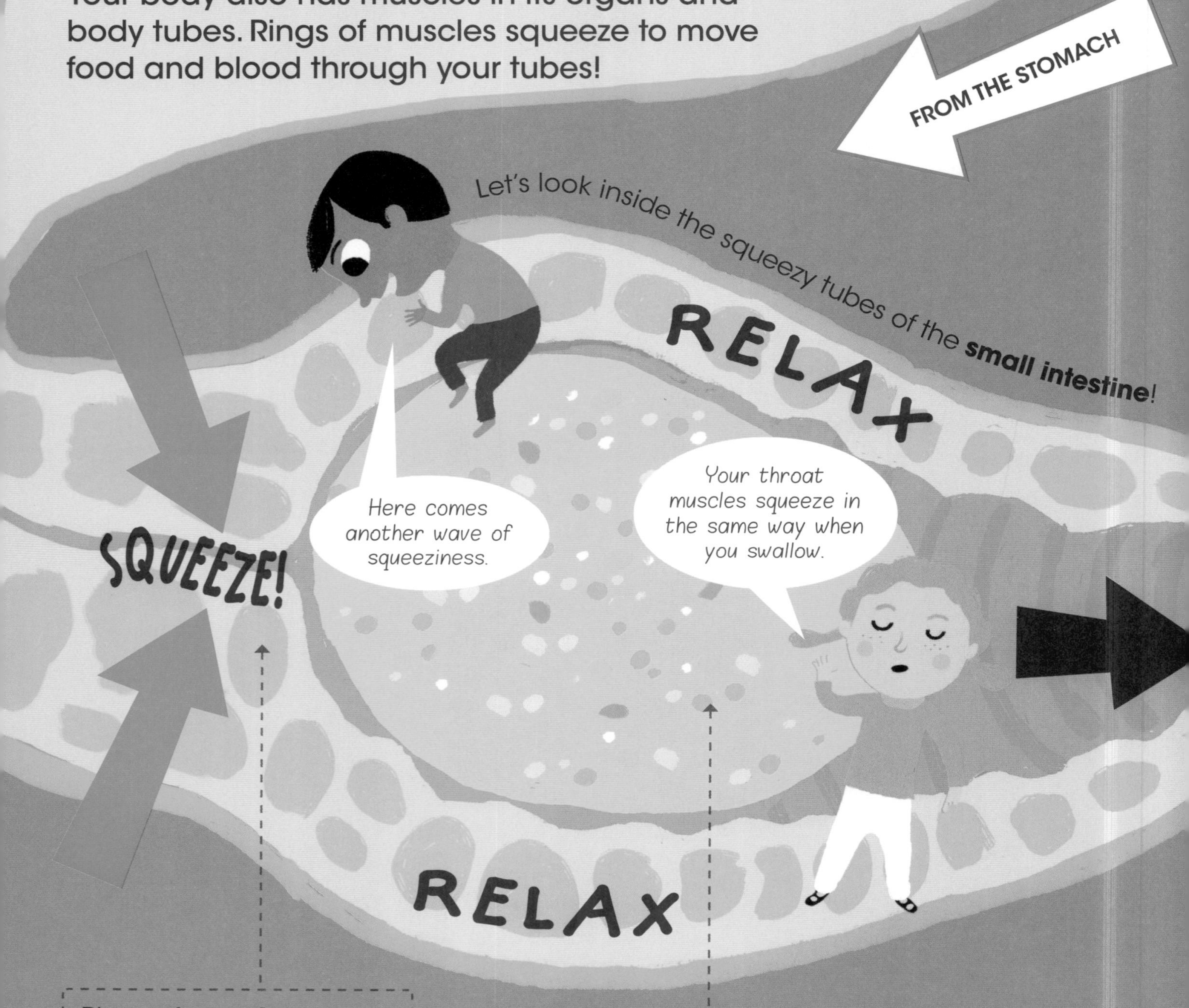

FROM THE STOMACH

Let's look inside the squeezy tubes of the **small intestine!**

RELAX

SQUEEZE!

Here comes another wave of squeeziness.

Your throat muscles squeeze in the same way when you swallow.

RELAX

Rings of **muscle** squeeze in turn. The squeezing moves along the tube in waves.

The squeezing pushes the mushed food forward towards the **large intestine**.

Squeezy pump

The heart is made of muscle, too, and it also works by squeezing. It clenches tight to pump blood around your body.

Put your hand on your tummy. This is where your small intestine is.

RELAX

SQUEEZE!

SQUEEZE!

Let's ride the squeezy wave!

Eeek! We're moving!

SQUEEZE!

RELAX

The waves of squeezing and relaxing muscles are called **peristalsis** (say: pear-i-stal-sis).

TO THE LARGE INTESTINE

31

Food for life

Eating food gives us the energy to live, move and grow. It also provides the raw materials that we need to build and repair our bodies.

Work out which groups these foods belong to. Then draw them in the gaps on the correct shelves.

Food groups shopping list

Foods like potatoes, rice, pasta and bread are packed with **carbohydrates** (say: car-bo-hi-drates) and provide us with energy.

Proteins help your body to grow and repair itself. Fish, meat, eggs, beans and nuts are all rich in protein.

Fats are found in butter, cheese and cooking oil and provide an energy store. A layer of fat under our skin keeps us warm.

Fruit, vegetables, fish, orange juice and milk contain **vitamins** and **minerals**. They are used to make strong bones or blood cells and help our body to work.

Your blood and all your cells are mostly made of **water.** We get water from food and drink to keep them healthy.

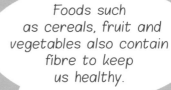

Foods such as cereals, fruit and vegetables also contain fibre to keep us healthy.

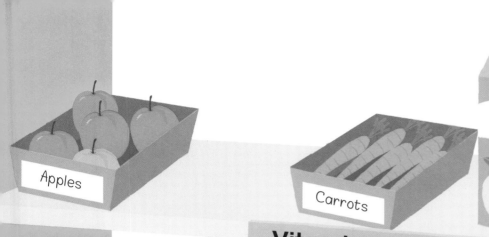

Apples

Carrots

APPLE
JUICE

Broccoli &
Cabbage

Vitamins and minerals

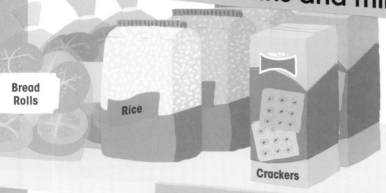

Bread
Rolls

Rice

Crackers

Chocolate
Lollies

Carbohydrates

Nuts

Beans   Beans   ans

Proteins

Butter

Butter

Olive
Oil

Olive
Oil

Milk

Fats

Water

33

Dinner time!

To stay healthy, we can't just eat our favourite foods all the time. We need to eat a balanced amount of different food types.

This plate shows roughly how much of each type of food we should eat.

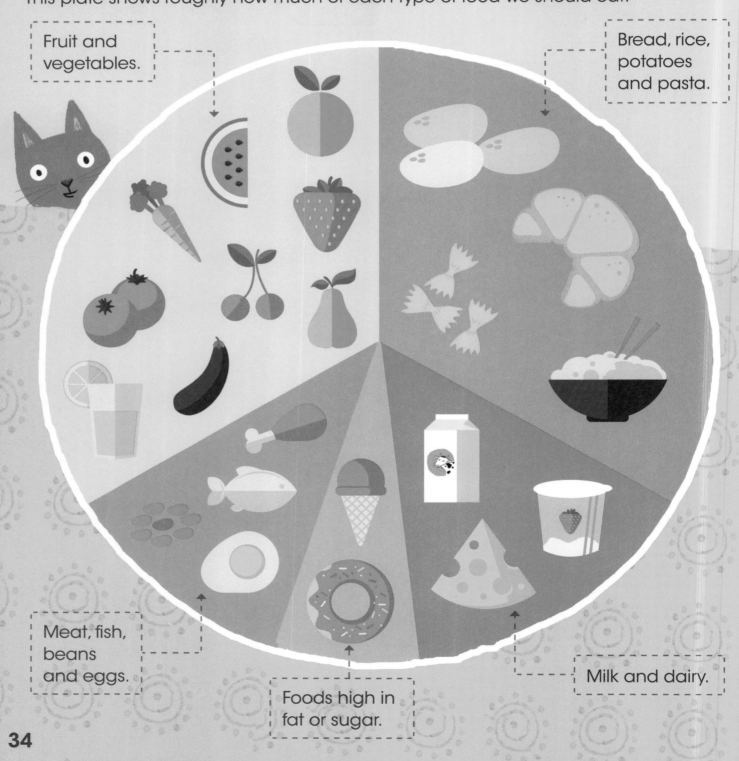

Fruit and vegetables.

Bread, rice, potatoes and pasta.

Meat, fish, beans and eggs.

Foods high in fat or sugar.

Milk and dairy.

Draw your favourite meal. What food types are there? Does it look like a healthy meal?

Your digestive system

When you eat your dinner, the food starts a long journey through your body's digestive system. It's a truly amazing food processor!

It's lunchtime!

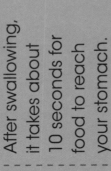

After swallowing, it takes about 10 seconds for food to reach your stomach.

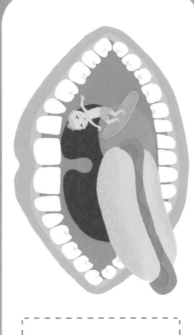

MOUTH
Most food is too big to be swallowed whole. Your teeth cut it into bite-size chunks and grind it into small pieces.

It takes about three hours for your stomach to process the food.

STOMACH
Your stomach squishes the food up with digestive juices to turn it into a liquid mush!

Liquid food spends about three hours passing through your small intestine.

It can take from one to three days for food to travel all the way here!

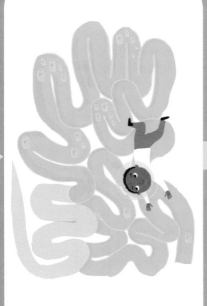

SMALL INTESTINE
When it arrives here, the food has been broken down into tiny bits that can be used by your body.

LARGE INTESTINE
Your large intestine turns the watery, leftover food waste into poo.

Quick digestion quiz

Food travels almost 9 metres through the tubes of the human digestive system.

TRUE

FALSE

Munching mouth

Hitch a ride with a mouthful of food to explore the body's digestive system. Your journey begins in the mouth!

Sharp front teeth are used to bite and slice up food.

I'm surfing a wave of yucky saliva!

Your back teeth are flat on the top. They grind food between them.

Salivary glands squirt out saliva, or spit, which mixes with the food and starts breaking it down or digesting it.

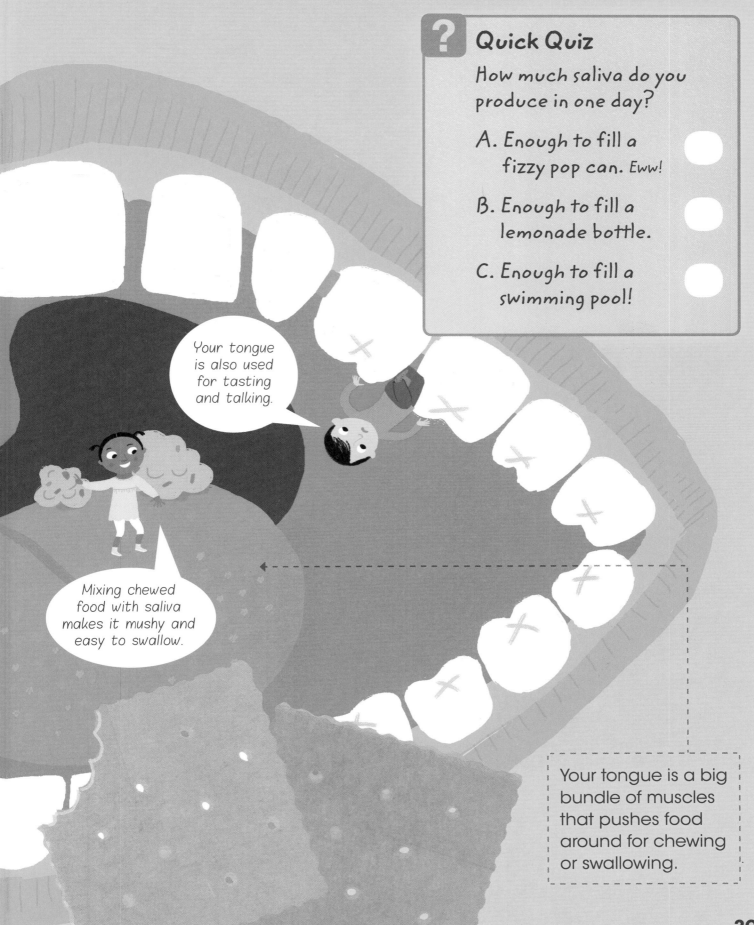

Quick Quiz

How much saliva do you produce in one day?

A. Enough to fill a fizzy pop can. Eww!

B. Enough to fill a lemonade bottle.

C. Enough to fill a swimming pool!

Your tongue is also used for tasting and talking.

Mixing chewed food with saliva makes it mushy and easy to swallow.

Your tongue is a big bundle of muscles that pushes food around for chewing or swallowing.

Squishy stomach

Once the food is chewed, your tongue pushes it to the back of your mouth and it gets swallowed. Next stop – the stomach!

Air travels down the **windpipe** to your lungs. Whenever you swallow, a flap closes off your windpipe so that food can't go the wrong way.

Your **throat** leads to your stomach, but you also use it to breathe in air.

Food is squeezed down a tube called the **oesophagus** (say: uh-sof-a-gus) until it reaches the stomach.

Quick, let's head for the stomach with the food.

Food this way!

Lung

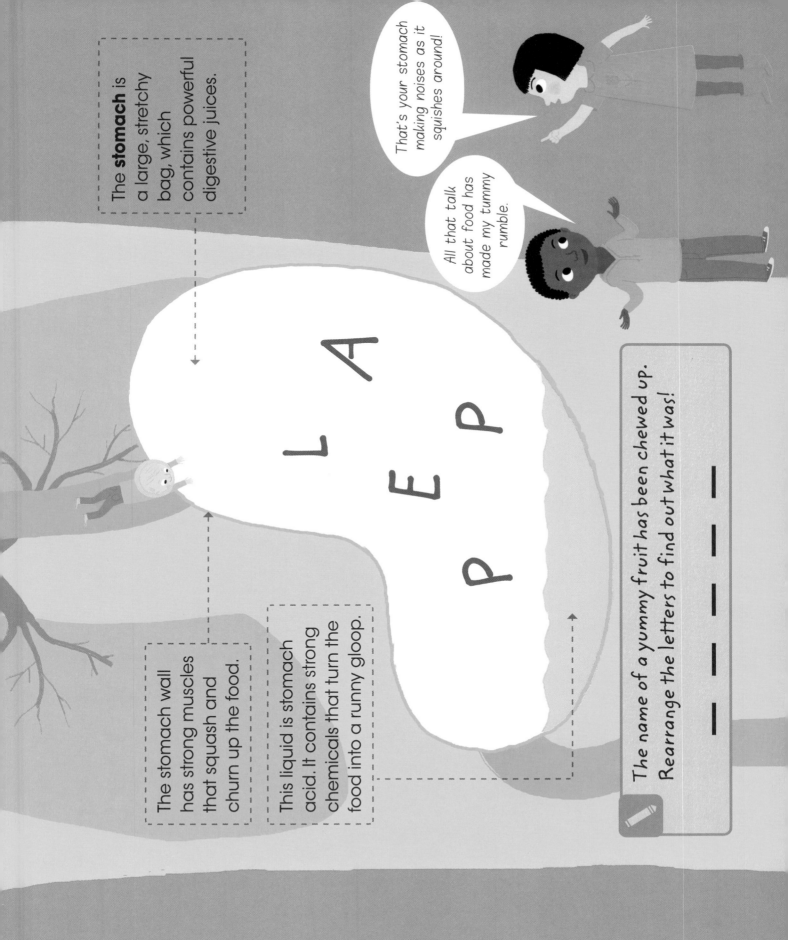

The **stomach** is a large, stretchy bag, which contains powerful digestive juices.

That's your stomach making noises as it squishes around!

All that talk about food has made my tummy rumble.

The stomach wall has strong muscles that squash and churn up the food.

This liquid is stomach acid. It contains strong chemicals that turn the food into a runny gloop.

L A
E
P
P

The name of a yummy fruit has been chewed up. Rearrange the letters to find out what it was!

_ _ _ _ _

When food goes wrong

PAARRRPP!

Eating is usually fun, but sometimes eating food can have unexpected effects on your body!

Food can make you **fart**, creating smelly gas in your large intestine that then escapes with an embarrassing noise and a stink!

If you eat food that's gone bad, or contains something harmful, your stomach knows. It takes action by making you **sick** and sending the food back up the oesophagus and out of your mouth. Yucky!

Sometimes, stomach acid goes the wrong way and comes back up from your stomach towards your throat. This causes **indigestion** – a horrible burning feeling in your chest.

A **burp** happens when gas or air from your stomach suddenly bubbles up out of your mouth. Sometimes this happens because you swallow air when you eat or drink too quickly.

BuuUrRpPpp!

Burping gets rid of one litre of gas from your stomach every day.

What embarrassing things have happened to you after eating or drinking? Keep a record here.

Today I drank a can of lemonade and burped in class five times! It was SO embarrassing!

Into the intestines!

After your food has been turned into gloop in the stomach, it sets off on a very long journey through the twisty tubes of your intestines, or guts.

Liquid food squeezes along inside the **small intestine**. The useful bits from the food are soaked up into your blood and travel to all the parts of your body, ready to be used.

I remember! Muscles squeeeeeze the food along.

Food can take up to six hours to pass through the small intestine into the large intestine.

This worm-like bit between the small intestine and the large intestine is the appendix. No one is sure what it's for!

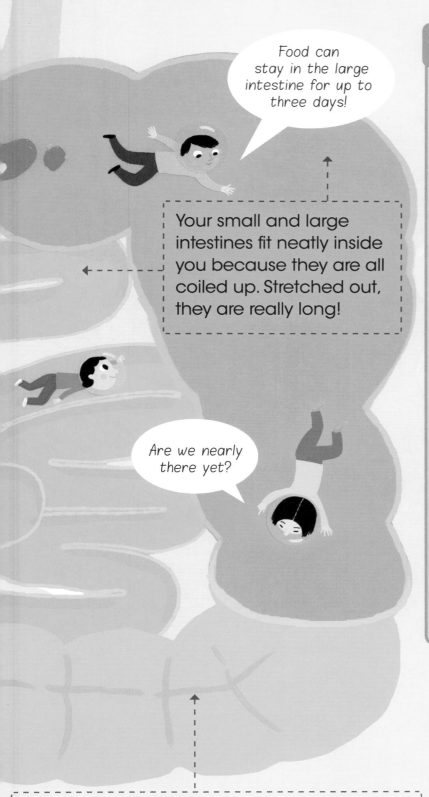

Food can stay in the large intestine for up to three days!

Your small and large intestines fit neatly inside you because they are all coiled up. Stretched out, they are really long!

Are we nearly there yet?

Gigantic guts

Follow the steps to work out how long your intestines are!

1. Measure your height:

   ....cm

2. Write your height x 4:

   ....cm

   (That's how long your small intestine is.)

3. Write your height x 1:

   ....cm

   (That's the length of your large intestine.)

4. Add the answers to 2 and 3 together to discover the total length of your intestines.

   ....cm

Wow, that is really LONG!

Once all the goodness has been taken out, the leftover food goes into the **large intestine**. Here, the waste bits of food collect into lumps, ready to leave your body.

45

The Gassy Guts Hotel

Meet the guests who live in your guts! It's true – your large intestine is a bit like a hotel, where billions of bacteria come to stay.

Bacteria are tiny creatures that live inside everyone. They help you to digest your food and turn it into useful things, such as vitamins. They also help to keep dangerous germs away.

As the bacteria feed on the food gloop in your guts, they release waste gases that bubble along your intestines and then escape from your bottom as stinky farts.

Travel around the Gassy Guts Hotel and answer TRUE or FALSE to the quiz questions.

1. Boys fart more than girls.
TRUE   FALSE

2. A fart's sound depends on the food it is made from.
TRUE   FALSE

3. You breathe in about a litre of other people's farts each day.
TRUE   FALSE

4. About a third of your poo is made of bacteria.

TRUE ⬤   FALSE ⬤

5. The older that you get, the more you fart.

TRUE ⬤   FALSE ⬤

Waste disposal

Remember that mouthful of food you were following? Now that all the goodness has been taken out, the leftover solid waste is ready to leave your large intestine – as poo!

LARGE INTESTINE

1. By the time food gets to your **large intestine**, your body has taken out all the useful bits. What's left are the bits you can't digest, known as fibre.

2. The intestine sucks water out of the waste food to dry it out.

3. It clumps into smelly lumps. As well as fibre, each lump contains gut bacteria.

RECTUM

Fibre is good for you. It speeds up digestion to remove waste from your body. Tick which two of these foods is high in fibre.

wholewheat pasta

vegetables

eggs

4. At the very end of the large intestine, the **rectum** stores the waste as poo until you go to the toilet.

5. The bacteria in poo are what makes it stinky. Watch out! The bacteria in poo can make you ill if they get into your mouth. ALWAYS wash your hands after going to the toilet!

EXIT THIS WAY

Waterworks

So, what happens to the water you get from food and drink? It travels from your small intestine into your blood and then to your kidneys.

Your body is mostly made of water. No matter how much water you take in, your **kidneys** make sure you have just the right amount.

They also control what chemicals are in your blood. The kidneys act like sieves to remove chemicals that shouldn't be there.

Extra water and waste chemicals travel out through the **ureter** (say: your-eat-er) to your **bladder** as **urine**!

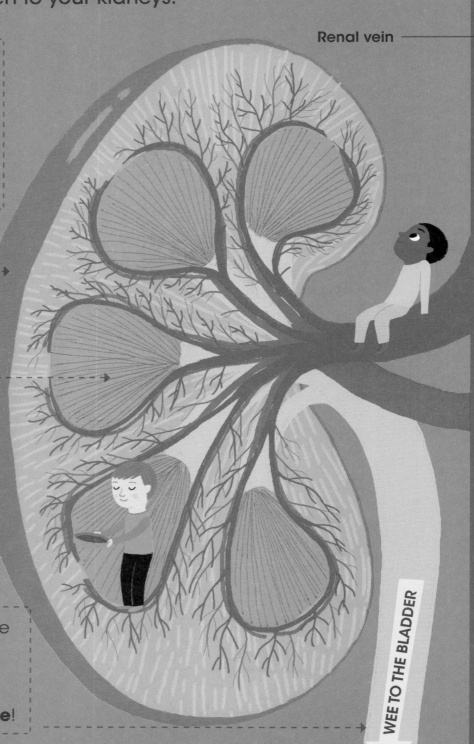

Renal vein

BLOOD TO THE BODY

WEE TO THE BLADDER

50

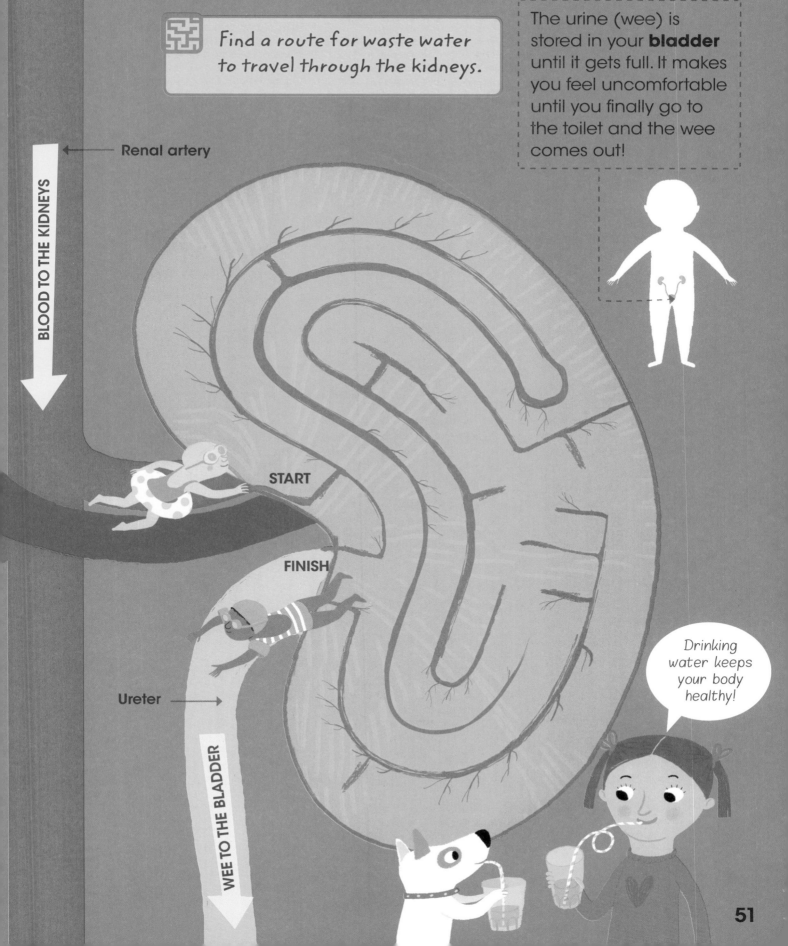

Your blood network

Each time your heart beats, it pumps blood all around your body. The blood flows through a network of tubes called blood vessels.

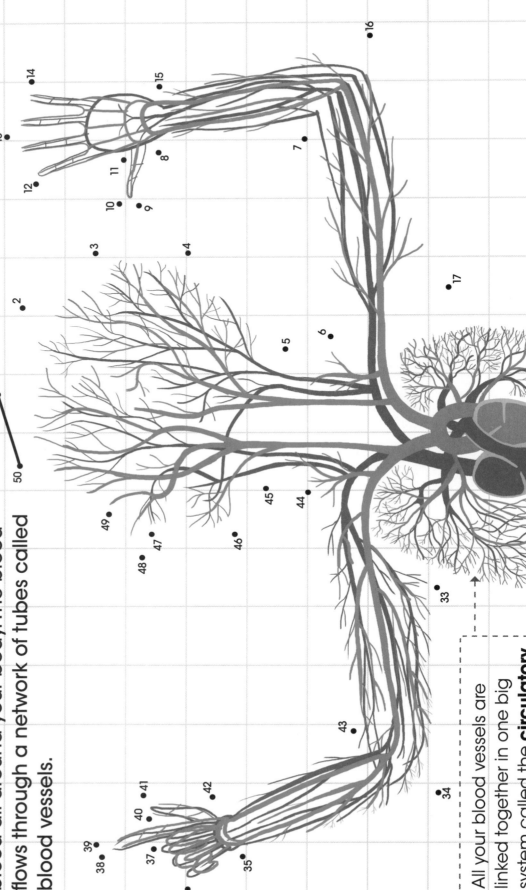

All your blood vessels are linked together in one big system called the **circulatory system**. It carries blood close to every cell in your body, from head to toe.

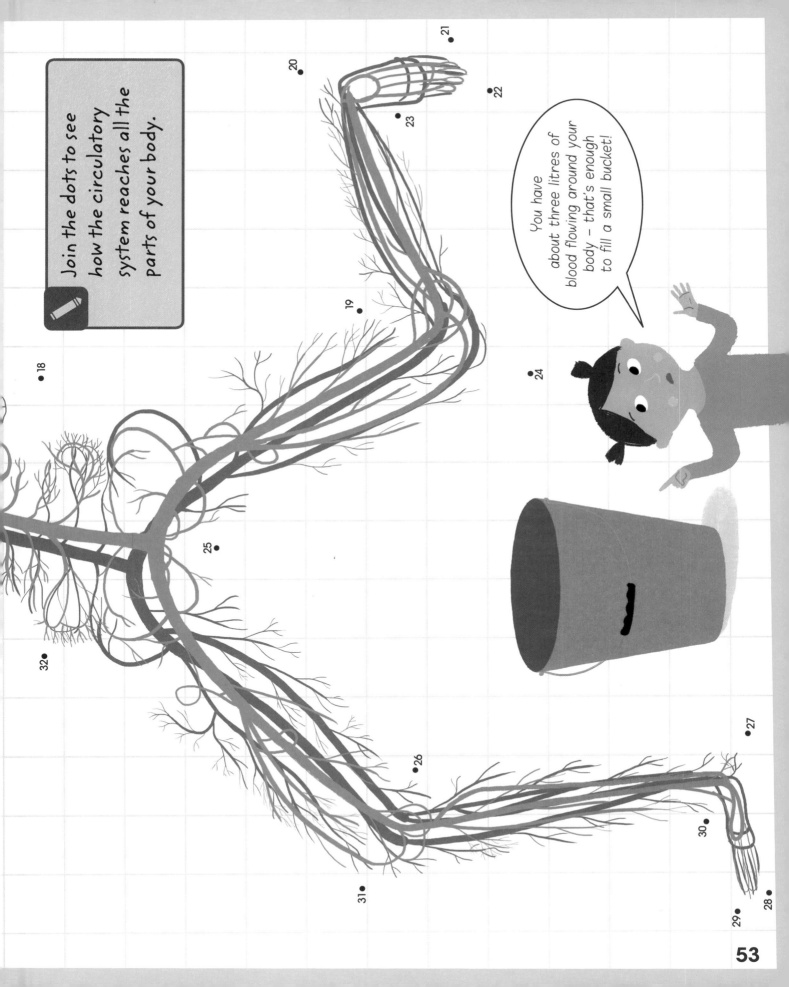

53

Blood vessels

Your heart pumps blood non-stop around your circulatory system. This network is so huge that if the **blood vessels** were laid out end to end, they would stretch around the Earth an incredible two-and-a-half times!

Blood vessels leading out of the heart are called **arteries**.

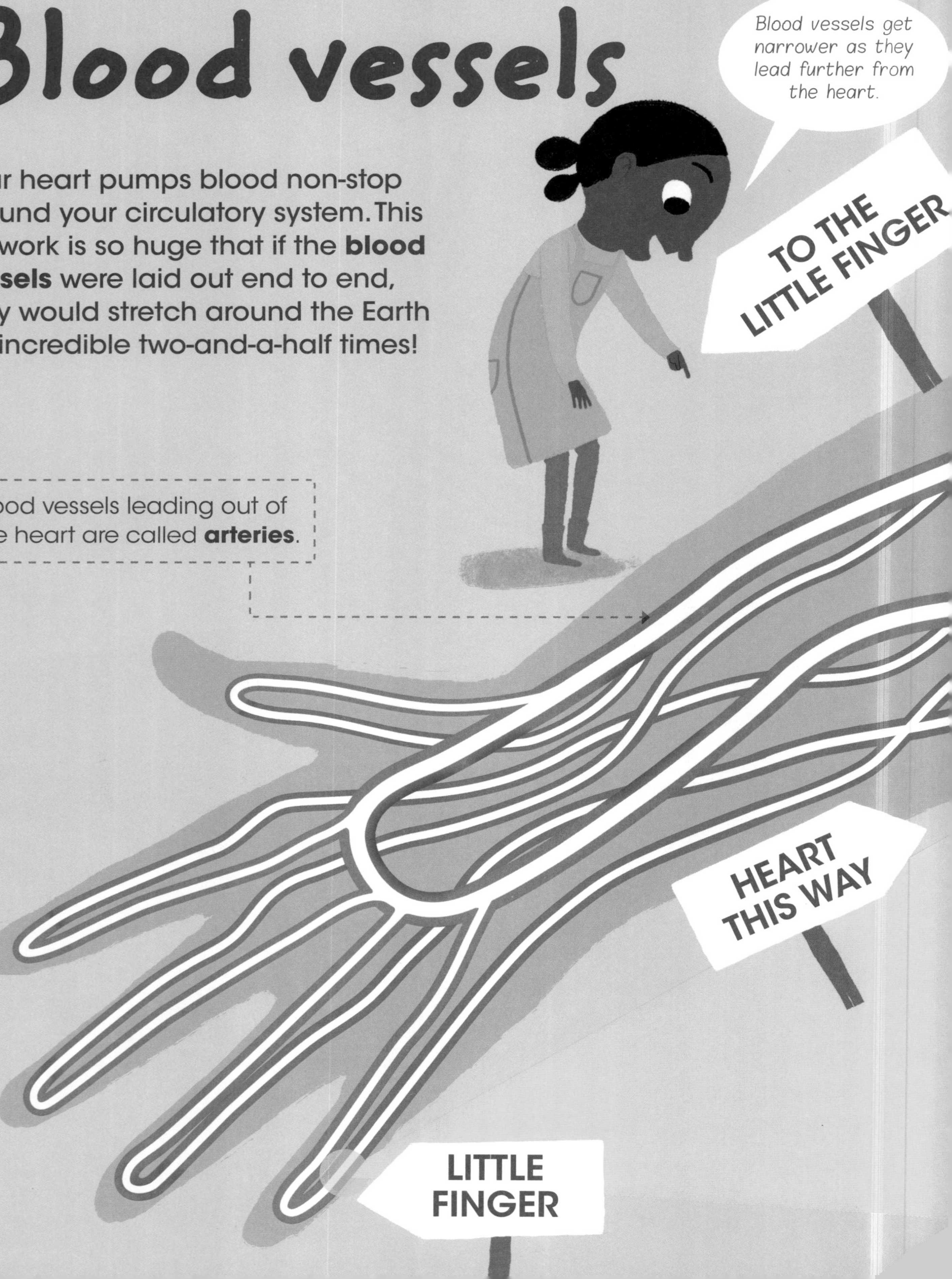

Blood vessels get narrower as they lead further from the heart.

TO THE LITTLE FINGER

HEART THIS WAY

LITTLE FINGER

54

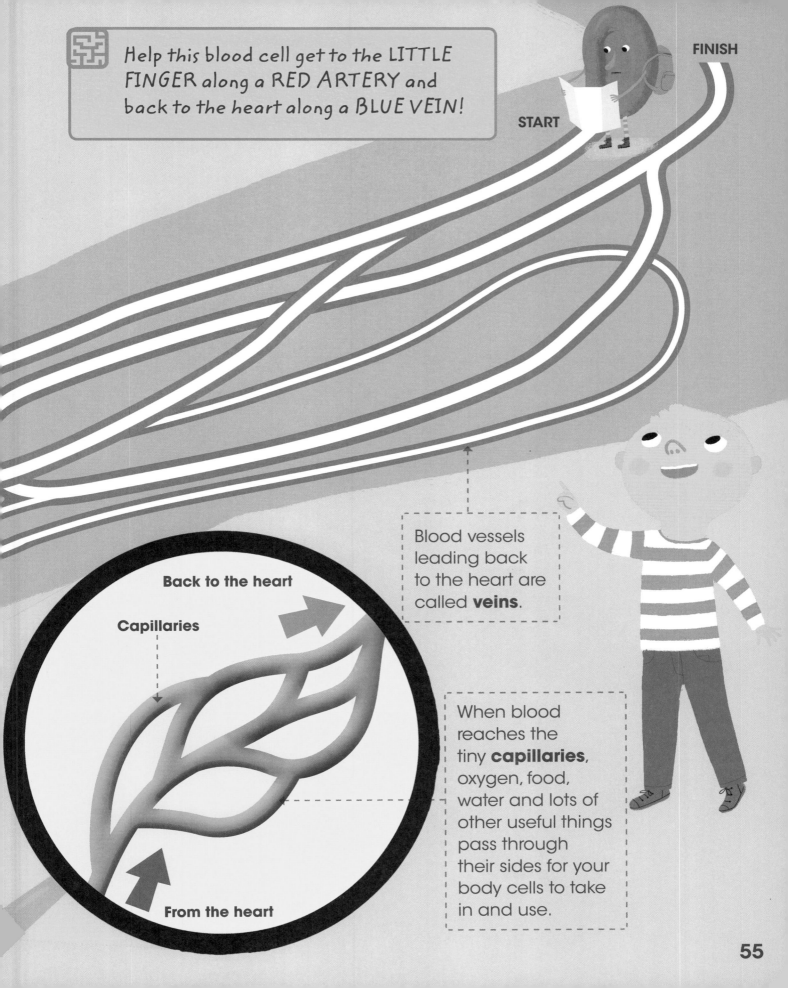

Help this blood cell get to the LITTLE FINGER along a RED ARTERY and back to the heart along a BLUE VEIN!

START

FINISH

Blood vessels leading back to the heart are called **veins**.

Back to the heart

Capillaries

From the heart

When blood reaches the tiny **capillaries**, oxygen, food, water and lots of other useful things pass through their sides for your body cells to take in and use.

Blood delivers

Around the clock, your blood delivers all the stuff your body needs. It does lots of other useful jobs, too. Discover what your blood delivery service carries around the body.

Oxygen is a gas in the air that we breathe in. Every cell needs oxygen to work.

Cells need **food** to make them work.

Cells need **water**. It is used to make things like tears, sweat, saliva – and blood, too!

Germ-fighting cells in your blood protect you from germs.

Your blood carries a **first-aid kit** to help repair wounds and make scabs.

57

Inside a drop of blood

Blood looks red and runny, but what's it actually made of? Let's zoom in and get to know the millions of microscopic cells that float about in a single drop of blood.

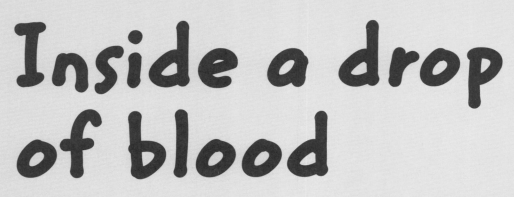

There's so much packed into just one tiny drop of blood!

Wow! Look at all those red blood cells.

Red blood cells

Cells in one drop: roughly 300 million.

Description: round, flat and, er... red!

Job: carrying oxygen and delivering it to all the cells in the body.

Platelets

Cells in one drop: up to 15 million.

Description: small, round and flat like a plate – they stretch out long fingers when they need to mend a wound.

Job: clumping together to build scabs and heal cuts.

58

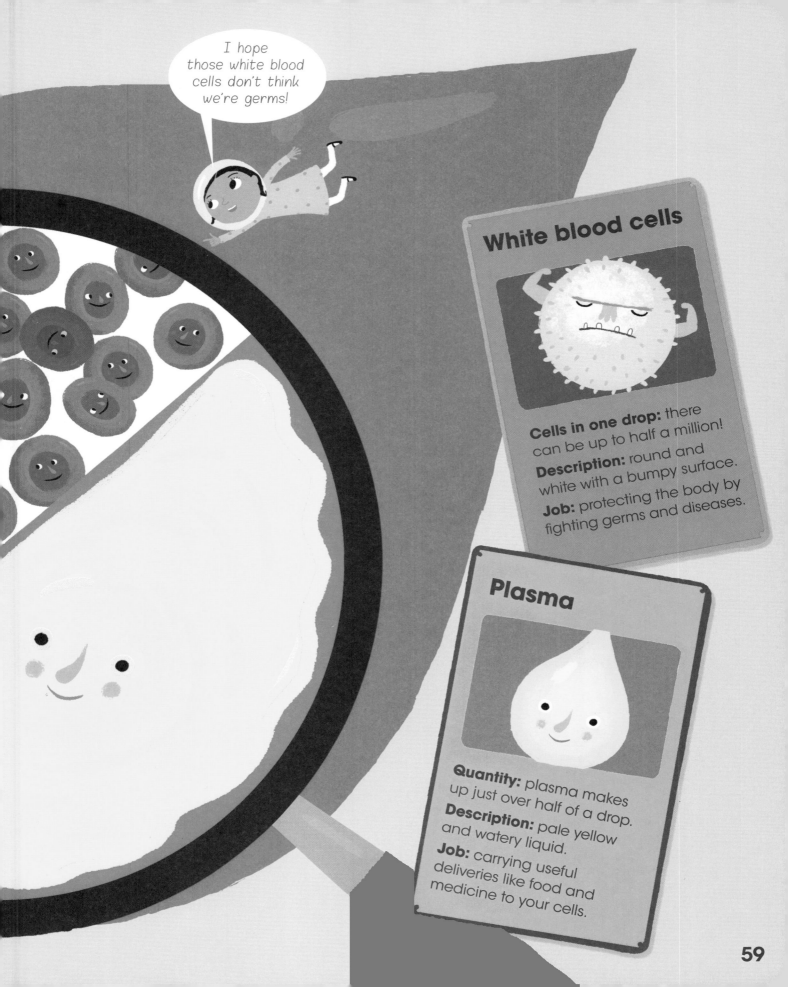

I hope those white blood cells don't think we're germs!

White blood cells

Cells in one drop: there can be up to half a million!
Description: round and white with a bumpy surface.
Job: protecting the body by fighting germs and diseases.

Plasma

Quantity: plasma makes up just over half of a drop.
Description: pale yellow and watery liquid.
Job: carrying useful deliveries like food and medicine to your cells.

From the heart

Your heart has two sides that work together.
They pump blood to your lungs to pick up oxygen.
Then they send the blood around the body.

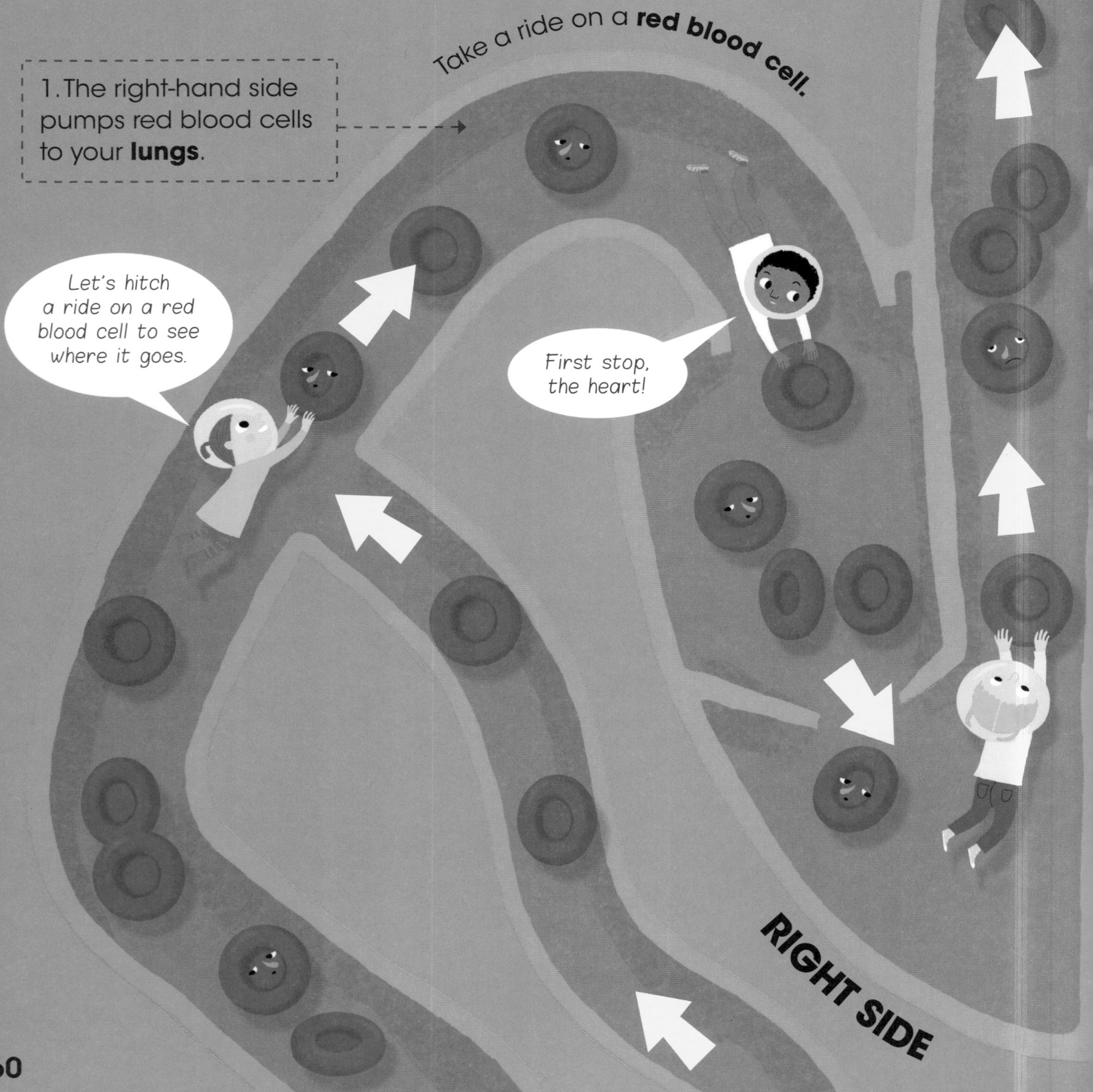

1. The right-hand side pumps red blood cells to your **lungs**.

Take a ride on a **red blood cell**.

Let's hitch a ride on a red blood cell to see where it goes.

First stop, the heart!

RIGHT SIDE

60

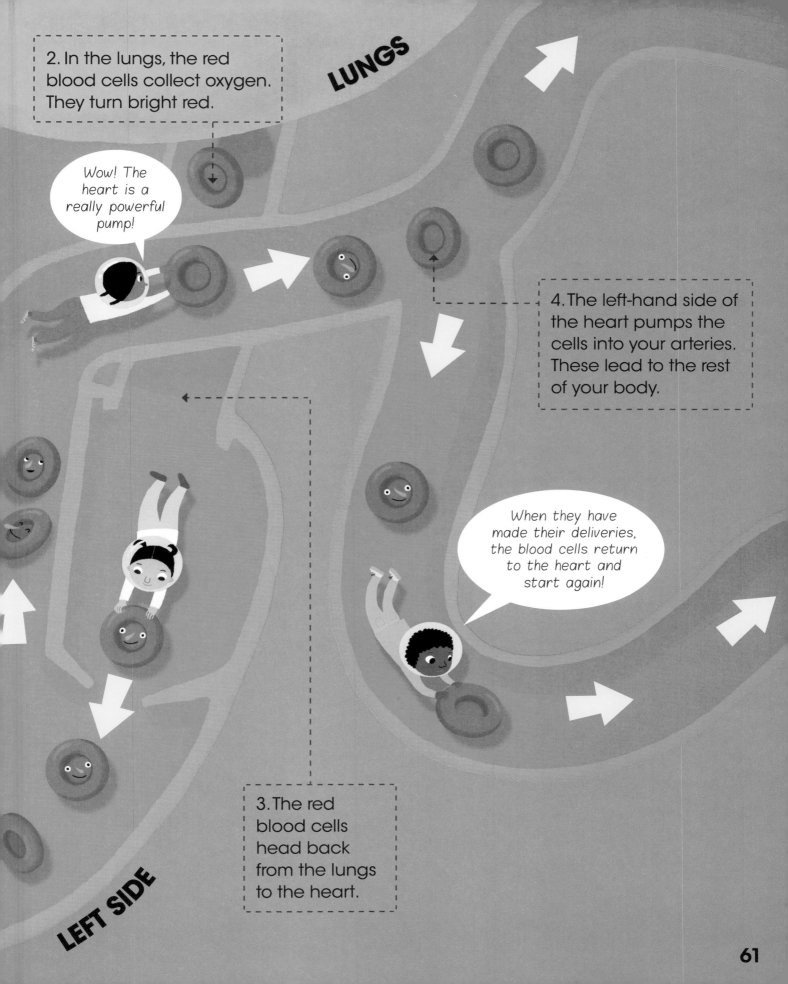

Your pulse

Every time your heart squeezes to pump blood around your body, it produces a heartbeat. Your pulse rate is the number of times your heart beats in one minute.

Your cells need more oxygen and food when you exercise. So your heart beats faster to pump more blood around your body.

 What happens to your pulse rate when you exercise? Do this fun experiment to find out!

First, find out your normal pulse rate. Stick out one hand, palm up, and press two fingers of your other hand onto the wrist, like this.

Can you feel a regular bump? That's your pulse. Use a watch and count how many times your pulse bumps in one minute:

_ _ _ beats per minute.

Now, take your pulse rate before and after each of these exercises. Rest for five minutes between each exercise to write in your results.

One minute of running

BEFORE: ....

AFTER: ....

One minute of skipping
BEFORE: ....
AFTER: ....

One minute of dancing
BEFORE: ....
AFTER: ....

One minute of star jumps
BEFORE: ....
AFTER: ....

63

Hard-working heart

Your heart is an incredibly hard-working muscle.
Even when you are sitting very still, it's hard at
work, beating around 70 times every minute.

Colour the 70 little heartbeats in red.
How many can you do in one minute?

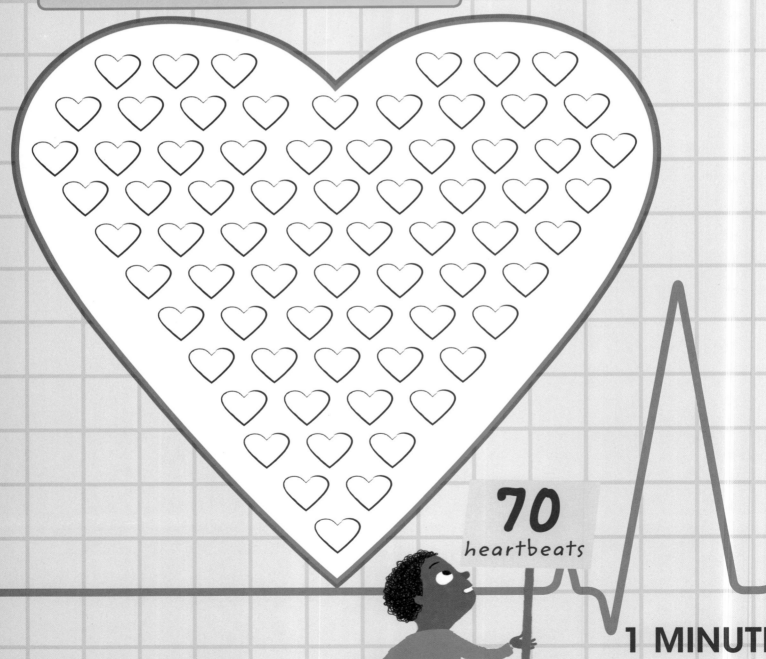

70 heartbeats

1 MINUTE

Doctors can listen to our hearts with a **stethoscope** to make sure that they are working properly. It makes the sounds louder and easier to hear.

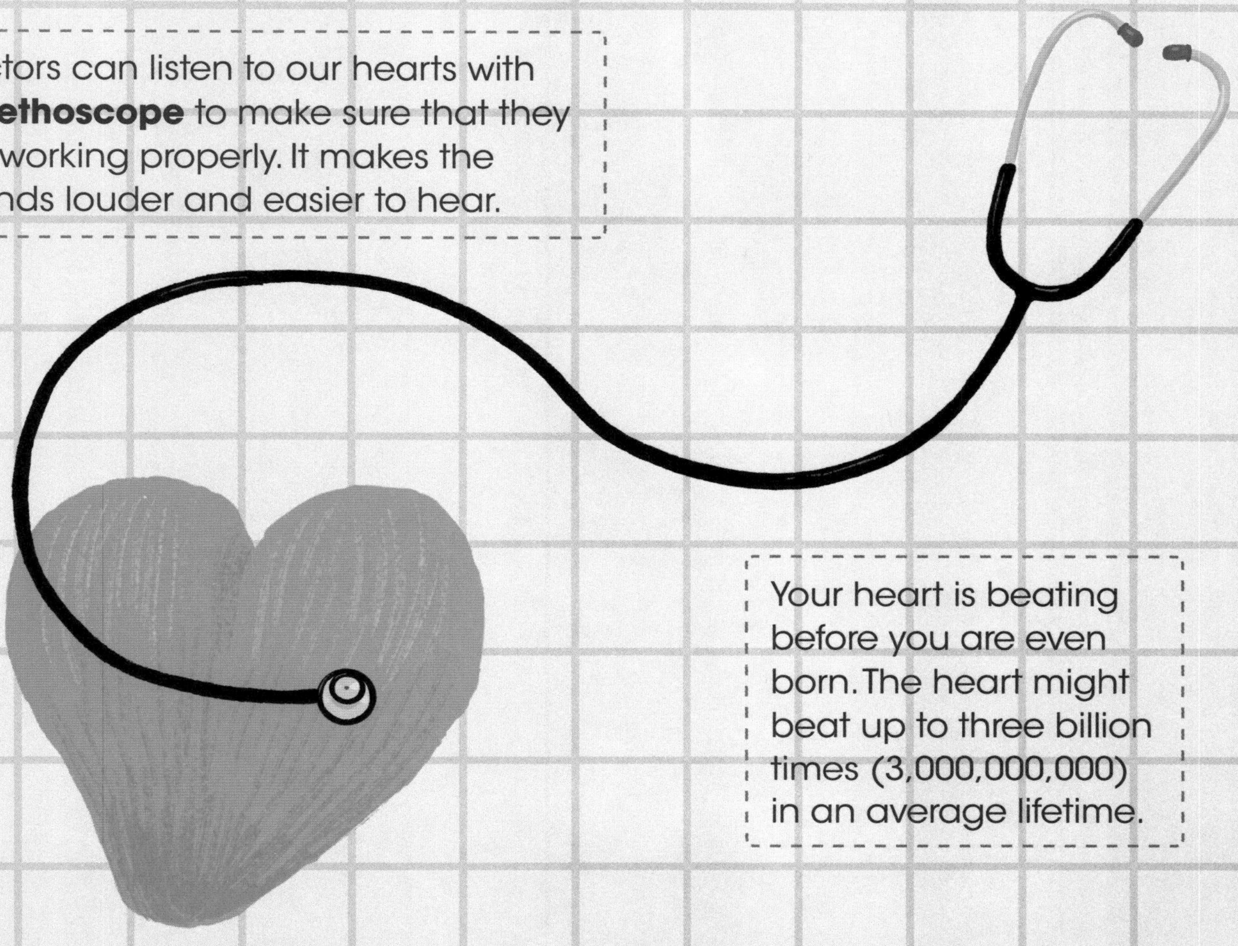

Your heart is beating before you are even born. The heart might beat up to three billion times (3,000,000,000) in an average lifetime.

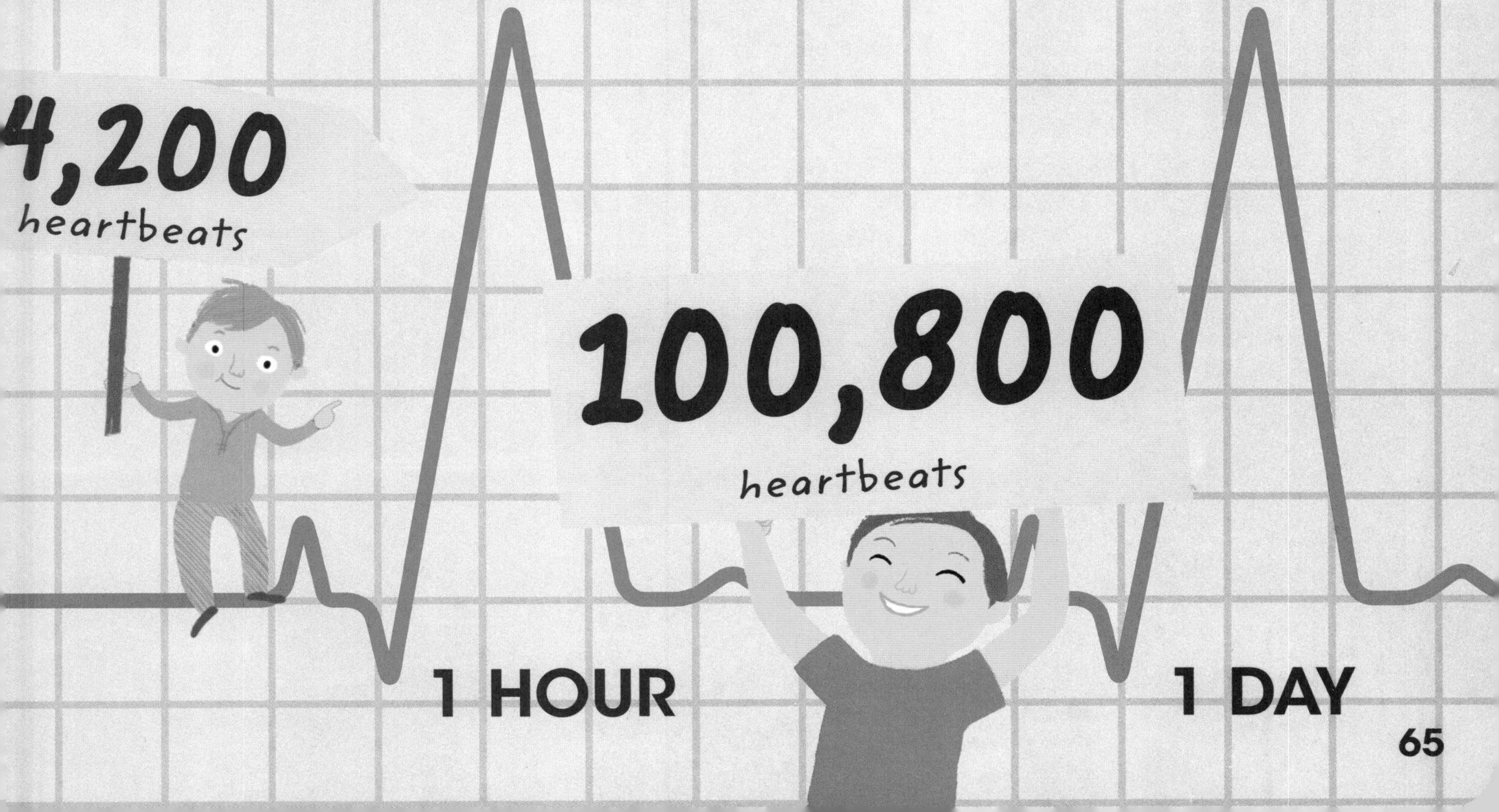

4,200 heartbeats

100,800 heartbeats

1 HOUR

1 DAY

65

Breathing

Take a deep breath. Your **lungs** have just filled up with air, and oxygen has been added to your blood. Now breathe the rest of the air back out!

AIR

1. **Air** gets into your body through your **nose** and **mouth**.

2. The air travels down your throat and then carries on through the **trachea** (say: tra-kee-a), or windpipe.

3. The trachea splits into two tubes, each leading into one of your two **lungs**. The tubes are called **bronchi** (say: brong-key).

4. The **bronchi** branch off into thousands of smaller tubes – the **bronchioles** (say: brong-key-oles).

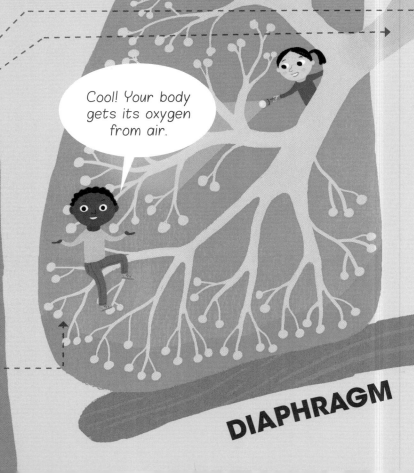

LUNG

Cool! Your body gets its oxygen from air.

DIAPHRAGM

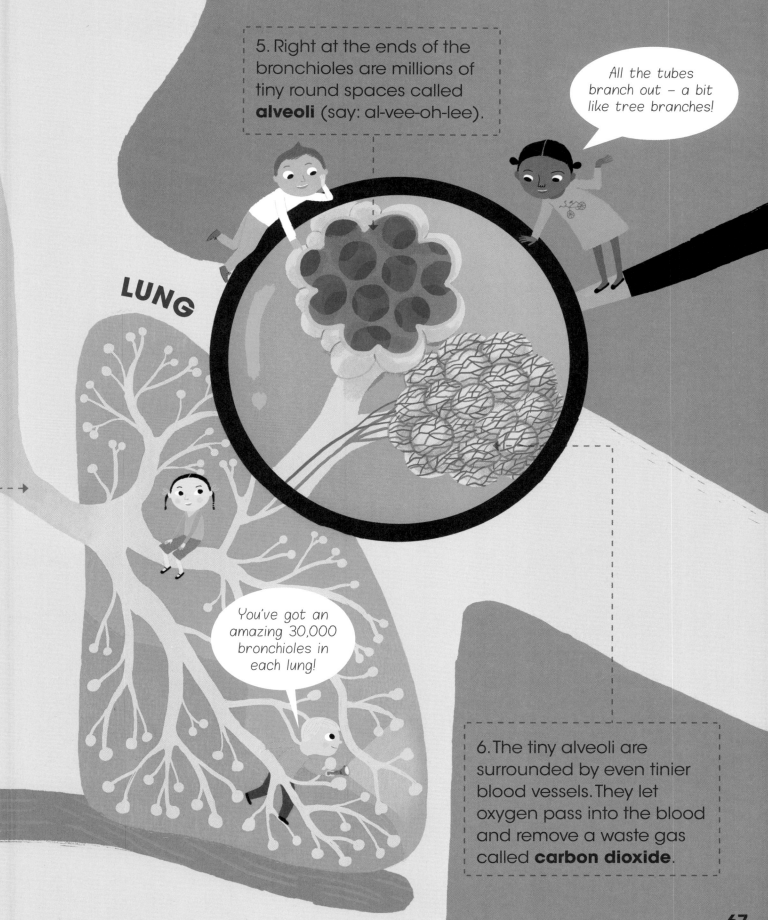

5. Right at the ends of the bronchioles are millions of tiny round spaces called **alveoli** (say: al-vee-oh-lee).

All the tubes branch out – a bit like tree branches!

LUNG

You've got an amazing 30,000 bronchioles in each lung!

6. The tiny alveoli are surrounded by even tinier blood vessels. They let oxygen pass into the blood and remove a waste gas called **carbon dioxide**.

Hiccups!

However hard you try, you can't stop a hiccup. It's a sudden, jerky breath that shakes your body from the inside. But why do we get hiccups?

1. Hiccups happen in a big, stretchy breathing muscle called the **diaphragm** (say "die-a-fram"). It's a dome-shaped muscle, just under your lungs.

2. To make you breathe in, the diaphragm muscle pulls down. This makes your lungs open to suck air in.

 Colour in this comic strip of ways to stop hiccups. Which have you tried? Did it work?

BREATHING IN

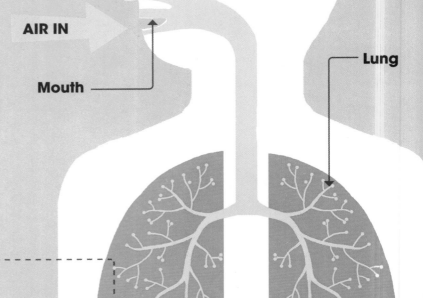

AIR IN

Mouth

Lung

Diaphragm

Hic!

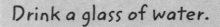
Drink a glass of water.

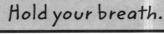
Hold your breath.

BREATHING OUT

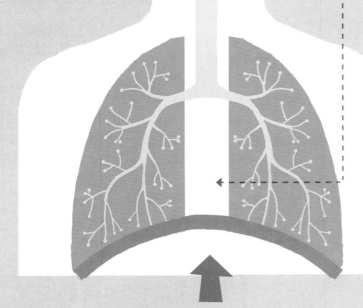

Hic!

← **AIR OUT**

Windpipe ————→

3. To make you breathe out, the diaphragm relaxes and moves back up. Your lungs get smaller and push air out.

4. If you eat or drink too quickly, the diaphragm can jerk up and down. This makes you breathe in suddenly. To keep you from choking in case you accidently breathe in food, your body quickly closes your windpipe. That's what makes the "hic" sound.

Hic! Woof!
Hic! Woof!

Sing!

A sudden surprise!

Brain and senses

Inside your head is the brain, which is the control centre for your body. The brain takes in information from your body and its senses, including your eyes, ears, nose, tongue and skin.

Your **brain** works like a computer. It receives information from your senses and uses it to decide what to do.

**Thinking...
deciding...
doing...
it's an apple!**

Instructions to body
1. Find money – it's in your pocket.
2. Buy apple.
3. Eat apple – yummy!

Another great idea of mine!

The brain sends out signals to make your body move, walk or talk. It really is the boss!

Controlling your heartbeat →

Storing memories →

Learning →

Ideas →

Planning →

Your **brain** is a supercomputer that handles thousands of pieces of information every second, such as ...

← Taking in messages from your senses

← Moving your muscles

← Understanding words

← Keeping you breathing

← Feelings

How good is your brain at remembering? Look at these 10 objects for 10 seconds. Cover them and write down as many as you can remember!

1..................... 6.....................

2..................... 7.....................

3..................... 8.....................

4..................... 9.....................

5..................... 10.....................

How did you score?

10/10 Super brain!

5 to 8 Totally brainy

1 to 4 Brain strain!

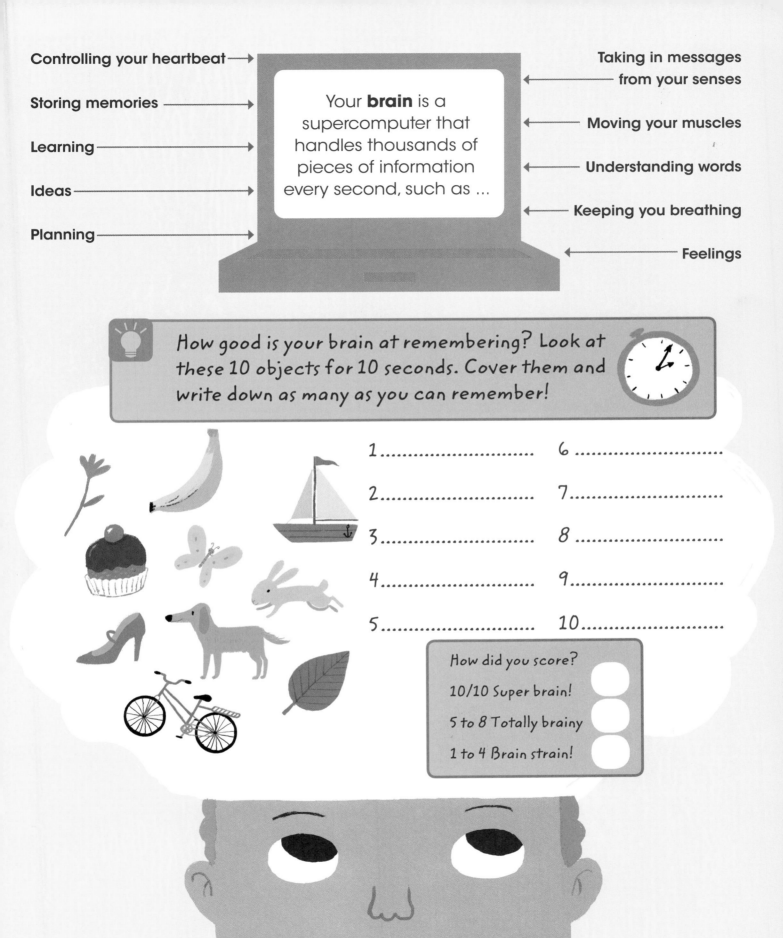

Take a brain tour

Your brain is made up of many parts and the brain cells in different areas of the brain have special jobs. Explore the brain with this map.

The **cerebrum** (say: se-ree-brum) makes up most of your brain. It controls your body when you choose to do things.

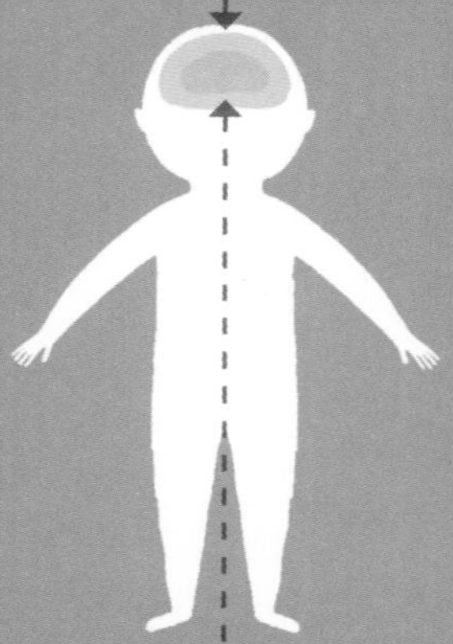

The bumpy, wrinkly outer layer of the cerebrum is called the **cerebral cortex** (say: se-ree-bral core-tex). It's used for sensing, thinking and learning.

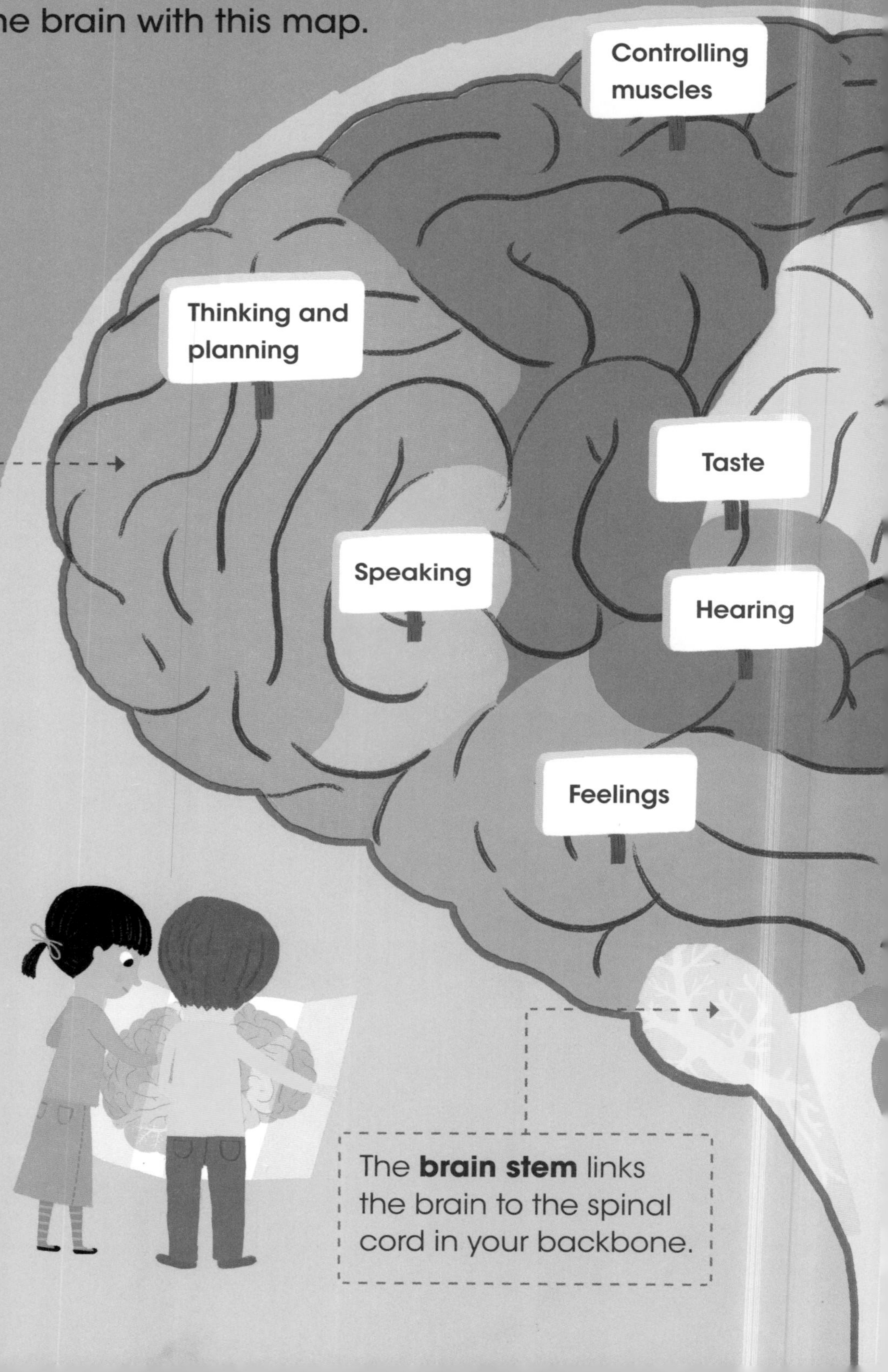

Controlling muscles

Thinking and planning

Taste

Speaking

Hearing

Feelings

The **brain stem** links the brain to the spinal cord in your backbone.

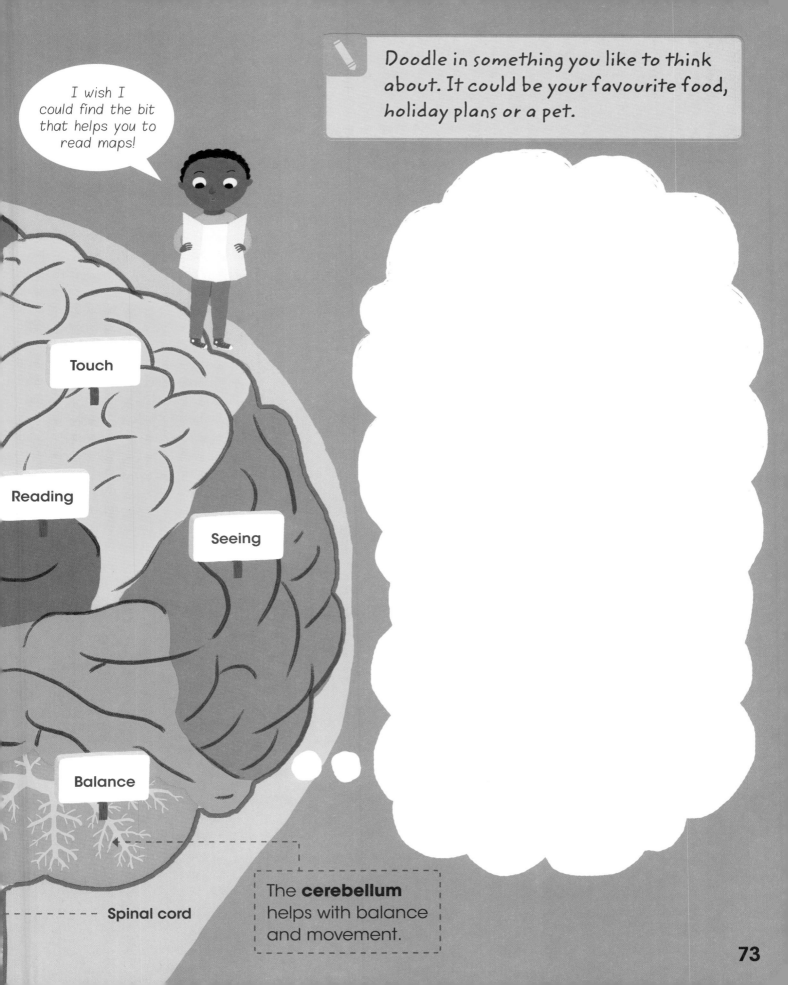

Brilliant brain cells

Your brain has billions of brain cells called neurons. Each neuron is like a tiny octopus, with lots of tentacles that reach out to link it with other brain cells.

Your brain must be very clever to send messages through this tangled maze!

 The alarm clock is ringing! Find a way through the tangle of neurons to choose what you'd like to do.

There may be one hundred billion **neurons** in the human brain.

START

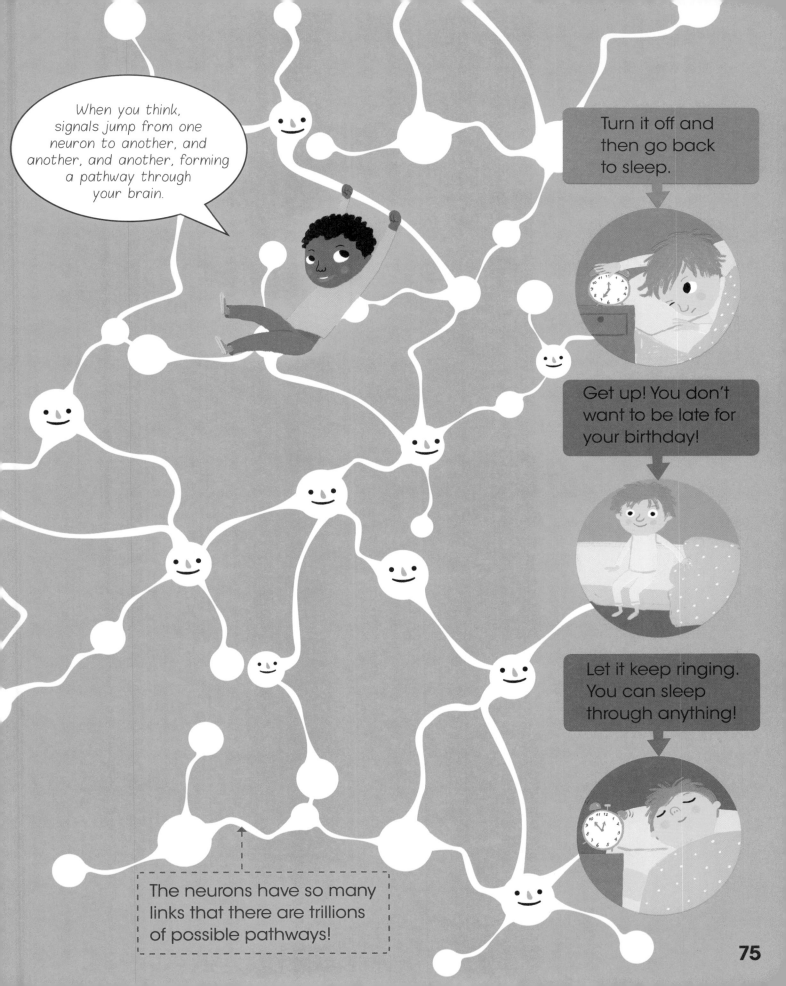

Your nerve network

A network of cells called nerves carries information and messages between your body and your brain. It's called the nervous system – and it's super-fast!

Nerves pick up information from your eyes, ears, tongue, nose and touch sensors all over your skin.

Your **nervous system** carries this information to your brain.

Your **nervous system** carries messages between your **brain** and your body.

You have just caught the ball!

The **spinal cord** is a big bundle of nerves that runs down your back, inside your backbone. Lots of smaller nerve pathways branch off from it.

Your nervous system stretches from head to toe.

Make those feet move!

Nerve signals can travel very fast – it can take just a fraction of a second for your brain to sense something, decide what to do, and act on it.

Your nervous system is made of neurons – the same as the cells in the brain.

Write a message from the brain to a part of the body. What will you tell it to do?

Message from: The Brain

To: _____ (body part)

Zzzzzzzzzz...

When you sleep, you don't seem to hear, see or notice things around you. But inside your skull, your brain is still working – right around the clock!

Your **brain** keeps working to control things like body heat, heartbeat and breathing. It also keeps alert to danger.

A really loud noise could signal danger, so your brain wakes you up.

Scientists think that while you sleep, your brain sorts through the things it has stored, keeping important stuff in your memory and throwing the rest away.

Your brain likes to keep things very organised!

78

You **dream** while you sleep. Dreams can be very weird! Scientists think that these strange stories happen as your brain sorts through your memories and feelings.

Dreams are often muddled and mixed up.

Magical or totally impossible things can happen in your dreams!

Dreams sometimes include people, places and events from real life.

Create a dream diary. Write down your dreams as soon as you wake up — before you forget them!

My weirdest dream: _____

_____

My funniest dream: _____

_____

My scariest dream: _____

_____

Inside your eye

From the moment you open your eyes in the morning to when you close them at night, they take pictures of the world around you and send them to your brain.

1. Light rays pass through the pupil and the lens.

Our eyes need light to see. Light rays come from the sun, light bulbs or even a torch. Rays of light bounce off things and into your eyes.

The **lens** works like a camera lens to bring images into focus.

The **pupil** is the dark circle in the middle of the eye. It can be made smaller or bigger to let more or less light in.

Now I see how it works.

The **iris** controls how much light comes into the eye by changing the size of the pupil.

Hey – it's all upside down!

What is this eye looking at? Join the dots — then turn the page around to find out!

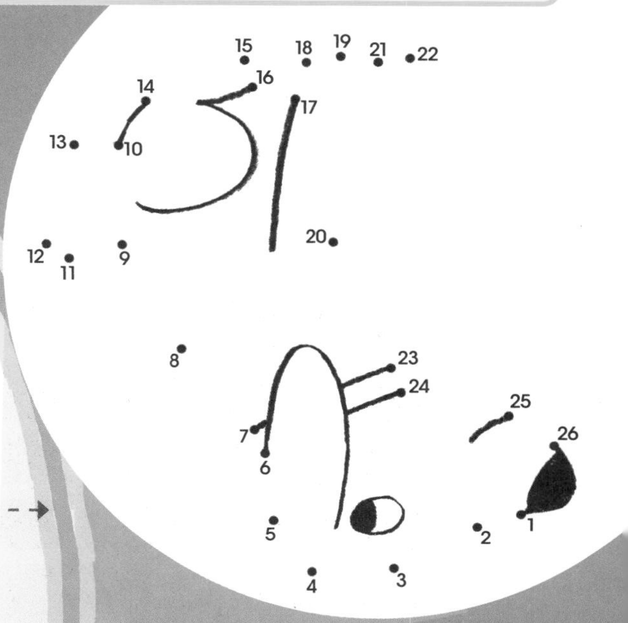

2. As light rays enter the eyeball, they cross over before they land on your retina to create an upside-down picture.

The **retina** at the back of your eye is made of light-sensitive cells.

3. Nerve cells in the retina turn the patterns of light into signals.

Your **eyeball** is filled with a clear jelly that lets light through.

4. The signals zoom along the **optic nerve** to the brain. It flips the picture the right way round and works out what it is.

TO THE BRAIN

Goofy gallery

Your brain is brilliant at sorting out all the signals from your eyes. But sometimes even your clever brain can't work out what it's seeing!

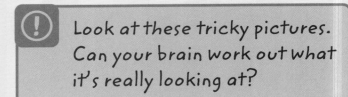
Look at these tricky pictures. Can your brain work out what it's really looking at?

Look at these squares. Can you see grey dots appear?

Which of the two blue trees is bigger? Measure them to find out.

Your brain knows that things should look smaller if they are far away, so it thinks the faraway tree must be the biggest.

82

Do the rows of tiles go across at different angles?

Do you see a duck or a rabbit? Or does it flip between the two?

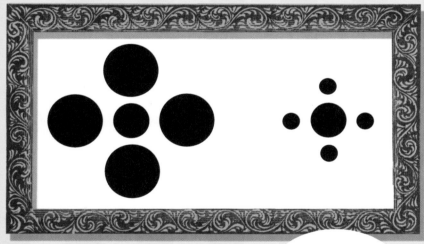

Look at the two dots in the middle of these patterns. Which one is bigger? Now measure them with a ruler.

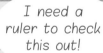

I need a ruler to check this out!

Listen up!

Your ears are truly amazing, picking up all the sounds around you, from soft sounds like the wind in the trees, through to loud noises like a drum.

The smallest bone in your body is found inside your ear.

The **ear canal** is a tunnel leading inside your ear.

Let's make some noise!

Sound travels as a series of ripples, or sound waves, in the air.

Your ears are dish-shaped to catch sound waves in the air.

Outer ear

84

Your **eardrum** is a thin, tightly stretched skin – like the skin of a drum!

When the sound waves hit your eardrum, they make it vibrate (shake to and fro).

Tiny hairs inside the **cochlea** sense the vibrations and turn them into nerve signals.

It sounds like it's dinner time!

Inner ear

The nerve signals go to your brain, which makes sense of the sound signals.

Middle ear

Tiny ear bones called **ossicles** (say: oss-ick-culs) carry the vibrations to the spiral-shaped cochlea.

La la la!

 Gently put your hand on your throat and sing or talk. Can you feel the sound vibrations?

Know your nose

Smells really do get up your nose! You smell things when tiny bits of them float into your nostrils. That's everything from fresh bread to stinky socks!

About seven centimetres inside your nostrils there is a patch of smell-detecting cells.

When something smelly touches the smell-detecting cells, they send signals along nerves to the brain.

Mmmmm! That smells like bread. Can I have a slice please?

Some very tiny pieces of bread make their way to your nose, especially when you breathe in.

The very tiny pieces of bread are far too small to see.

The smell of this freshly baked bread is actually made of tiny molecules of bread that float into the air.

Nasty smells are useful too. They tell us when something is rotten, burning – or needs a wash!

Sense of smell experiment
Collect some smelly things from the list here and put them in separate plastic cups.

1. Ask friends or family members to take turns putting on a blindfold and then sniffing each smelly thing.

2. Can they tell you what each one is just by sense of smell? Write down their answers.

How many did they get right? Who has the best sense of smell?

You will need

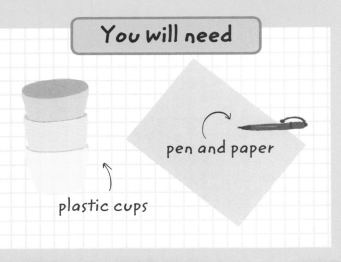

pen and paper

plastic cups

Smelly things

vinegar

coffee

chocolate bar

lemon

rose petals

pencil and pencil shavings

banana

onion

peppermints

orange

Mmmm, I'm smelling my favourite smell. CHOCOLATE!

Tasty!

You have about 10,000 tiny taste buds on your tongue. The nerves in your taste buds send signals to your brain about what's in your mouth.

Taste buds

Your tongue has tiny bumps all over it. The **taste buds** are in these bumps. When you eat, saliva (spit) washes food into the bumps and it touches the taste buds.

More than three-quarters of what you taste actually comes from your sense of smell. As you eat, you smell your food too. That's why your food isn't as tasty when you have a cold – your smell cells are blocked with snot!

Yum! Salty like salt flavour crisps!

Umami – that's savoury, like strong cheese!

Sour like lemons!

I can't taste a thing!

Your taste buds can sense five main tastes: sweet, sour, salt, bitter and umami (say: ooo-ma-me).

88

Sweet like honey!

Bitter like dark chocolate!

Doodle in your favourite food for each of the five main tastes.

Salt

Sweet

Sour

Bitter

Umami (savoury)

Keep in touch

Just imagine touching something really hot if you didn't know it was hot! Sensors in our skin keep us aware of danger – they also help us to feel the world around us.

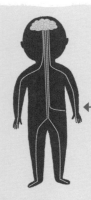

The skin all over your body is full of touch sensors, made of special cells that send information to your brain.

? Match the children to what their sense of touch is telling them.

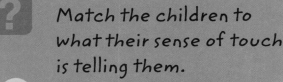

Pain .... *Ouch! That's spiky.* ⬭

Cold .... *Ahh, lovely and cool.* ⬭

Heat........ *Phew! I'm hot.* ⬭

Pressure ... *I'm being pulled along!* ⬭

Your skin has touch sensors to feel cold, heat, pain and pressure.

Your senses really keep you in touch with the world.

91

Quick reactions

How quickly you can react depends on how fast your brain can tell your body what to do. Your body also has superfast automatic reactions, called **reflexes**.

Reaction time test

Test how quick your reactions are with this fun experiment!

1. Ask a friend to hold a ruler, with the low numbers at the bottom end.

2. Hold your hand open around the bottom of the ruler.

3. Ask your friend to drop the ruler. As soon as you see it fall, grab it!

4. The number you grab gives you a score. Lower numbers mean faster reactions.

Try it three times and write down your results. Then try testing different people to see who is the fastest.

Reaction results

Name:	Number: 1	2	3
Me _ _ _ _ _ _ _ _ _ _ _	◯	◯	◯
_ _ _ _ _ _ _ _ _ _ _ _ _	◯	◯	◯
_ _ _ _ _ _ _ _ _ _ _ _ _	◯	◯	◯
_ _ _ _ _ _ _ _ _ _ _ _ _	◯	◯	◯
_ _ _ _ _ _ _ _ _ _ _ _ _	◯	◯	◯

Who has the fastest reactions?

_ _

Reflexes are reactions that you don't control. They can automatically protect you when there's not enough time for messages to get to your brain and back.

Your blink reflex makes you automatically close your eyelids when something comes near them.

Reflexes help to protect us in emergencies.

Test your blink reflex

Stand behind a window and ask a friend to go on the other side and throw cotton wool balls towards your face.

Can you resist your blink reflex and keep your eyes open the whole time?

Under your skin

Your skin provides a tough, flexible covering for your body. It does lots of useful jobs, too. In fact, there's a lot more to your skin than what you can see on the surface!

Yuck! I've just stepped in some sweat!

The thinner top layer of your skin is called the **epidermis** (say: ep-i-der-miss).

The surface of your skin is a layer of dead, flattened cells. These flake off and get replaced by more from below.

The thicker layer underneath is called the **dermis** (say: der-miss).

There's a lot to see under your skin!

Sweat glands make and release sweat to holes on the surface called **pores**.

Blood vessels bring food and oxygen to your skin cells and carry away waste.

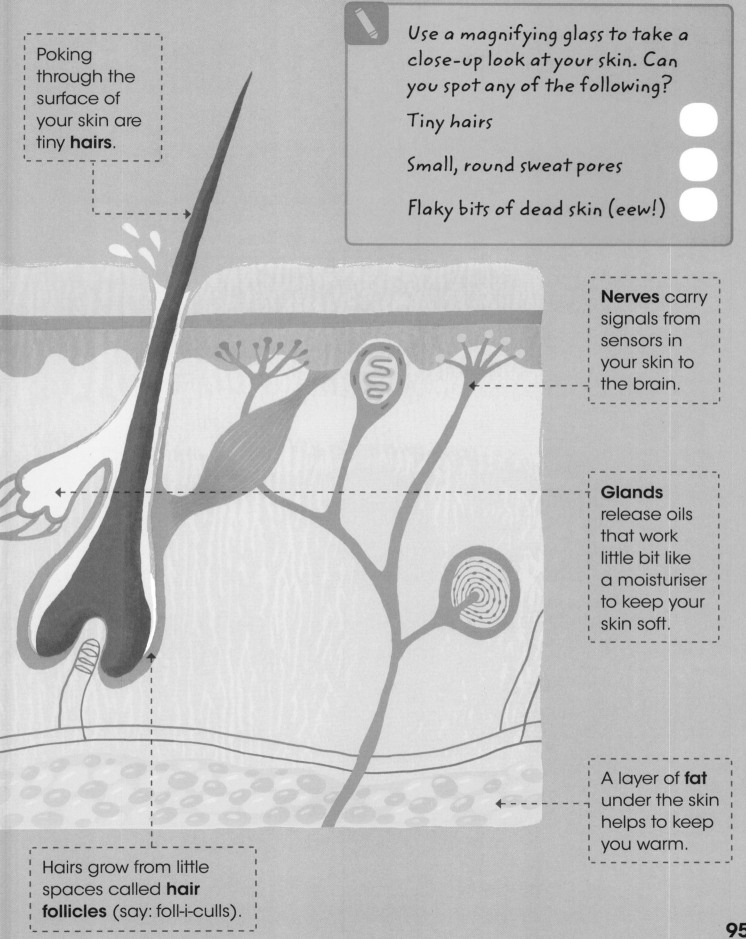

Poking through the surface of your skin are tiny **hairs**.

Use a magnifying glass to take a close-up look at your skin. Can you spot any of the following?

Tiny hairs

Small, round sweat pores

Flaky bits of dead skin (eew!)

Nerves carry signals from sensors in your skin to the brain.

Glands release oils that work little bit like a moisturiser to keep your skin soft.

A layer of **fat** under the skin helps to keep you warm.

Hairs grow from little spaces called **hair follicles** (say: foll-i-culls).

95

Your super skin

Groups of cells make up organs with special jobs to do, such as your heart. Did you know that your skin is your body's largest organ, with lots of important jobs to do?

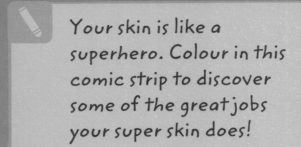

Your skin is like a superhero. Colour in this comic strip to discover some of the great jobs your super skin does!

It keeps your body parts safe inside and stops them from drying out.

It keeps dirt and germs out of your body.

It helps you to sense the world around you.

It's super-flexible so you can pull all those fancy superhero moves.

It can keep you warm and help you to cool down.

Get a grip!

The skin on the palms of your hands and the soles of your feet has little ridges to give you better grip. The best way to see this is to take a close look at your fingertips.

Everyone has their own special pattern of lines and ridges on their fingertips.

The ridges have lots of sweat pores. They release sweat to keep the skin very slightly damp. This helps us to grip the surface of some objects.

Most of your body is covered with small hairs, but not your fingertips, the palms of your hands, or the soles of your feet.

Compare your fingerprints with family or friends. See – they are all different!

Use a washable pen to colour the top part of your thumb. Then press it down on the space below. Do the same for the rest of your fingers.

			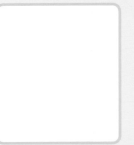	
THUMB	**FINGER 1**	**FINGER 2**	**FINGER 3**	**FINGER 4**

START

FINISH

Can you find a way through the fingerprint maze?

First-aid kit

A scab works a bit like a sticking plaster!

If you cut yourself, blood flows out from under your skin. Luckily, your skin has its own first-aid kit. It makes a scab to stop the leak and starts healing the cut.

First-aid Kit
Ingredients for making scabs:

- Red blood cells
- Disc-shaped platelets
- Stringy, sticky fibrin threads

It can take from five days to six weeks for a cut to heal.

1. Emergency! A net of sticky fibrin threads and small, plate-shaped cells called platelets plug the leak.

A cut breaks blood vessels under the skin and red blood cells pour out.

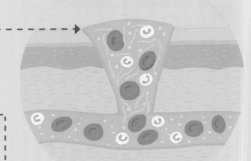

2. Stop the leak. The cut is properly sealed off as the mesh of ingredients starts to dry out, forming a thick clot.

The net holds back the red blood cells.

White blood cells fight any germs in the area.

3. Making a scab. Protected by the scab, the skin beneath repairs itself. When it's done the scab falls off.

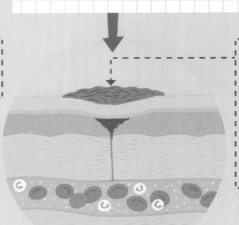

The surface of the clot dries and hardens to form a scab.

100

Make your own gross scab by following the steps below. Then show it to your friends!

Don't worry banana, you'll make a full recovery!

You will need:

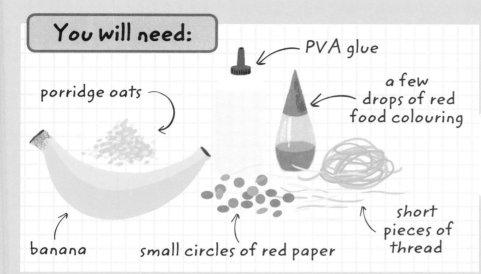

porridge oats

PVA glue

a few drops of red food colouring

banana

small circles of red paper

short pieces of thread

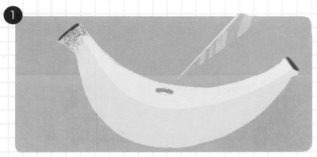

1 Ask a grown-up to help you make a hole in a banana (leave the skin on). This is the "cut" you will fix!

2 Mix some PVA glue with the thread and red food colouring to make the fibrin.

3 Add porridge oats for platelets and the small red paper circles as red blood cells.

4 Mix all the scab ingredients together. Then use the mixture to fill and cover the hole.

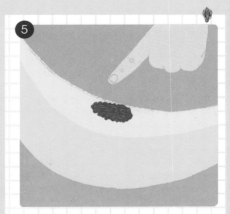

5 Let it dry and watch it form into a crispy scab. Gross!

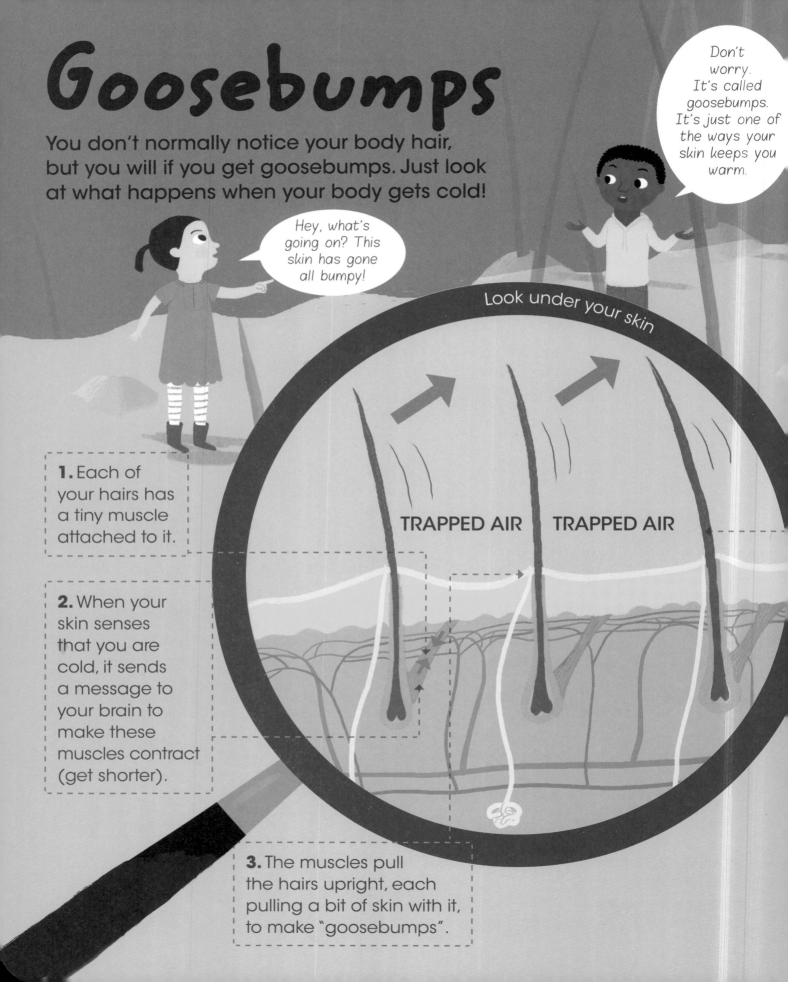

All the little hairs are standing up!

You get goosebumps when you feel scared, too. Your hairs stand up to make you seem bigger.

Animals get goose bumps, too. Look at this scaredy cat!

4. The hairs stand on end and trap air next to your body to keep you warm, like a woolly jumper.

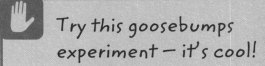

Try this goosebumps experiment — it's cool!

Pour some tap water into a bowl and add ice cubes. Wait until the ice has made the water really cold.

Dip a finger in and use it to dribble a few drops of the icy water down your back. Brrrr!

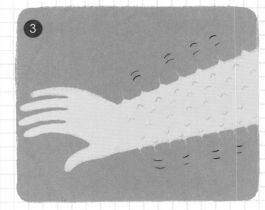

Watch the hair and skin on your arms. Did you get goosebumps?

103

Hot and cold

To keep healthy, your body needs to stay at about the same temperature. If you get too hot, your skin has some cool tricks to turn down the temperature!

When it's hot, the hairs on your skin lay flat. It's like taking a jumper off on a sunny day!

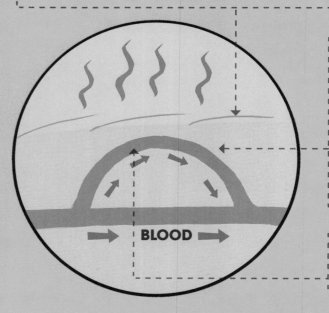

BLOOD

Blood vessels near the surface of your skin become wider, letting more blood flow through.

Blood near the surface loses heat, cooling you down.

Your skin is covered with millions of tiny holes called **sweat pores**. These lead to **sweat glands** under the surface of your skin.

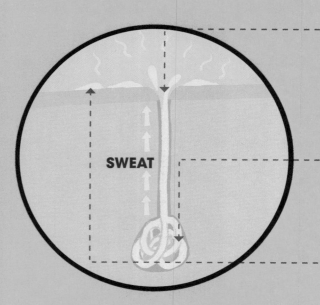

SWEAT

Your **sweat glands** regularly release liquid sweat onto the surface of your skin. When you get hot, they can produce up to a litre of sweat in an hour.

As the **sweat** dries off, it cools down your skin and your body.

BLOOD

When it's cold, your body keeps blood away from the surface of your skin, where it would lose some heat.

Blood vessels become narrower, so less blood can flow through. This can make you look paler.

? Quick Quiz

Chill out or work up a sweat by ticking the correct answers below!

1. You sweat all the time, not just on hot days.

TRUE ○ FALSE ○

2. Sweating releases hot water onto your skin to keep you warm.

TRUE ○ FALSE ○

3. Your skin is covered with more than two million sweat pores.

TRUE ○ FALSE ○

Hair safari

Most of us have hair on our head, but we've also got tiny hairs all over our body. The thickest and longest hairs are found on the head. Take a closer look!

Most of your hair is not living cells. It's made of a tough material called keratin (say: care-a-tin).

Eek! This hair is flexible and wobbly!

It's like a jungle down here.

A typical person has about 100,000 head hairs.

The hairs on your head are very close together, with up to 300 hairs in every square centimetre.

Hair types salon

Some people have straight hair, while others have wavy or curly hair. The type of hair you have depends on the shape of the hairs and how they grow out of your skin.

Draw in the different hair types for the people below.

Draw in some straight hair.

STRAIGHT HAIR

Straight hairs have a round shape. They grow from hair follicles with a round shape.

Let's get styling!

Draw in some wavy hair

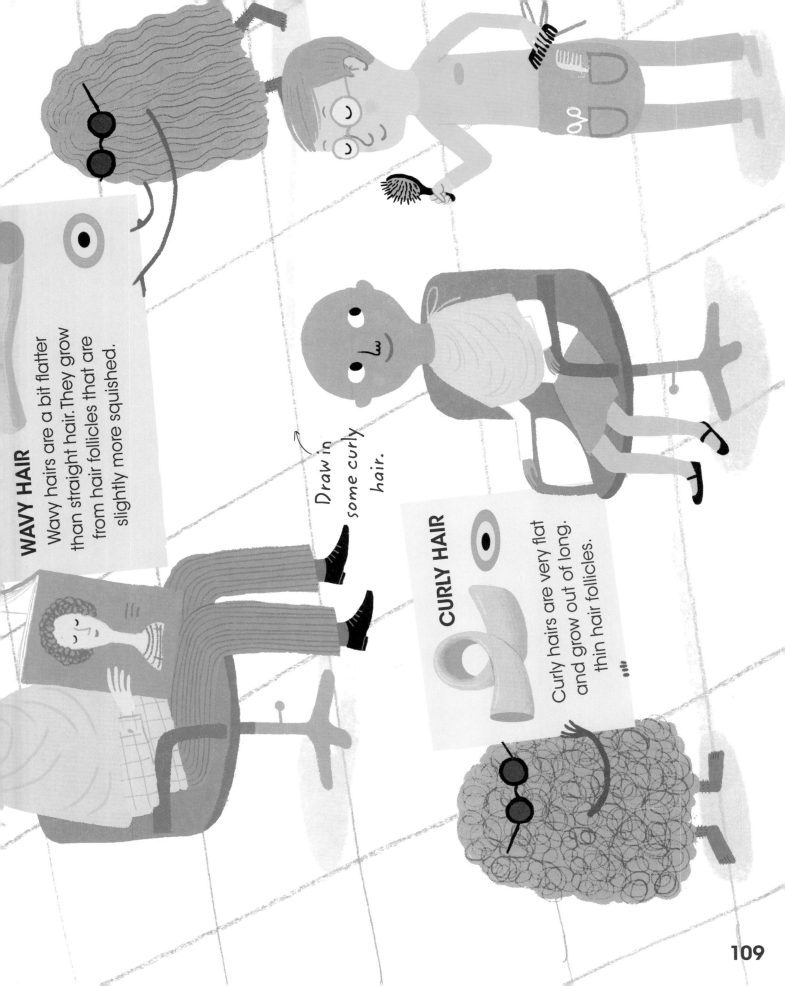

WAVY HAIR

Wavy hairs are a bit flatter than straight hair. They grow from hair follicles that are slightly more squished.

Draw in some curly hair.

CURLY HAIR

Curly hairs are very flat and grow out of long, thin hair follicles.

Nifty nails

Tigers have claws, horses have hooves, but humans have fingernails and toenails. These hard coverings help to protect the tips of your fingers and toes.

New nail cells grow out from an area called the **nail root**.

This end of the nail is called the **free edge**. It's the bit that sticks out more as the nail grows.

Just like your hair, your nails are made out of super-strong **keratin**.

Cuticle

Toenails grow more slowly than fingernails.

The hard surface of the nail is made of dead cells and is called the **nail plate**.

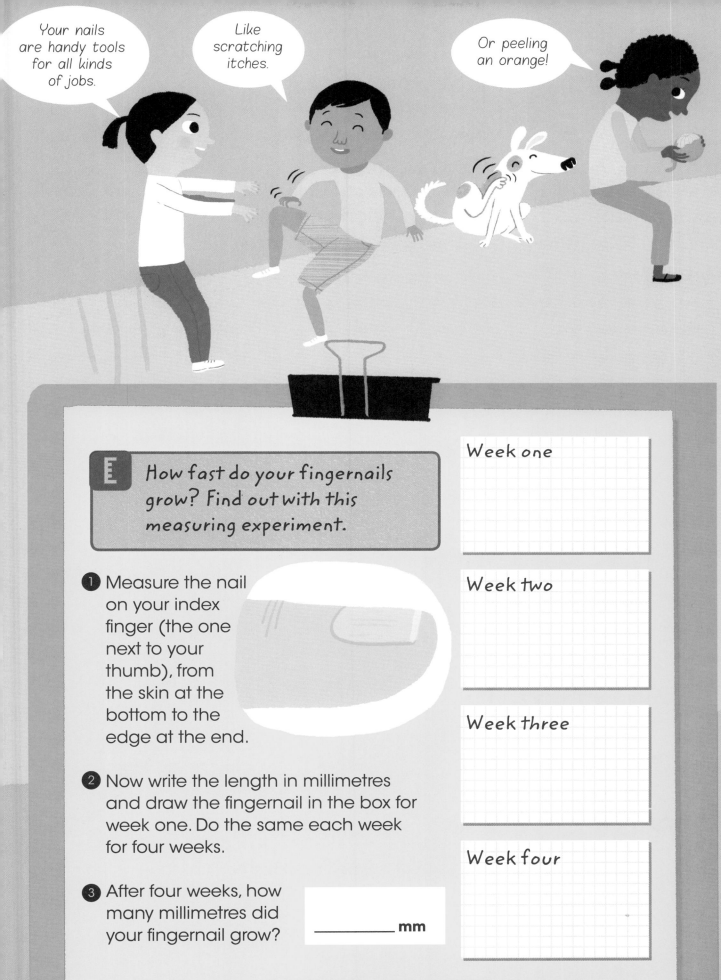

Your nails are handy tools for all kinds of jobs.

Like scratching itches.

Or peeling an orange!

How fast do your fingernails grow? Find out with this measuring experiment.

1 Measure the nail on your index finger (the one next to your thumb), from the skin at the bottom to the edge at the end.

2 Now write the length in millimetres and draw the fingernail in the box for week one. Do the same each week for four weeks.

3 After four weeks, how many millimetres did your fingernail grow?

_____ mm

Week one

Week two

Week three

Week four

111

Inside a body cell

Cells are the building blocks that make up your body. We are each made from trillions of tiny cells. Each cell has its own job to do and there are 200 types of cell doing 200 different jobs!

Now let's take a closer look inside just one body cell!

You've discovered many different types of cell on your journey around the body.

Most of your body cells have a control centre in the middle called the **nucleus** (say: new-clee-us).

These shapes are **mitochondria** (say: might-oh-con-dree-aa). They generate most of the energy a cell needs to do its work.

Such as red blood cells, muscle cells and skin cells!

The outer part of the cell is called the **cell membrane**. This is the cell's skin. It lets water, food and useful things pass through.

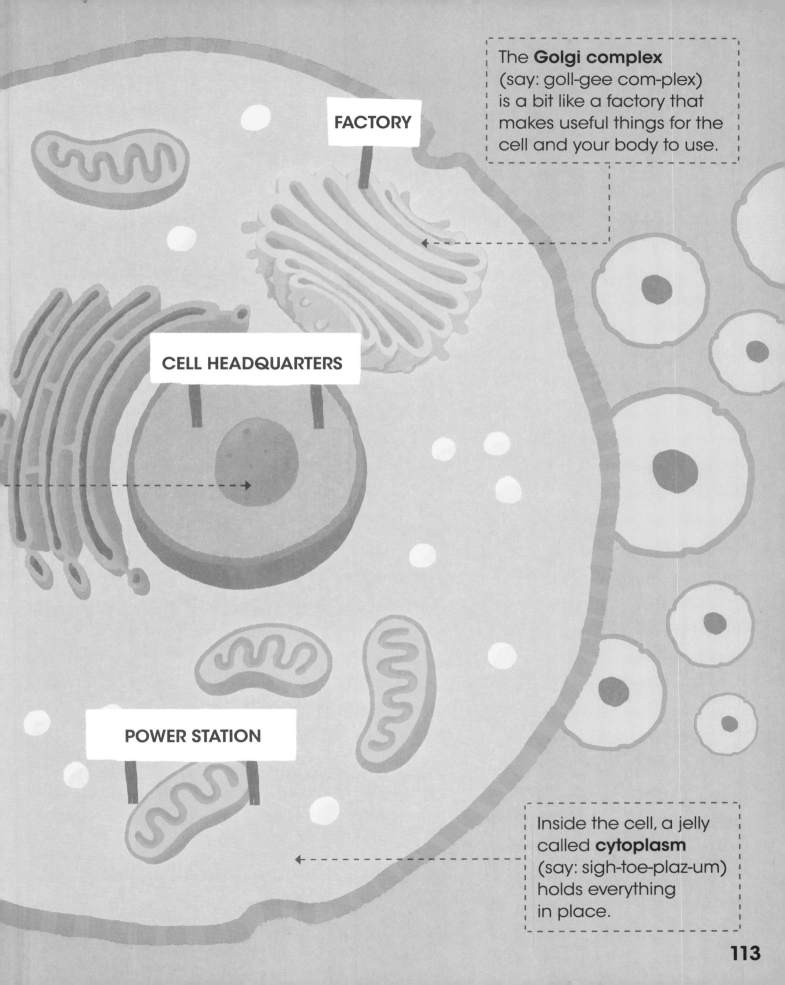

FACTORY

The **Golgi complex** (say: goll-gee com-plex) is a bit like a factory that makes useful things for the cell and your body to use.

CELL HEADQUARTERS

POWER STATION

Inside the cell, a jelly called **cytoplasm** (say: sigh-toe-plaz-um) holds everything in place.

Genius genes

Your body is made of many different types of cell, but how does it know how to make and look after them? The answer lies in your **genes** – a clever secret code, hidden inside your body cells.

Each **chromosome** is made of a long, twisted string of **DNA**.

Inside the **nucleus** of your body cells, there are 46 tiny strands called **chromosomes** (say: crow-mo-sow-mm-s).

Chromosome

Body cell

Nucleus

The chromosomes sometimes form X shapes. If you're a boy, one of them forms a Y shape.

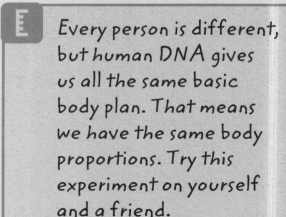

Every person is different, but human DNA gives us all the same basic body plan. That means we have the same body proportions. Try this experiment on yourself and a friend.

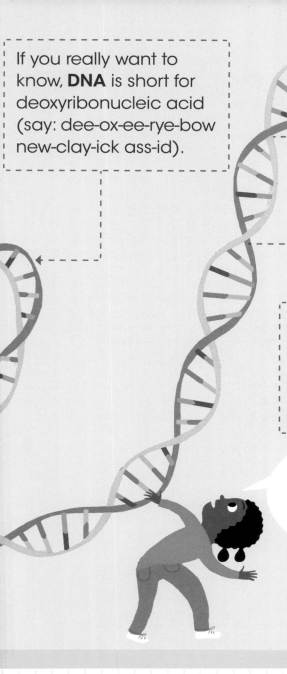

If you really want to know, **DNA** is short for deoxyribonucleic acid (say: dee-ox-ee-rye-bow new-clay-ick ass-id).

Genes are little sections of your DNA. There are hundreds of genes lined up in a row along each DNA string.

Genes are instructions that tell your body cells what to make or do. Together, they are like the plans for building all the different body bits!

What does a cell do when it needs to make something, such as a new skin cell?

It finds the right bit of DNA in its nucleus and then follows the instructions!

① Measure the distance from your wrist to your elbow. It should match the length of your foot!

② Stretch your arms out wide. The distance between your fingertips should roughly match your height.

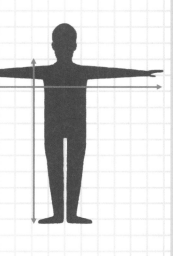

DNA roller coaster

If you stretched out all your body's DNA in a long line, it would reach to the sun and back more than three times. Let's take a roller coaster ride on some human DNA!

Each string of **DNA** is actually made of two strands, which are joined together like a twisty ladder.

The coded instructions of your **genes** are contained in these links between the strands.

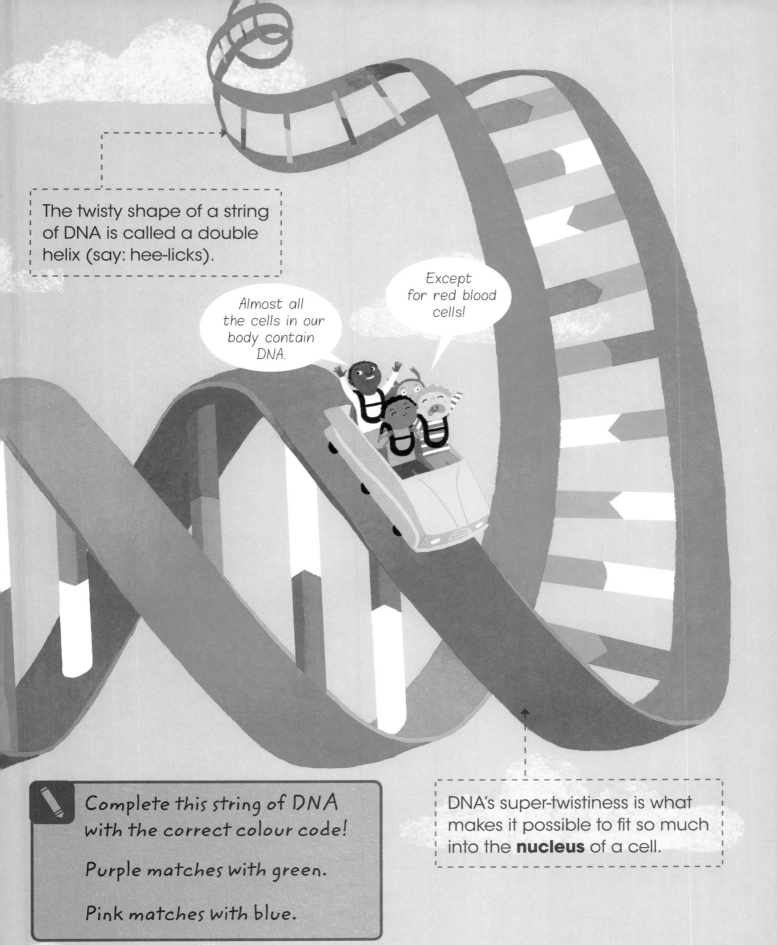

The twisty shape of a string of DNA is called a double helix (say: hee-licks).

Almost all the cells in our body contain DNA.

Except for red blood cells!

Complete this string of DNA with the correct colour code!

Purple matches with green.

Pink matches with blue.

DNA's super-twistiness is what makes it possible to fit so much into the **nucleus** of a cell.

Your genes

Genes are what make people look the way they do. They decide many of the things that make you look one-of-a-kind, from head to toe!

Complete the following to reveal how your genes have made you YOU!

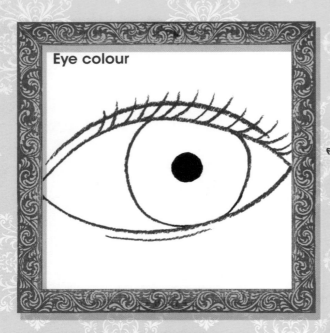
Eye colour

Skin colour

Colour in your eye and skin colour.

Hair colour

Scribble in your hair here.

Shape of your ears

Draw in an ear. Either one!

118

Right- or left-handed?

Colour in the hand you write with.

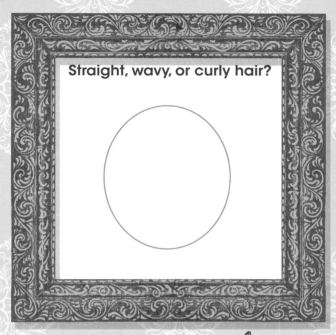

Straight, wavy, or curly hair?

Draw yourself and your hairstyle in the mirror!

Identical twins look exactly the same because they share exactly the same genes. Can you draw in this girl's identical twin?

Passing it on

Ever wondered why you've got freckles or curly hair? Well, you can blame your parents, or even your grandparents, for passing them on. It's all down to genes and DNA again!

Babies get a mix of DNA with genes from the cells of the father and the mother.

The way the DNA mixes means that any brothers or sisters get a different mix of genes.

From just one cell with a mix of genes from its parents, a baby grows up to become a totally new person.

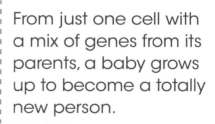

That means you might have your mum's curly hair, while your brother might be tall like your dad!

Grandparents pass on some features to their children, who pass some on in turn. Mix up some family features to add a girl and a boy to the family tree.

You could give her red hair like her grandma.

You could make him freckly like his dad.

121

Growing up

Your body is amazing. It starts out as just one cell and ends up as trillions of different cells all working together. Follow the timeline to see how you grow up.

DAY 1
You are just one cell. The cell splits into two and then keeps going.

9 MONTHS
You are a newborn baby. Welcome to the world!

5 YEARS
Your brain is learning a lot. Your milk teeth start falling out to make way for bigger teeth.

10 YEARS
You get much taller. But you're still growing!

Whoa! It all begins with just one tiny cell.

What do you want to be when you grow up? Write a note here to your future self. Remember to check back when you've grown up!

15 YEARS
You get bigger and stronger, and your body changes as you turn into a grown-up.

20 YEARS
Your bones are long and you have reached your full height. Your body stops growing.

60 YEARS
As you get older, your skin gets wrinkly and your hair gets thinner and turns grey.

To: _____

Date: _____

_____

My plan for when I grow up: _____

_____

_____

123

Glossary

You can check out the meaning of lots of amazing body words here!

Artery Blood vessel that carries blood away from the heart.

Bacteria Tiny living things that can sometimes cause diseases.

Blood vessel Tube that carries blood around the body.

Capillary Tiny blood vessel that delivers oxygen and food to cells and carries away waste.

Carbohydrate Type of food that gives your body energy.

Carbon dioxide Gas made as a waste product by the body's cells.

Cartilage Tough, rubbery material found in joints and some other parts of the skeleton.

Cells Tiny units that living things are made up of.

Cochlea Snail-shaped part inside the ear.

Diaphragm Muscle under the lungs that pulls down to help you breathe in.

Digest To break down food and soak up the useful parts of it.

Genes Instructions in cells that control the way they work.

Gland Body part that releases a substance, such as sweat or saliva.

Joint Connection between bones.

Kidneys Two organs that filter the blood and remove waste water and chemicals.

Ligament Tough cord that links bones together at a joint.

Minerals Non-living substances that the body needs, such as calcium.

Muscle Body part that gets shorter and pulls to make the body move.

Nerve Pathway between the brain and body that signals travel along.

Neuron Type of body cell that makes up nerves and the thinking parts of the brain.

Organ A complex body part that does a particular job, such as the brain or lungs.

Oxygen Gas found in the air that body cells need in order to work.

Peristalsis Squeezing action that pushes things along inside tubes in the body.

Pores Openings in the skin that let sweat out.

Protein Type of food that is used to build and repair body parts.

Pulse Your heart rate, or the number of times the heart beats in a minute.

Rectum Tube at the end of the large intestine that carries poo out of the body.

Reflexes Automatic body reactions, such as blinking when something comes near your eyes.

Retina Area of light-sensitive cells inside the back of the eyeball.

Senses Ability to detect different things outside the body, such as seeing, hearing and smelling.

Skeleton Framework of bones that support the body.

Spinal cord Big bundle of nerves in your back, connecting the brain to the rest of the body.

Sweat Liquid released from the skin to help you cool down.

Taste buds Tiny taste-detecting organs found in the tongue.

Tendon Strong cord connecting a muscle to a bone.

Ureter Tube that carries urine from a kidney to the bladder.

Urine Waste liquid collected by the kidneys.

Vein Blood vessel that carries blood towards the heart.

Vitamins Chemicals found in food that the body needs in small amounts.

X-ray Type of photograph that can show some of the parts inside the body.

I'm using one of my body's senses to read these words.

Index

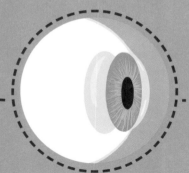

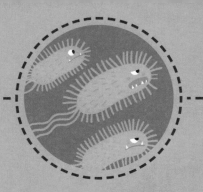

Answers

Page 21

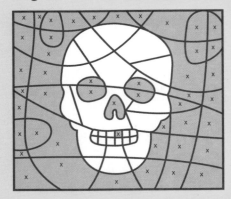

Page 27 25 muscles!

Pages 32–33 Meat – proteins, cheese – fats (but also proteins), orange juice – vitamins and minerals (but also carbohydrates), pasta – carbohydrates.

Page 37 True

Page 39 B

Page 41 Apple

Page 46–47 1. False, 2. False, 3. True, 4. True, 5. True.

Page 49 Wholewheat pasta and vegetables are high in fibre.

Pages 50–51

Pages 52–53

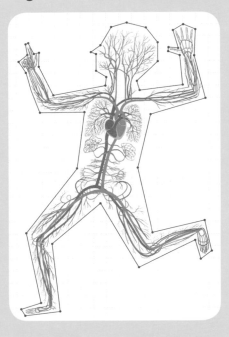

Pages 54–55

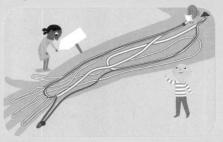

Page 57 1.  2. 3.

Page 81 A dog.

Pages 82–83 The two blue trees are the same size. The rows of tiles go straight across - it is an illusion. The two dots are the same size.

Pages 90–91 Pain – D, Cold – B, Heat – A, Pressure – C.

Page 99 One possible route is:

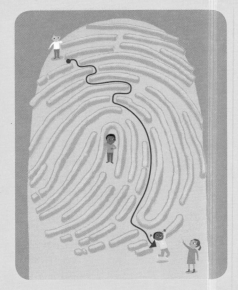

Page 105 1. True, 2. False, 3. True.

Page 111 Your fingernails will have grown about 3mm in one month.

Page 116